Praise for *Relationshift*

"Blaney has written a must-read primer for understanding how relationships make us into the people we are, and how we can shape our future selves by deliberately selecting the people in our lives and cultivating our relationships with them."

—**Ramez Naam, award-winning author of *Nexus***

"If you are looking for a self-improvement book, consider the topic of improving your life by improving your relationships. *Relationshift* is packed with practical advice and is one of the most unique and interesting books I've come across this year."

—**James J. Talerico, Jr., CMC (R), Nationally Recognized Small Business Expert**

"I found this book, and the examples Justin used, to be intriguing, recognizable and relatable in a way that gave me new perspective on how I want to approach my best life and support those around me to do the same."

—**Samantha Buhr, Director, Strategic Consulting Programs at University of Washington**

"Interesting and inspiring. This book could transform your life"

—**John E. Anderson, Chapter President of Pacific Northwest Institute of Management Consultants and President of Be Cause Business Resources, Inc.**

"It's amazing how different a life can be when a person gets a good grip on the "steering wheel." You can't make the bumps in the road go away, but you sure can choose how to navigate through them. Justin's book does a great job making the concepts of a "deliberate life" come alive. This is a must-have personal play book."

—**Frank E. Coker, CMC**

"As this book so wonderfully explains, understanding relationships unlocks life's grandest possibilities. Life is a game worth playing and this is a great playbook with winning strategies and tactics. Justin has done an outstanding job on how we became who we are and how to use this knowledge to change into who we want to become."

—**Henry DeVries, columnist for Forbes.com and bestselling author of *How to Close a Deal Like Warren Buffett***

"Relationships have a critical impact on your work and professional life. Blaney offers solid strategies to open up your thinking, uncover positive mentors, and build a network that propels you to greater success and more life satisfaction."

—**Robin Ryan, author of *60 Seconds & You're Hired* and *Soaring on Your Strengths***

"Justin Blaney and *Relationshift* explore a simple idea—that we become like the people we spend time with—in surprisingly helpful ways that I feel I can use every day to improve my personal and professional life. Without a doubt, this is a unique self-improvement book that weaves the author's personal journey with the stories of other living and historic examples and visual illustrations to make the concepts come to life. Many would benefit from practicing these principals more often."

—**David Carroll, VP at Banner Bank, Business Coach and Co-Founder of Cantillon**

"A single relationship can transform your life. We know this to be accurate, but Blaney's characterizations and systemic view of our relationships give us the intention to lean into the best paths for each of us individually and affiliate with the tribes that will provide us with meaningful connections that give our lives purpose. And the higher you climb, the more possibilities you can see, so you need to know the right people for your pillars of purpose, and you don't end up viewing from the wrong mountain! This book helps you reflect on who you are becoming by who surrounds you. The mentors that shaped my life did so by accident, yet I am still thankful to them every day. This book gives that journey intention and influence to help lean your path in the desired direction."

—**Kris Fuehr, Founder and SMB Advocate, Paulson Exchange**

"I have relied on relationships for my entire career to build my business. Even with decades of experience, *Relationshift* surprised me with practical strategies for taking my networking to the next level. Justin Blaney argues effectively that there is far more value in our relationships than most of us imagine or make use of. By tapping into that power, we can achieve almost anything. This book could be helpful to anyone: whether you're debating a career change, looking to quit a bad habit, aiming to get into better physical or mental shape, or desiring to achieve your highest potential in any area of life. I highly recommend *Relationshift*."

—**Doug Hall, Founder, Resources for CEOs**

"It's not what you know, but who you know". This adage has proven itself time and time again. Justin Blaney's new book, *Relationshift,* builds upon that strategy and improves it with fresh tactics. The *Relationshift* principles are illustrated with examples of famous people overcoming challenges by using this powerful technique. Lessons taken from Justin's own life experiences solidify the idea. After describing how and why *Relationshift* works, he reveals ways to integrate it into your own routines for attracting success. No matter your chosen career or desires, this book can move you closer toward your goals. It can also cause a powerful paradigm shift in your life. It's an enjoyable read with valuable insights!"

—**E. Doyle Edgerton, Jr., President, Kinetic Data Systems, Inc.**

RELATIONSHIFT

Also by Justin Blaney, D.M.

Whispers Willow
Famously Helpful
Will Post for Profit
Innovation and Influence
Evan Burl and the Falling

RELATIONSHIFT

Unleash the Surprising Power of Relationships to Change Yourself, Remake Your Life, and Achieve Any Business Goal

JUSTIN BLANEY, D.M.

Matt Holt Books
An Imprint of BenBella Books, Inc.
Dallas, TX

This book is designed to provide accurate and authoritative information about personal development. Neither the author nor the publisher is engaged in rendering legal, accounting, or other professional services by publishing this book. If any such assistance is required, the services of a qualified financial or other professional should be sought. The author and publisher will not be responsible for any liability, loss, or risk incurred as a result of the use and application of any information contained in this book.

Relationshift copyright © 2022 by Justin Blaney

Published in association with the literary agency of Legacy, LLC, 501 N. Orlando Avenue, Suite #313-348, Winter Park, FL 32789.

All rights reserved. No part of this book may be used or reproduced in any manner whatsoever without written permission of the publisher, except in the case of brief quotations embodied in critical articles or reviews.

BenBella Books, Inc.
10440 N. Central Expressway
Suite 800
Dallas, TX 75231
benbellabooks.com
Send feedback to feedback@benbellabooks.com

BenBella and *Matt Holt* are federally registered trademarks.

Printed in the United States of America
10 9 8 7 6 5 4 3 2 1

Library of Congress Control Number: 2022013472
ISBN 9781637741849
eISBN 9781637741856

Editing by Joe Rhatigan
Copyediting by James Fraleigh
Proofreading by Michael Fedison and Lisa Story
Indexing by Amy Murphy
Text design and composition by PerfecType, Nashville, TN
Cover design by Justin Blaney and Brigid Pearson
Cover image © Shutterstock/AlenaPo
Author photo by Natalia Sakhnova
Printed by Lake Book Manufacturing

Special discounts for bulk sales are available. Please contact bulkorders@benbellabooks.com.

To those who inspire me most: Lily, Emma, and Mackenzie

CONTENTS

Introduction 1

PART I
How You Became You and How to Change
Chapter 1   Becoming You   13
Chapter 2   How Relationshift Works   37
Chapter 3   Key Relationships   79
Chapter 4   Specific Paths   103

PART II
Who Do You Want to Become?
Chapter 5   The Game   145
Chapter 6   Viral Ideas   173
Chapter 7   The Purpose of Your Life   207

Conclusion   251
Appendix   261
Acknowledgments   267
Definitions   269
Endnotes   279
Index   301

INTRODUCTION

I was born on a sunny November morning in Los Angeles, the youngest son of a drug-dealing con man. That might sound like a strange childhood, but to me, it was normal. I built a tree house with my dad, performed in talent shows, and went to the fair like countless other children—with a few differences. For instance, when the tree house was finished, Dad showed me how the high vantage point made it easier to spot police or rival drug dealers with plenty of time to run out the back gate. For my first-grade talent show, my father encouraged me to try my hand at magic. He must have figured this was the perfect opportunity to teach his son a bit of the family trade.

"When it's time to choose an assistant," he said, arm around my shoulder, "pick the prettiest girl in the audience. You want everyone watching her instead of you. It's a lot easier to fool people who are distracted."

Dad used a bit of the same misdirection for our first visit to the county fair. We didn't go in the front gate like all the other families. We waited until it was Take Your Child to Work Day. Dad dressed as a maintenance worker and, with a fake name badge, snuck us in the employee entrance.

I wouldn't realize how much these experiences had shaped me until I was much older. As far as I knew, suckers were born to be conned, and corners were made to be cut.

. . .

When I was seven, my mom woke me, my brother, and my sister in the middle of the night. She handed me two duffel bags, already packed with my clothes, toothbrush, and Nintendo games.

"We're going on an adventure," she said.

Turns out we were only going across town to live with her sister. Earlier that night, Mom had discovered Dad with another woman. He confessed to cheating for years, and she had had enough. Except for the time he gave me a stolen wallet for my tenth birthday, I wouldn't see my father again until I was well into adulthood.

I can't say that I thought much about whether I wanted to be like or unlike my dad. As with most people, life just sort of happened to me. I made my choices, usually to the best of my ability at the time. Some decisions resulted as I intended; others, not so much. I didn't consider where these choices came from or why I thought about them the way I did. Looking back, I can see myself making many of the same mistakes again and again without realizing the habits I'd fallen into. More than thirty years passed before I began to discover just how much my relationship with my dad had affected me.

When a child shares similarities with their parent, people say, "The apple doesn't fall far from the tree." But what causes apples to fall nearer or farther from the tree? Why do we become like our parents in some ways but not in others? And what of other relationships—with teachers, politicians, religious authorities, or favorite podcasters? Some people encourage us to chase after life with their good example. Others inspire us to pursue a better life because they've made a mess of theirs, and we don't want to end up anything like them. Still others can lull us into complacency, foster hate in our hearts, or draw us into a life marked by bad choices, sadness, or apathy. Every interaction with another human has the potential to shape us, for better or worse.

This book is built on a very simple idea: we become like the people we hang around with. Not just our parents but every person we are exposed to has the potential to change us. And although, at some level, we all understand the power of what one might call peer pressure, this commonly understood force for change is far more potent than most of us realize. With practice, we can use this force to our advantage to transform ourselves faster, more dramatically, and with less effort. We can use this understanding of how relationships work to grow rich, reduce anxiety, conquer bad habits, learn a language, get into better shape, enjoy a more fulfilling sex life—even expand what we believe to be possible. I call this process of tapping the power of human connection *relationshift*. Nearly anything you want to change can be accomplished by better understanding how relationships pull us in one direction or another.

What's in This Book?

Relationshift explores how we are shaped into who we are and how we can make the most of relationships to control who we are becoming. Since the moment we were born, we have been playing a game—and make no mistake, this game is not fair. The range of advantage to disadvantage into which we are born is vast. However, regardless of our birth circumstances, we have far more control over our lives than we might imagine. Many of life's rules can be bent. Some can be broken. But how?

The answer is straightforward. When we want more from life, to change and grow, to improve the possibilities for ourselves or others, we change through relationships.

"Rules should always be bent, if not broken. It's the only way to have any fun."

Alyson Noël

I became who I am today because of my relationship—or lack thereof—with my dad and countless other people who came and went through my life. Connections bring us opportunities, but they also spark something far more fundamental: relationships change us. They make us who we are, and we can leverage them to become nearly anything we want to be.

Understanding this unlocks life's grandest possibilities. If life is a game, this book offers shortcuts to level up easier and faster. Over the last five years, I have been on a mission to better understand the ideas I'll present here—to examine how we became who we are and how to use this knowledge to change into who we want to become.

After reading this book, you should have a deeper understanding of how you became the person you are today. You will see more clearly your path to a more exciting future. You will gain tools to shape who you are becoming, to take greater control of your life, to turn your path whichever way you most desire. And you will better understand how to connect with people who can help you become the best version of yourself.

In the coming pages, we will explore many stories to see these principles in action. We will learn about British explorer Gertrude Bell, a remarkable woman who was instrumental in establishing the nation of Iraq; Frederick Douglass, the abolitionist hero who escaped slavery and went on to become the first African American to be nominated vice president of the United States; a young man who gave up his kingdom to start a religion; a trio of brothers who were separated from one another for nearly twenty years as part of a secret and illegal scientific study; a twenty-two-year-old video blogger who drew eleven thousand fans to a spontaneous meetup at a mall in Dubai; and the Jewish diamond-trading empire in New York City.

These stories are my foundation for exploring the concepts necessary to understand and apply relationshift. Each chapter builds upon the last in a specific order. You may feel some sections don't apply to you or that you already know the material. However, as I elaborate in the coming pages, sometimes we don't know what we think we do (I've been guilty of this on countless occasions). Other times, we understand an idea up to a point, believing this is all there is, only to discover a much deeper level of understanding is possible. In light of this, I highly recommend keeping an open mind until you read the complete story. You may find this leads to breakthroughs in your life in areas you didn't even realize needed a breakthrough.

What's in Each Section

Part one is a survey of the essentials of relationshift. We will dive straight into what you need to know to employ these principles to pursue whatever changes you might want to see in yourself or your life.

>**Chapter one** explores how you became who you are today. Before you can get directions to someplace new, you must understand your starting point. This chapter covers topics like nature versus nurture, how our past choices affect our current options, and the problem with second-guessing past decisions.

Chapter two shows you relationshift in action. We will discuss how to build a tribe of mentors, peers, and protégés who together can help us become whatever we want. We will review strategies for recruiting mentors, influencers, and other high-caliber people to be a part of our journey. This section also includes a survey of social capital—a scientific research area that considers the value of relationships and how to get more from them, and a topic essential to making the most of relationshift in our lives.

Chapter three examines high-impact relationships such as romantic partners, parents, teachers, faith leaders, and bosses. We will attempt to understand how each of these critical relationships uniquely affects us and how to maximize the benefits we can receive from them while minimizing any potential for negative relationshift.

Chapter four surveys ten specific paths that you may be interested in pursuing, such as how to get a better job, achieve fitness goals, or become famous. I'll give you hands-on advice for these goals, and by taking it all together, you will better understand how to pursue almost any desired change, no matter how unique or audacious.

Part two takes a new direction, one imperative to getting the most out of this book. Whereas part one covers how to use relationshift for change, part two will help you better choose what kind of person you want to become. Because we all have points we overlook and are motivated in ways we don't always consciously understand, this section is a guide to the critical elements of unlocking your maximum level of happiness, contentment, and fulfillment. It will enable you to release the instincts and motivations that could be making you miserable without you even realizing it so you can become freer to embrace a life that is filled with purpose as your most enlightened self defines it.

Chapter five dives into our evolutionary instincts, those that have been handed down from our ancestors over generations. We will look at how these instincts came to be and how they affect us today. Many of these drivers were helpful in getting our species to where it is today but no longer serve us. We must understand where our inner thoughts and subconscious motivations came from, and how they affect us, if we want to maximize our ability to write our own rules and better construct a life that suits our goals.

Chapter six continues by analyzing what we can do to overcome the outdated instincts covered in chapter five. We will learn how these ideas are passed between people and generations. You will learn tools for overcoming blind spots and bias to uncover entirely new possibilities that you can't yet perceive. Perhaps most importantly, we will discuss how you can distinguish between good and bad advice, truth and untruth, and wisdom that can help you achieve your goals versus input that will only distract you or empty your wallet.

Chapter seven helps you better define your purpose for living as you let go of any instincts and motivations that have been holding you back. Building on the works of more than twenty experts on the topic, we will consider how our purpose can be split up into various aspects of our life—spiritual, physical, emotional, and occupational—and how better understanding these directions can help us make use of the principles of relationshift to guide our relationships.

Following the conclusion, we will discuss several common objections, questions, and ethical concerns about the concepts of relationshift. Through it all, we will find the common threads that help us apply these ideas to our life in the most straightforward and practical terms.

The Curated Psyche: Learning to Emulate Traits You Want to Embody

All my life, people who know me have suggested that I might be on the autism spectrum. As a child, I didn't always understand other people, and they often seemed to misinterpret my feelings or behavior. I was unable to convey my emotions or meaning accurately through nonverbal communication and would easily become hyperfocused on whatever caught my attention. Rather than playing with other children, I'd spend hours creating complicated mosaics of blocks that would stretch across the living room and down the hallway. When assigned the homework in second grade of drawing a boat, I spent the entire weekend barely eating because I was engrossed in creating a fifty-foot-long battleship that required an entire roll of white butcher paper to complete. It was so heavy, my mom had to help carry it to school. Through childhood into my mid-thirties, I never really had many friends—acquaintances and colleagues, sure, but no one close enough that they might, say, invite me to their birthday party or wedding.

I've never been officially diagnosed with autism, but all my life I've felt there was an anchor of some kind tied to my ability to relate to people—some mental block preventing me from ever truly understanding many of the basics of human interaction. Like why no one ever seemed to be able to tell if I was joking or being serious. I'm not disturbed by the possibility that I might have autism because I like who I am and I've learned to have a happy, friend-filled life. Also, this book wouldn't exist if I hadn't struggled with many of these aspects of existence.

From the youngest age, I had to learn to relate to people. Of course, everyone has to learn these lessons to some degree. The difference with me was I often didn't understand the principles I was trying to adopt. Sometimes, it feels like I'm memorizing the lyrics of a song in another language without ever really understanding what the words mean. I do certain things in specific ways because I've learned that's how people are supposed to act, but these actions might never really make sense to me.

I've had countless opportunities to practice observing and adopting what I see other people do. A while back, I went out for drinks with a new acquaintance I'd met briefly at a party. Halfway into our conversation she blurted, "You're so much more serious than I thought you would be." I was surprised because I thought we'd been having a lighthearted and fun conversation. This incongruence between how she saw me and how I felt bothered me, so I spent the next few days observing people having conversations. I noticed that when someone is talking, the listeners often smile a little. I assume this is an instinctual attempt to show the speaker that they are being heard and what they're saying is interesting. I then started to pay attention to whether or not I did the same. As you might expect, I realized that my face felt very neutral to me but appeared to others to be bored, tired, or stoic. So now I try to remember to smile more often when other people are talking. It's not entirely natural for me yet, but the more I think about people doing this and the more I practice it, the more it becomes second nature to me.

This example of emulation is like a quick-start guide to relationshift. You can use it every day to begin adopting changes in your attitudes, beliefs, skills, and abilities. In fact, you could consider that these people are *relationshifting* you into a version of yourself you prefer to the person you are today.

Think about a trait you might want to be a stronger part of who you are. Who do you know that embodies this trait best? The next time you get the chance to practice it, channel in your own thoughts and actions the way this person lives out the characteristic. You don't have to copy them completely. Just think about how they might act in the situation you're in or about to enter. Then do your version of it, whatever that means to you.

For example, when I want to be more confident, I recall a good friend of mine who has the most unshakable confidence of anyone I know. Thinking about this person and how they might handle the situation I am facing helps me embody more confidence. When I want to give a toast at dinner, I think about a mentor of mine who always gives the most captivating toasts. Then I emulate his vocal pace, how he works vivid stories in, and so on. When I give one of my team members a performance review, I think about a boss I once had who always did the best reviews. Picturing the person and recalling how they manifest the trait I want to have more of myself helps me make these traits my own.

This takes a lot of practice, so don't worry if it feels unnatural or ineffective at first. In time, you can learn to authentically embody almost any trait you like by blending and curating the positive aspects you see in others. This is just one example of how people in your life can relationshift you into a more ideal version of yourself. We'll be covering much more on the topic over the remainder of this book, of course—yet the simple concept of emulating the way you've seen others embody a trait you want more of in your own life is perhaps the best way to begin to make use of relationshift without reading another page. Give it a try for yourself!

• • •

If you take one lesson away from this book, I hope you remember this: you are able to consciously curate your personality and life situation by being more intentional about who you spend time with and how you approach these relationships. But who should you choose to be part of your community? Why choose one person over another? And what if you're not even sure what you might want to change about yourself? These are just some of the questions we'll explore over the coming pages.

Most importantly, anyone can make use of relationshift to improve their life. You don't need to have been born rich, smart, or free. You may have just lost your job, gone through a divorce, or filed for bankruptcy. You don't need to have a network of powerful people to help you, or even any friends at all. You don't even need ambition or direction. All you need to do is turn the page and begin.

PART I

How You Became You and How to Change

"Show me a successful individual and I'll show you someone who had real positive influences in his or her life. I don't care what you do for a living—if you do it well I'm sure there was someone cheering you on or showing the way. A mentor."

Denzel Washington

CHAPTER 1

Becoming You

"Who and what we surround ourselves with is who and what we become. In the midst of good people, it is easy to be good. In the midst of bad people, it is easy to be bad."

—Karen Marie Moning

After completing high school in 1979, Edward "Eddy" Galland enrolled at Sullivan Community College in New York. But, with just one year complete, Eddy told his friends he wasn't returning in the fall. His friends were therefore ecstatic to find he had changed his mind when he appeared on campus the following September.

The only problem was that Eddy didn't seem to remember any of them. He was shocked to have students shout, "Welcome back!" and even more surprised when a young woman he didn't know ran up and kissed him. But what surprised him most was that everyone insisted on calling him Eddy.

His name, in fact, was Robert Shafran. The situation became clear when someone asked if he was adopted. Eddy and Bobby discovered they were twins adopted by different families. They had been living less than one hundred miles apart for nineteen years without ever realizing someone else shared their DNA. When they reunited, they quickly became media favorites, appearing in newspapers and on television talk shows. Everyone was happy to hear the story of how the twins found each other—no one more so than David Kellman.

David was reading the paper one morning when he saw a seemingly impossible photo: two stocky men with bushy brown hair laughing as they posed for the camera. They looked so much like David that he might as well have been looking in a mirror. To everyone's surprise, David was the third identical brother of the trio. The triplets had been born to a teenage mother in 1961—a prom night mistake. She gave them over to an adoption agency called Louise Wise Services. In turn, this agency placed the three children in different homes, neglecting to inform any of the families of the connection.

The first time all three brothers met each other, they immediately felt as if they had been best friends for life. They discovered similarities: all three brothers smoked the same brand of cigarettes, enjoyed wrestling, and had the same taste in women.

Eventually, the brothers and their families confronted the executives of Louise Wise Services to discover why the agency separated the children. The director told the families that placing three children in one home would be too difficult. But this answer didn't satisfy anyone. The parents recalled how the boys would bang their heads against their cribs and cry inconsolably in the first few weeks after adoption—clear signs of acute separation anxiety. The families were outraged and felt certain there was more to the story. They were right.

In the second half of the nineteenth century, an author and part-time scientist named Francis Galton became interested in the idea that one could study twins to determine which traits are the result of genetics and which are determined by nurturing. Identical twins, after all, have the same genetics. Galton argued that similarities between twins could be attributed to heredity, while their differences should be the result of outside influences.

His findings, however, were largely dismissed due to a flaw in the method.[1] One hundred years later, Dr. Peter Neubauer came up with an idea to fix Galton's twin study. Similarities between twins raised by *different* parents could more accurately be attributed to genetics. The biggest problem with this idea was finding a large sample of identical twins raised by different parents—importantly, twins raised by parents who didn't realize they were part of a study.[2]

Finding such a situation in the wild would be enormously improbable. If Neubauer was going to have any hope of completing the study in the way he envisioned, he would have to create the circumstances artificially. Louise Wise Services agreed to work with Neubauer and his assistants, who placed an unknown number of twins and triplets with different families. The adopting parents knew only that their children would be interviewed by a researcher twice per year to determine how the adoption process was affecting the child. No one was told that identical siblings were being separated and studied. Eddy, Bobby, and David became unwitting parts of this research.

Everything seemed to be going great for the triplets, until even more disturbing details of the experiment unraveled. As the brothers shared details of their lives, they realized that all three had struggled with mental health. Eddy and David had both been admitted to psychiatric hospitals as teenagers. Bobby was on probation after a series of tragic decisions related to a robbery that had ended in a woman being murdered. They compared notes with other twins who had been used in the study. It ended up that Neubauer wasn't just interested in comparing genetics and childhood development generally. The research team specifically selected twins and triplets who had been born to parents with mental health difficulties. Furthermore, they placed the twins and triplets with parents of various socioeconomic backgrounds—working, middle, and upper class. Neubauer studied how

---

1. Among other reasons to revisit Galton's methods (including the aforementioned flaw in his research approach) was his being a founder of the eugenics movement and a proponent of racist science.

2. Research shows that people change their behavior when they know they are being studied. In order to determine an accurate result from a study, it's important to set up the methods so the subjects don't know the purpose of the study—or, ideally, that they are being studied at all.

genes and the socioeconomic situation in which children are raised affect the passing of mental health challenges from parent to child.

The brothers' difficulties with mental health continued as they grew older, especially for Eddy. David and Bobby grew closer while Eddy felt more and more like an outsider and showed increasing signs of bipolar disorder. He struggled in private more each year, until, in 1995, he took his own life.

We will never know if Eddy would still be alive today if Neubauer hadn't selected him as a study subject. No doubt his life would have been different if one set of parents had raised the three brothers, and if they knew about their mother's struggle with her mental health.

It is difficult to draw accurate conclusions from a single case such as the story of Eddy, Bobby, and David. Peter Neubauer died in 2008. The study's results will be locked in a vault at Yale University until 2065—which might sound like an Indiana Jones plot point if it weren't so tragic. Louise Wise Services went bankrupt. Living researchers involved in the research claim to know little of the results or refuse to answer questions. TV producers turned the story of the brothers into a documentary titled *Three Identical Strangers*. This public exposure has increased pressure for the researchers to release their records, but as I write this, they haven't done so.

...

If you're like most people, there are aspects of yourself or your life that you might like to change. You may wish for a fatter wallet, a better sex life, or freedom from addiction. But regardless of what you want to improve about yourself, you must start by understanding who you are now and how you became that way. To skip this step would be like getting directions to someplace without knowing your starting point. In other words, you will be far better equipped to move from point A to point B if you fully understand what it means to be at point A and how you got there in the first place.

To help you explore who you are today, we will survey a number of theories that explain how we came to believe what we do, starting with a discussion on the ways natural and nurturing forces work together to form much of our physical and mental state. Then we will unpack how a third force—our previous choices—affects us in ways over which our current self has little control. Last, I'll share a case study of these principles in action by telling a story from my personal journey.

Nature vs. Nurture

The twin study method pioneered by theorists like Galton and Neubauer seeks to understand how much of our selves would remain if we had been raised differently. In the case of Eddy, Bobby, and David, the brothers would have had different lives if they had been raised together. But how different? Researchers frame the answer to the question of the origin of our worldview as a battle between *nature* and *nurture*, which can be depicted as the two overlapping sides of a Venn diagram.

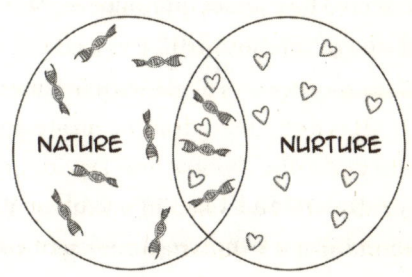

What kind of person would you be if you had lived from birth to this day in complete isolation from all human contact? What if you hadn't had access to books, movies, paintings, music, and oral traditions? You might find yourself grunting and making cave drawings instead of sending text messages or driving a car. Even the DNA of a genius like Leonardo da Vinci would do little good for a person with no one to learn from. Quite a few Maya Angelous and Sonia Sotomayors have likely come and gone from our planet without history taking notice because they happened to be born in the wrong time and place.

Imagining how different we might be under such dramatic circumstances isn't challenging, but what if you had lived during the Crusades? Would you have supported the slaughter of millions of people so Christians could take Jerusalem from the Muslims who lived there? Your answer likely depends on whether you had been born Christian, Muslim, or any number of other possibilities at the time. If you had lived in Japan during World War II, would you have cheered or mourned the destruction of Pearl Harbor? Or, if you lived in Germany, would you have supported or opposed Nazism?

Most people agree that the time and place of our birth affect who we become, but this line of thinking becomes very uncomfortable for many when they carry it through to the logical conclusion. If you had been born into different circumstances, you might have found yourself crossing nervously to the opposite side of the street upon seeing this alternate version of you approaching. This other you might hate the people you love. You might even find yourself and your variant on opposite sides of a religious war, one in which you both label the other as evil. It's difficult to accept that a version of you born in a different year and location might see you as a depraved soul. And while time and place affect who we become, *the real contrast between all these circumstances is the people in them, and how they would influence you.* All of these examples of how we might be different had we been raised in different circumstances highlight aspects of ourselves that are possible to change through relationshift.

The Blank Book

To understand the impact of relationshift further, imagine that each of us is born a blank book. We are a finite resource and each life contains a certain number of pages. As we move through life, we loan these empty sheets to those in our proximity: the people we associate with, listen to, or sleep with; the people whose manifestos we read and whose music we listen to; the actors and writers of the movies we watch; and the politicians we support.

As we moved through early adolescence, the adults in our life controlled access to our book. In these pages, our mom or dad or our friends, siblings, and teachers wrote. So also did our abusers, crushes, bullies, mentors, and spiritual advisers. Over time, most people take control of their lives by granting or limiting access to their pages. If they choose, a fifteen-year-old can take their book away from their guardians and give it to whoever they like. However, what we do with our pages as we take control of them is affected by what exists in our book. Children who are treated well by their parents are unlikely to take many pages away, even after realizing they can.

Inversely, children who hate their mothers or fathers already might have given their pages to other influences before the parents even realize it. Whoever has possession of our pages may write whatever they wish, as long as we allow them. And so life continues this way until we meet Death, who signs her name on our final, incomplete page.

In some cases, the people who write on our pages may leave an unintentional story behind. Your parents might attempt to write about love in your pages by telling you how to find a suitable partner and how to treat them with respect. But if they act hatefully toward each other, the story they write will be very different from what they intend—perhaps that relationships can be dangerous to your mental health. If your dad is kind to your mom, he is writing in your book about how we expect husbands to treat their wives in a loving relationship. Or, if we hate him because he wrote abuse into our pages, then we might read what he wrote about his love of our mother as hypocrisy or as a mask of a false perfection to cover up a secret black heart.

Most of us simply allow whoever happens to have acquired our pages over time to write whatever they wish, whether good or bad. When certain people write awful things therein, we can find it difficult and uncomfortable to reclaim our pages from them. This is the case with negative peer pressure, but it's also what enables many abusive relationships. Great courage is required to wrest our book from these hurtful people's hands and give it to someone who will write kinder things in our pages. Sadly, because of what is in our book, many of us cannot do this difficult task independently—and so, tragically, we are stuck. Too many of our pages are in the hands of people who are using them for ill—and worse, the abusive people writing these terrible things are experts at making sure their victim's book remains entirely in their control.

> "Keep away from people who try to belittle your ambitions. Small people always do that, but the really great make you feel that you, too, can become great."
>
> **Mark Twain**

The impact people have on us is reflected in what they write in our pages. Whether we are aware of this process doesn't change the fact that we are being shifted by those around us, in one direction or another. Making the most of relationshift means that we can better control who we are becoming by growing more aware of what we allow to be written in our pages and adjusting who has access to them, according to who we desire to become.

> ### A Note on How to Regain Agency Over One's Pages in Difficult Situations
>
> If someone in your life is in this situation, you may find that your best chance of helping them is to do the best you can with the limited number of pages you can access. Focus on gaining more access to their book over time and writing good things there, words of strength and truth. And if you are personally stuck in this situation, seek whatever help is necessary to give you the edge you need to sever others' control over your pages and reclaim your book. If you have no friends, family, or mentors to lean on, look elsewhere. Books, nonprofits, and hotlines—even mental health influencers—may be able to help when we have no one else. Make a positive move, no matter how small, whether that's seeking the help of a nonprofit or calling a free hotline to speak to a trained professional. Once you have done this, make another small positive change, then another, until you find yourself gaining momentum toward a healthier situation.

Pause to reflect

- Who has authored the most impactful pages of your book?
- What passages in your book have formed the most foundational elements of your life and personality?
- Are there passages in your book that are holding you back or hurting you? What can you do to minimize the impact of these pages going forward?
- What are you writing in the pages of those who have allowed you to write in their book?
- Can you grow in your positive impact by changing what you're writing in the books of others?

Relationships and Human Evolution

We gape in awe at all that we humans accomplished. Space flight. The Large Hadron collider. We may not have self-driving cars yet, but you can be damn proud that we at least have self-driving vacuum cleaners. We've been so successful as a species that we're on the verge of destroying our habitat and everything in it—something of a mark against our superiority, but that's another book. We especially love to credit our superior intelligence as the reason we've been able to overcome our weaknesses and move from being cave dwellers in the middle of the food chain to the most dominant life form in the known universe. But that's not the only reason. A primary factor in our success as a species is that we have refined the art of relationships.

Go far back in time, to when humans didn't yet have language skills. We had not quite become the preeminent species that we are now. Before we discovered fire or invented the first weapons that allowed us to kill at a safer distance, our survival was far from assured. At least ten varieties of humans didn't make it to modernity. We survived because we had one surprisingly simple edge over other animals at the time: being the world's best communicators.

Humans are not unique in their ability to communicate. Initially, we were just a little better at it than our fellow earthlings, but this small edge made it possible to practice and develop our skills. Soon we gained more advanced abilities for sharing detailed information. This enabled us to invent systems to maximize these abilities, such as a symbol schema that makes possible the sharing of unlimited volumes of information to billions of people instantly, with excellent accuracy.

As our ability to coordinate more extensive groups of people improved, our small tribes began to grow into villages, towns, and then cities. We learned to travel farther to trade goods and information. What we picked up from the people we met, we taught to our children. Over many thousands of years, we slowly discovered or invented every aspect of our modern world, from political systems and religion to ever more efficient technology and even the ability to extend our lives with science. With each year that passes, we use our advantage to widen the gap between us and the world from which we evolved. Yet we are largely the same biologically as we were one hundred thousand years ago. So our dominance as a species was born not from our natural intelligence alone but because we used the small edge we possessed to influence and learn from each other.

The difference between modern civilization and the circumstances of the first humans was enabled largely by our ability to influence each other in complex ways. Relationships between humans are responsible for our transformation from an animal barely more advanced than a chimpanzee to what we are today—capable of building a Wi-Fi-enabled toilet that, upon verbal command, will shoot water at your bum. How far we've come!

Peer Pressure in Action

Since your first breath, people have been nurturing you to think a particular way. This programming process, or "domestication," as many put it, is uncomfortably similar to how we train animals. If you return home to find that your cat has peed on your pumps, you might put on a big frowny face and say things like, "Bad Fluffy! These are Mommy's shoes. You're supposed to pee on this copy of the *New York Post*." In fact, over thousands of years, humans selectively bred and trained many animals to fit better within human society.

We succeeded in making animals act more like humans, but we didn't stop there. Pruning plants is another form of nurturing. We do this to make them healthier, produce more fruit, and shape their growth. We even domesticate fields to optimize them for farming. As long as humans have been humans, we have been engaging in this same process with pretty much anything we can get our hands on, including each other. Though we may not call it by this name, we are always trying to relationshift each other.

For many millennia, being cast out of our tribe was a death sentence. So we evolved to crave the feel-good chemicals that get pumped through our brain when we feel accepted. This is why we so often go to great lengths to fit in. Studies have shown how enormously powerful this desire is. In one, researchers showed a group of actors and one study participant three lines of various lengths, then asked them to identify the longest. The actors all confidently choose the wrong answer. The study participant, who went last, chose the same wrong answer as the actors 75 percent of the time. (So the next time someone asks you if you would follow your friends off a cliff, you can answer with a relatively high level of confidence, "Three times out of four, yes!") In another study, researchers quizzed volunteers on various preferences for cuisine, hobbies, politics, family planning, and so on. The participants were later observed in a speed-dating scenario. Researchers found that many volunteers changed their preferences to match the person they were speaking with. This is peer pressure in action.

We also limit access to certain peers to control what people believe. Many cults and religions teach adherents that they should be careful about spending time with those who do not have the same belief system. That's one reason why religious schools and universities exist: to ensure younger generations aren't drawn away through exposure to different views. Many religions and cults forbid partnering with or marrying nonbelievers. Some cults go as far as physically isolating their followers in camps and compounds far from any urban area. This is a critical factor in ensuring members maintain their views.

Remember when your mom didn't want you hanging around *those* kids—the ones who smoked cigarettes, wore too much makeup, or had a key to their parents' porn cabinet. She knew the power of relationships—how likely you were to pick up the habits, characteristics, language, and life direction of whoever you spent time with. Entrepreneur and author Jim Rohn famously posits, "You're the average of the five people you spend the most time with." The idea is so ubiquitous now that almost anyone could have said it—even your mom.

> "Tell me with whom you associate, and I will tell you who you are."
>
> Johann Wolfgang von Goethe

Fortunately, we don't pick up just the bad habits of our friends. Their healthy traits inspire us, too. Research shows that our peers can make us more ambitious, creative, intelligent, and hardworking. Having athletic friends can help us lose weight—a little bitterness goes a long way—and spending time with strong-willed people can help us gain self-control. Academics have shown that the practice of investing in our network is the number one way to increase our financial success. Our peers even influence our physical appearance. The clothes we wear, whether we have tattoos and piercings, the way we style our hair, the makeup we may or may not put on, and our weight are all influenced over time by the people brushing their teeth next to us each morning, those we meet for lunch, and the cranky uncle we argue with during holiday dinners.

Humans use many tools to teach each other how we feel people ought to behave. Oral tradition, discipline, politics, judicial systems, mentoring, storytelling, pop culture, music, art, and religion are just a few. Some of our codes are agreed upon across a political entity as laws. But even laws are continuously debated because we all have a different idea of how the world should be. This is because each of us has a unique set of experiences and combination of inputs that lead to our current position on any given subject.

The next time you hear a song, listen to how the writer has embedded societal messaging that stems from our evolutionary instincts into the lyrics—instincts we will explore in much greater detail in chapter five. Musicians package their way of seeing the world, or at least a way of seeing the world they feel their audience wants reinforced, into a danceable groove with a catchy melody optimized for memorization. When we find ourselves singing in the shower,

> "Most people want so desperately to be an individual yet are so easily shaped by the media."
>
> Criss Jami

we are reciting the artist's prescribed worldview to ourselves. The same process of promoting ideas about how to live happens in every movie, novel, sermon, and stump speech.

Of course, hardly any of this is conscious. It's not as if musicians and Hollywood are coordinating with political leaders to control the population. And yet, any number of examples show how an artist's worldview is part of their creative work. Among many lessons, the movie *Goodfellas* initially seems to teach us that crime is exciting and, of course, not to cross Joe Pesci. But in the end, the film concludes all the fun was in vain because everyone will eventually die, go to jail, or, in the film's last line, "live the rest of my life like a schnook." In *The Communist Manifesto*, Karl Marx teaches us that we should all come together and share resources to ensure that everyone is taken care of equally. George Orwell wrote *Animal Farm* to teach us that overthrowing a dictator can result in yet another ruling class exploiting the masses for personal gain. And in the song "Wet Ass Pussy," Cardi B and Megan Thee Stallion argue that women should celebrate their sexuality, success, and power as a counterpoint to the male-centric messaging of most rap music. One could debate any of the above interpretations, but the fact remains: the creators of these works are making a statement that is designed to influence their audience.

The people in your life and the society you've lived in have programmed you into the person you are. But the power of relationshift lies in more than just understanding how we became the people we are today. Rather, we want to learn to use this understanding to change who we are becoming. Once we grasp how relationships affect the way we see our options, we can begin to make better use of relationshift to change the way we see the world, and in so doing grow more into the person we want to be. This is the subject we will explore next, beginning with a story from my own life.

> "People make you. People break you. People heal you. People save you."
>
> Ritu Ghatourey

The Third Force

A few months after we ran away from my dad in the night, my family moved to Vista, California, where we found a stepdad, two stepsisters, and Jesus. Religion provided me a simple framework through which to understand the world. Going to church is good. Sneaking into the county fair without paying is bad. Making my complex world feel understandable was an attractive feeling. And my Sunday school teachers were persuasive, especially when they brought us jelly doughnuts. They explained that my dad did bad things because he didn't have Jesus inside to help him make the right decisions. Accepting religion was not only a way to fit in and please the mentors in my life, but also a way to guarantee I wouldn't become like my dad. How could I, if the creator of the universe himself was willing to help me be a good boy? This is a clear example of how authorities in my life were relationshifting me by filling my blank pages with what they believed would help me live a happier life.

The religious influences around me wanted me to be an apple that fell far from the tree—to be a better man than my dad had become. This might seem to imply that I would focus on becoming a moral man of God. But my interpretation was a little different. My dad was a petty drug dealer, so I decided to become what I considered to be the most opposite of him that I could imagine: a successful businessman. But as is usually the case with a son trying to be different from his dad, the child usually ends up quite a bit more like his father than he would like to admit.

Around sixth grade, I started selling Lemonheads and Red Hots in the back row of math class. Before long, a competing eighth-grade candy dealer got jealous of all that coin rattling around in my pockets. He ratted me out, and I got to experience my first of many school suspensions. My dad was a con man who used his genius to devise moneymaking strategies like buying something at Walmart on sale, then returning it to Target later that day for a tidy $10 profit. I had my own ideas—like forging a driver's license so I could sign up for online gambling at age fourteen. I found a few "proven systems" on message boards and quickly lost $500—the first of many times I've lost my entire life savings.

By the age of seventeen, I had not made much progress in my plan to differentiate myself from my father. And now I had an entirely new difficulty on my hands, leading directly from my own poor decision making. My girlfriend, Anna, was pregnant. The stats on teenage pregnancy are stark. Fewer than half of adolescent parents graduate high school, and only one out of fifty gets a college degree. Two out of three families that start with a teen pregnancy become permanently poor. Despite these facts, my pastor assured me that God was able to help me turn this situation around.

> "I am today what I should have been in the past, however, it was the past that has made me into the person I am today."
>
> **David Kreger**

I had four options: marry Anna, ask her to get an abortion, share custody as single parents, or avoid my responsibilities and disappear. I don't remember considering any alternative but the first. Perhaps I thought back to those Sunday school flannelgraphs that featured the most famous teenage parent of all, Mary—since it had worked out for her, well, it might work for me. Somehow, I knew there was only one option: to marry Anna and begin raising my family. But why did I "know" this to be the right choice? More than five hundred American teenagers face a similar decision every day. Internationally, that number rises to more than twenty million per year. Of those four alternatives, adolescent American would-be parents split just about evenly. Approximately one-quarter chooses marriage. One-quarter decides on abortion. A third quarter chooses cohabitation or shared support. And in the final 25 percent, teenage fathers avoid supporting or maintaining contact with their child.

If my course was so apparent to me, why do 75 percent of people take another? My choice was the result of my worldview, arising from a combination of genetic makeup and the impact of people in my life up until that point—the messages those people had written into the pages of my life. But something is missing from this equation. Long before I decided to marry Anna, I had become a Christian. This decision was partly due to religious exposure through my relationships—Sunday school teachers, parents, mentors, friends, and other family members. Yet this was a decision I made, and it affected the way I would view my options from that day forward.

In the following years, I became more interested in what the Bible and my pastors said about how I should act. This, and many other influences, led to a string of decisions, each one affecting the next. As a result, when faced with a significant life decision ten years later, I didn't consider three of my four options as viable alternatives. This example sheds new light on our two-sided Venn diagram model for understanding the origin of our worldview. We become the person we are today not because of two forces, but three: *nature, nurture,* and *previous choices,* each of which affects the other.

THE THREE FORCES THAT FORM US INTO WHO WE ARE

NATURE • NURTURE • CHOICES

Weighing Our Options

During many decisions, our subconscious is a lot busier than our conscious mind. Often without realizing it, we weigh each factor in the decision by importance, then choose the option that, at that moment, we perceive as most important to us. As we reflect on these scenarios of choice, a counterintuitive truth emerges: we always do what we want. Even when we feel we are doing something we'd rather avoid, our subconscious mind drives us to satisfy deeper ingrained desires.

Grocery choices are one example. Let's say I've committed to getting into shape but find a package of Double Stuf Oreos in my basket when I reach the checkout. Did I mistake them for a vegetable? Or did the temptation of glorious carbohydrates temporarily weigh in as a higher priority than losing those love handles? I may tell myself I'm committed to getting into shape, but when I placed cookies in my shopping cart, I was choosing what I wanted most at that moment: to satisfy my sweet tooth instead of trimming my waistline. In another example, one might be forced to decide whether or not to euthanize their cat. Few people want to terminate a beloved family pet. Yet we do it because we would rather not see the animal suffer. So we actually do want to. We want to help the animal avoid suffering more than we want to avoid the emotional pain of losing our pet.

> "Free will is an illusion. People always choose the perceived path of greatest pleasure."
>
> Scott Adams

Yet when two people experience the same choice under similar circumstances, they do not necessarily both choose the same option. One person

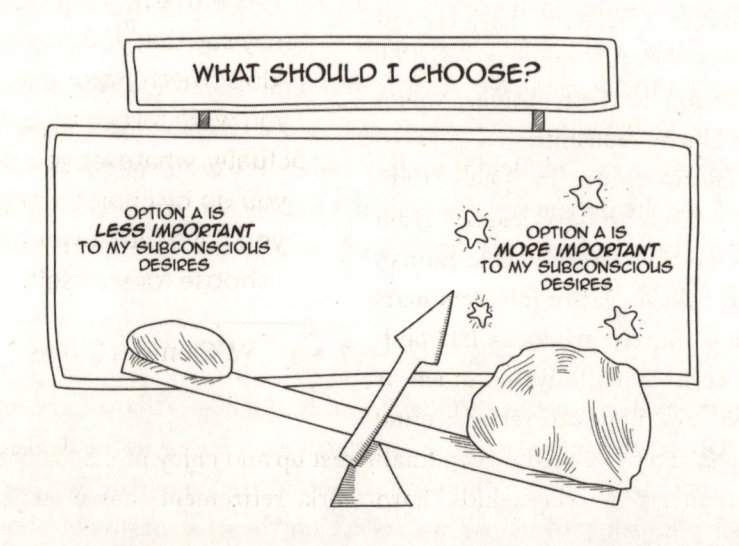

SHOULD I EUTHANIZE MY CAT?

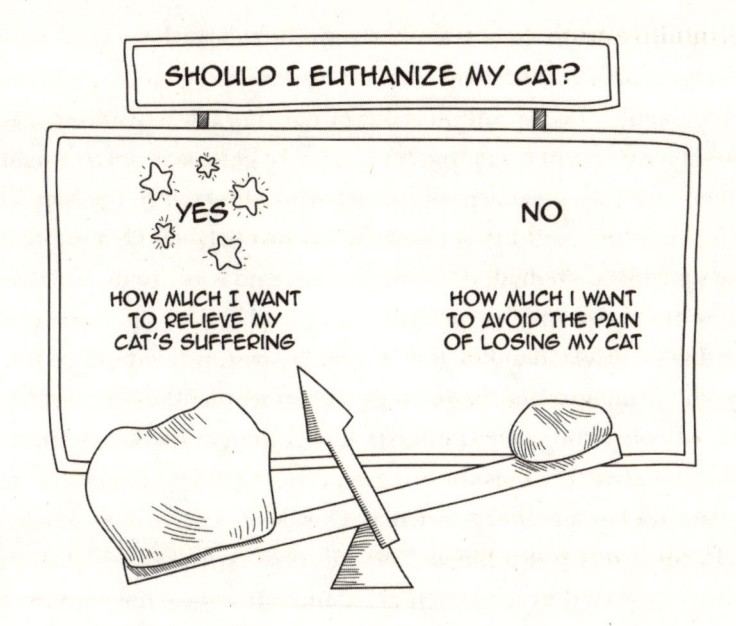

YES — HOW MUCH I WANT TO RELIEVE MY CAT'S SUFFERING

NO — HOW MUCH I WANT TO AVOID THE PAIN OF LOSING MY CAT

gives more weight to saving an animal from suffering by ending its life, while another chooses to let their pet's fate play out naturally. One employee assigns more value to staying at a job they hate to maintain their income, while another quits without the security of already having a better job lined up. The difference between these various scenarios is in the value assigned by each person to their options, values affected by relationshift.

Someone born in 1960s California is likely to have learned from childhood that a responsible human goes to college, gets a job, gets married in a church, produces 1.93 children, works hard, buys as much as possible, and hopes to retire around the age of sixty-five so they can finally rest up and enjoy life. Each of these goals—college, marriage, kids, hard work, retirement—has a subjective

> "You always do what you want to do. This is true with every act. You may say that you had to do something, or that you were forced to, but actually, whatever you do, you do by choice. Only you have the power to choose for yourself."
>
> W. Clement Stone

value that depends on the person. Whoever is taught these goals are valuable will give them precedence over other options.

Many people believe college is out of reach or a waste of time because their peers have taught them that the option of college is not as valuable as another choice, like getting a job. Many who skip college don't make this choice because they think higher education isn't helpful. They choose a job because without immediate income, they have no way to eat—simple math. Programs or options may be available that could help this person keep food on the table while earning a degree, but such possibilities don't exist for the person who is unaware of them. To gain that information, we must secure access to people with greater understanding about available options.

Not only does relationshift give us access to new ideas; it also affects how we see the options we're aware of. Our desires drive us to assign more or less value to our possibilities. These desires come primarily from how we've been nurtured by friends, family, and our tribe. Our parents, confidants, and mentors teach us that some things are good and others are bad. We see our friends wearing shorts with ironic statements on their butts like "Fauci" or "Daddy's Girl," and we may become more likely to want to wear similar fashions. We hear about a popular political candidate or the newest tech gadget and are likely to want to learn more, just because many other people seem interested.

> "Life is a matter of choices, and every choice you make makes you."
>
> John C. Maxwell

These influences aren't usually conscious. Rather, they are often instinctual, subconscious responses, ones into which we will delve further in chapter five. For now, let's say that much of this effect arises through our desire to earn the love or respect of parents, siblings, friends, bosses, partners, leaders, and even strangers by adapting our personality, preferences, and positions to fit in.

Facing a teenage pregnancy, I didn't consider the options chosen by 75 percent of people in my situation (abortion, abandonment, or raising the child separately) because I saw the world through a different lens than those who chose another path. As a result, I weighed my options differently than they did. This is true of any choice we face, whether we're deciding where to spend our retirement or scrolling for a show to watch on Netflix when we can't sleep. We rarely consider all our options, and those we do deliberate will be evaluated through a personal lens built on what has been written in our pages.

This can all be difficult to analyze in real life. Our journeys include countless decisions that have all been affected by myriad other forces—any of which could have a far-reaching impact on how our lives unfold. And every time we make a choice, our available options change, as well as the values we assign to them. So the most we can ever do is make the best choice we can, given where we are at in life, when these options are presented. But we can give ourselves access to more possibilities, and value those paths with greater accuracy, by spending time with people who have the knowledge we need to do so. Making the most of relationshift requires us to do just that.

Current Choices Affect Future Options

We can make better use of relationshift by understanding how much impact our current choices have on the options we will have available to us in the future. But before we can make the most of this power, we must fully accept that we cannot change the past, and we do ourselves no favors wishing we could.

Life is not like the movie *Back to the Future*. Once I discovered I was becoming a father at the age of seventeen, I could not go back and undo the decisions that had led to that moment. I could only decide based on my current situation with the knowledge, personality, preferences, and worldview I possessed at that time. When we return a pair of pants that don't fit, we're not undoing the decision to purchase the pants. Likewise, when we go back to work for a company we had previously quit, we're not undoing the decision to leave. We're making a new decision based on our current options.

> "Your life changes the moment you make a new, congruent, and committed decision."
>
> Anthony Robbins

The human system is what is known as a *type II chaotic system*. That's just an academic way of describing how we react to information that changes our next outcome.[3] But we never perfectly know what will and won't work before we try. This can lead us to base false conclusions on the outcomes of our decisions. For example, let's say your parents advised you to go to college to get a better job. So you earn a degree in computer science and begin working as a programmer at Netflix. On the way to work one day, you meet someone at a coffee shop who ends up partnering with you to start a company that is unrelated to your degree. Should you be angry with your parents for giving you bad advice about going to college? After all, you spent four years learning about computer science and now use none of that knowledge. On the other hand, you wouldn't have met

> You can't go back and change the beginning, but you can start where you are and change the ending.
>
> C. S. Lewis

TYPE II CHAOS SYSTEM

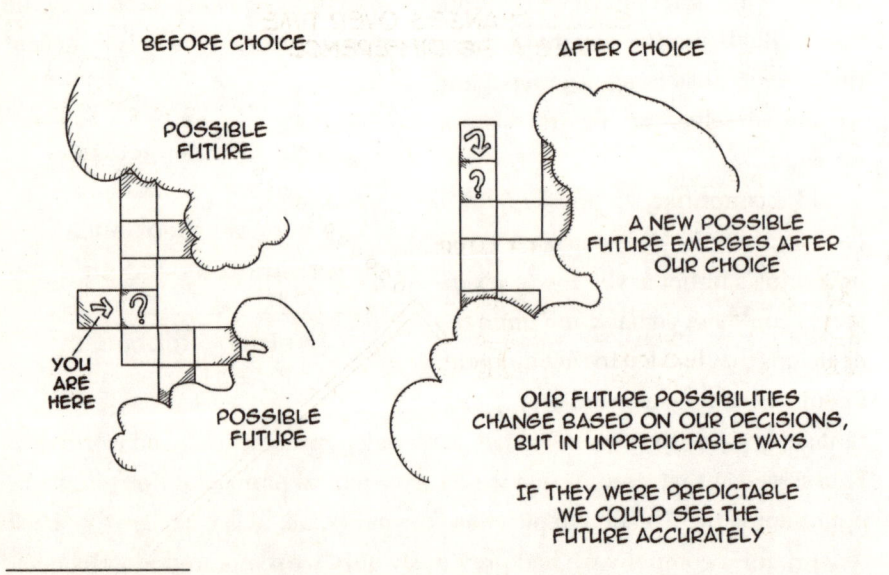

BEFORE CHOICE

POSSIBLE FUTURE

YOU ARE HERE

POSSIBLE FUTURE

AFTER CHOICE

A NEW POSSIBLE FUTURE EMERGES AFTER OUR CHOICE

OUR FUTURE POSSIBILITIES CHANGE BASED ON OUR DECISIONS, BUT IN UNPREDICTABLE WAYS

IF THEY WERE PREDICTABLE WE COULD SEE THE FUTURE ACCURATELY

---

3. In contrast, a type I chaotic system does not respond to predictions or choices. Weather is an excellent example of first-order chaos.

this business partner if you hadn't gotten a job at Netflix, one that required a college education.

Every choice changes our possibilities, often in unpredictable ways. Not only does this describe our past and how we became the person we are today, but it shows us how we can dramatically improve our future with the decisions we are making right now. We don't usually create radical change by leaping straight from where we are to where we want to be. We tend to make big improvements to our life with small, strategic decisions that compound over time in much the same way as a ship leaving San Francisco could end up in either Japan or Australia with just a few small adjustments to the rudder. Certain people can help you see your options today in such a way as to give you access to even more helpful people, who, in turn, help you see possibilities that you can't even

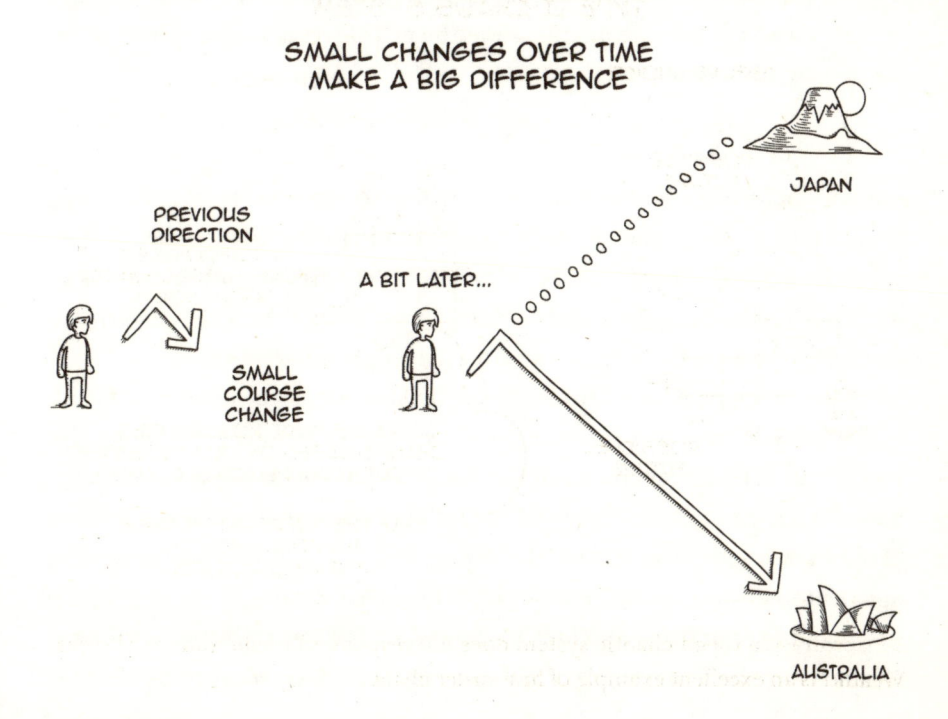

> "Every now and again your life's course can turn on one simple thing, some small decision the import of which isn't at all obvious at the time."
>
> — Debra Hamel

SMALL CHANGES OVER TIME MAKE A BIG DIFFERENCE

PREVIOUS DIRECTION

SMALL COURSE CHANGE

A BIT LATER...

JAPAN

AUSTRALIA

conceive of now, and so on. That's the kind of positive, self-reinforcing cycle that can transform you into almost anything you want to be, no matter how audacious your dreams are.

Pause to reflect

- What are some ways you can increase the number and quality of your options?
- Do you regret any past choices in a way that is negatively affecting you today? How can you let go of these regrets?
- Think about an important choice you face and the possible paths you are considering. Why do you view each option the way you do? Are there options you aren't considering? Why? Whose influence affects how you view these options? Do you think your current approach is the best way to weigh your possibilities, or are you simply reflecting the views of whoever influenced you, for better or worse?
- What choices can you make today that will have a significant positive impact on the well-being of your future self? What changes can you execute in the short term that you might someday be thankful you made?

• • •

A month before my hastily planned wedding to the mother of my coming child, I met with my pastor Clyde to tell him I was having a baby. He had a dark beard and aviator glasses. When not preaching, he often dressed in worn-out Carhartt jackets and Dickies jeans. Tools, like a nail gun and a worm drive saw, filled any gaps around the edges of his room.

A long silence followed my confession. After a while, Clyde simply said, "I thought you were better than this." I cried. We talked a bit longer. He hugged me as I left and promised that God could redeem me, even amid my darkest sins—something I'd heard before but hadn't yet experienced. Jesus could walk on water and raise the dead back to life, but it was becoming apparent that I was too difficult a case for him to take on.

About forty friends and family showed up for the marriage ceremony. We held it in the living room of my soon-to-be in-laws' country home. Our wedding presents fit neatly on an end table. The cake was from Costco. Smiles were scarce. I could almost hear the whispers of people debating how long our relationship would last. Most of those in attendance were Christian, as was nearly everyone I knew. No one seemed to know how to respond to the situation. Our belief system was based on the idea that God loved everyone, no matter how much of a sinner they were. But in my circumstance, the most important people in my life apparently felt I needed a different kind of love—more like that of a father who spanks his children when they misbehave in order to correct a character flaw.

Our church was small, so Pastor Clyde worked construction on the side to pay the bills. He taught me how to build just about anything, skills that would shape my life in ways I couldn't have imagined at the time. My friends and I attended church youth group events at Clyde's house. As our church didn't believe in sacraments, Clyde liked to joke that chips and salsa were our communion. We played billiards and listened to artists like Nickelback, Smashing Pumpkins, and Alanis Morissette. Yes, blasting "Rockstar" was part of some of the happiest times of my teenage years. It was the nineties. Don't judge.

After the wedding, I hoped things could remain much as they were before—the chips and salsa, the friends, billiards, and grunge music. But when I sat in the pews each Sunday, I felt invisible to everyone I'd grown up around. I think they tried to love me, but in the end their actions spoke louder than words. It was clear I didn't belong anymore.

My church's reaction hurt me for many years, but no longer. Today I believe they did the best they could, given the course of events that had led to who they were when I intersected with their lives. Their response was affected by their worldview, which was formed from past decisions, nurturing forces, and the situation into which they were born. We simply cannot approach any situation without bias that has been built by many factors outside our control. This lens is central to who we are.

This book is about exploring who we are and how we can change into someone new. Some may wish to form new habits, achieve a goal, or reach the next step in their career. Others may simply want to live a happier, more fulfilling life. No matter who you would like to be, we know that who we are today is a factor of nature, nurturing, and previous choices. We also understand that each of these forces affects the others. The nature side of us—our

DNA, where and when we were born, and so forth—changes how people nurture us. How we are raised affects how we view and make choices. Even our genes can be affected by choices and how we are nurtured.

We've discussed how you can curate the traits you want to embody by channeling those you know who best live them out. You can take control of who is writing in your pages to ensure you like what is being written there and that these influences are helping you become more of the person you want to be. And yet, ultimately, all you have control over is your current choice, as constrained by your bias and worldview. This, in turn, affects how you view your possibilities. You can learn through relationships to expand your opportunities and to see your alternatives more accurately. This, in turn, creates an even more expanded worldview that opens the doors to connections that can help you grow even further. All of this takes time and effort and many small choices that you hope will pay off—but you can never be quite sure until you get a little further down the road. The process can be messy, non-linear, and unpredictable, but it can also be positively transformative beyond your current ability to imagine.

This is *relationshift*.

CHAPTER 2

How Relationshift Works

> "If I have seen further it is by standing on the shoulders of giants."
>
> Isaac Newton

New York City, 1981.

Sixteen-year-old Mike was lucky to have intellectuals for parents. As long as grades didn't suffer, he could do nearly anything he wanted. Drinking, smoking, and dive bar shows late on school nights were common. One of those nights would change Mike's life forever—and as a result, the future of music, too.

The Washington, DC–based hard-core punk band Bad Brains was about to take the stage at Botany Talk House in Manhattan's Chelsea neighborhood. Mike showed up in homemade bondage pants and a spray-painted eighty-nine-cent shirt. Hard-core wasn't remotely mainstream in the early eighties, but Mike was still surprised to find just a dozen or so kids gathered near the stage. Only one seemed close to Mike's age: a skinny boy in a trench coat with a few homemade buttons and combat boots. His name was Adam.

Bad Brains was raucous, loud, and irreverent—everything the small audience craved. Perhaps that would have been it: just a fun night. But after the show, Mike gave his phone number to Adam. Being a couple of the only kids in the world who were into hard-core punk at the time, they were soon fast friends.

The two boys soon met another kid with similar tastes in mix tapes and torn skinny jeans. His name was Adam, too. These three middle-class teenagers were born to unknown sixties-era New York artists. Their friendship was not particularly remarkable. Though each was undoubtedly talented in his own right, it seems doubtful we would know their names if they had not become friends.

The band they went on to create was initially known for offensive lyrics and pissing off audiences in the hopes of being more memorable. Villainized by middle America, banned by preachers and parents but idolized by teenagers around the world, they brought an entirely new sound to the masses, selling more than twenty million albums. Separate from each other, Mike Diamond, Adam Horovitz, and Adam Yauch were just three small fish in a massive pond. But together, they became rich and famous, playing a significant role in the popularization of hip-hop—an entirely new genre of music at the time. They were, of course, the Beastie Boys.

> "There's an even rarer friend: the one that gets you motivated. The one that not only gets themselves going and doing great things but says: we should all get together and do this. And then does it. Adam Yauch was that type of friend."
>
> **Adam Horovitz**

Early on, after the band lost interest in hard-core, they turned to rap. They wrote a few songs and performed a couple of shows. With their local popularity growing, the industry started to take notice. Adam Horovitz's DJ friend Rick Rubin introduced the Beastie Boys to Russell Simmons—then the world's top hip-hop manager. He pitched the Boys to Freddy DeMann, manager of a young rising star by the name of Madonna. Freddy wanted

Run-DMC as the opening act, but their price was twenty thousand dollars a show. Russell said the Beastie Boys would take the gig for five hundred bucks. Soon they were touring with Madonna and riding the success of her breakout hit "Like a Virgin."

The band knew this was a once-in-a-lifetime chance to make their mark on the music world. But lots of groups open for big-time artists and never make it on their own. The Beastie Boys knew they needed to maximize this exposure by being as memorable as they could. Imagine all the different ways you might approach this opportunity. You could get singing lessons or coaching to improve your stage presence. You could dress flamboyantly like Lady Gaga and barbecue your meat dress at the end of each show to celebrate. You could write hypersexualized music. You might even attempt to parachute into the stadium, landing on the stage right at the start of your set. And if it goes badly, you might need to be airlifted out.

The Beastie Boys had their own simple plan for becoming memorable: they would master the art of obnoxiousness. They taunted the crowd and generally acted like asses during their entire set. Then, for their final song, a large box opened on the stage behind the band. Out of it popped a ten-foot-tall penis.

Their plan must have worked, because here we are talking about them more than thirty-five years later. But before the Beastie Boys could enjoy their success, countless pieces had to fall into just the right places, including someone thinking up a unique way to become memorable when opening for a bright new star. While we may not know the exact path each of these factors took to appear, we do know that the forces responsible for the rise of the Beastie Boys are the result of a particular string of connections (see figure on next page).

It's easy to miss the importance of relationships because they are such an everyday aspect of life. But you would never have heard of any of those seven people if not for the connections that made them who they became. As the old proverb goes, "It takes a village to raise a giant hydraulic penis." And their story is an excellent example of how we can be positively relationshifted by the people we surround ourselves with.

In this chapter, we are going to deconstruct the basics of using relationshift to change into the person you want to be. We will dive deeper into how the particular "village" detailed in the story of the Beastie Boys propelled them to such phenomenal success. We will delve into how to get

Mike Diamond + Adam Yauch + Adam Horovitz + Rick Rubin + Russell Simmons + Freddy DeMann + Madonna = Big Break

high-caliber people to help you transform yourself, and we will unpack the key facets of an academic principle known as social capital. This construct defines the value one can extract from one's relationships, and you must master it to make your journey toward relationshift most worthwhile. But first, let's discuss a critical concept I call transformational gravity—or simply gravity—which can help you move further and faster toward your most audacious goals.

Transformational Gravity

No basketball team had ever come back to win a championship after being down three games to one in an NBA final series until the Cleveland Cavaliers beat the Golden State Warriors of San Francisco in game seven of the 2016 NBA finals. This astonishing win was all the more impressive after Cleveland dropped three of the first four games to a team with better players, a better record, and all the momentum. Every expert predicted the Warriors would win the series. They had several of the world's best players, including Stephen Curry, newly dubbed the first unanimous league MVP in NBA history. So, if winning was such a lock, why didn't the Warriors close the deal?

In the movie *Moneyball*, a math whiz with limited sports knowledge used statistics to improve baseball. I realize this sounds like a terrible premise for a film, but it was actually pretty good. Using these principles, the NBA developed a player-comparison method that didn't just look at their basic stats—points, rebounds, assists, steals, and so on. One particular rating emerged as critical to understanding how each player affects the team's chances of winning: the plus/minus. This statistic measures the number of points scored while a particular player is on the court, regardless of who else might be playing. For example, if Stephen Curry has a +10 rating, this means his team scores ten more points than their opponents over an average one hundred possessions. This statistic is valuable because it measures a player's impact equally, whether they focus on offense, defense, or even boosting the other players on the court with their energy. In short, the plus/minus rating shows how much a player improves his teammates.

When a team loses a game it should win, it's most often because their star player can't play. Yet Stephen Curry played all seven games of the series. In fact, it was the team's center, Draymond Green, who didn't play game five. Can you guess who had the best plus/minus stat on the squad for the first four games of the finals? Draymond Green. While few would consider this big center the best player on the team, he affected their games' outcomes more than any other player. Green was relentless on defense and a great passer. But more than that, he was the team's emotional linchpin. His energy inspired the players around him. Cavaliers superstar LeBron James understood this and capitalized on his absence. By losing game five, San Francisco gave Cleveland one of the most dangerous gifts in sports—hope. The Cavaliers made the most of the Warriors' loss and went on to win the championship.

> "No matter what, no matter how I feel, always bring effort."
>
> **Draymond Green**

The plus/minus statistic is a measure of instant relationshift. The way we change each other isn't just a long-term effect. We can change the people around us or be relationshifted by someone else while we're in each other's presence. As one negative example, consider how normally law-abiding citizens can get caught up in the emotion of a riot and make bad decisions that follow them throughout their lives. This shows how the power of peer pressure can make us better or worse versions of ourselves, and how changing just one relationship can make the difference between being a champion and going home empty-handed.

Another interesting correlation exists between the plus/minus statistic and relationshift. In basketball, some players have more extraordinary talents and can control the outcome of the game more than others. Relationshift has a similar construct: transformational gravity. Some people have the ability to change you more than others, for better or for worse. If someone can pull you toward them with great power and velocity, they have strong gravity. If they don't affect your course or outcome much, their gravitational pull is weak. Think of your personal journey as a dotted line between who you are today and who you want to become. Mentors—people who are further along the journey you wish to travel—pull you toward themselves, and your goal, through the relational tie that binds you.

There are, of course, slow and fast ways to get between two points. Let's say a couple of shivering Canadians wish to enjoy the warm beaches of Zihuatanejo on a two-week holiday in December. They could walk to Mexico, but it will be summer before they arrive. They might drive and enjoy the scenery along the way. This trip would take about a week, giving them just enough time to dip their toes in the ocean before getting back in their car for the weeklong trip home. Or they could take a morning flight and arrive in time for jalapeño margaritas at sunset. Velocity can make the difference between enjoying a lovely holiday on the beach or not arriving at all.

The same is true with life goals. If you want to learn to make better cocktails, hanging around with a friend who is just a little better than you

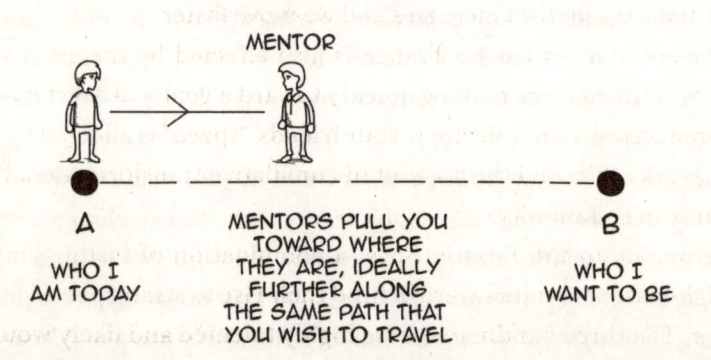

MENTOR

A — WHO I AM TODAY

MENTORS PULL YOU TOWARD WHERE THEY ARE, IDEALLY FURTHER ALONG THE SAME PATH THAT YOU WISH TO TRAVEL

B — WHO I WANT TO BE

LESS PULLING FORCE

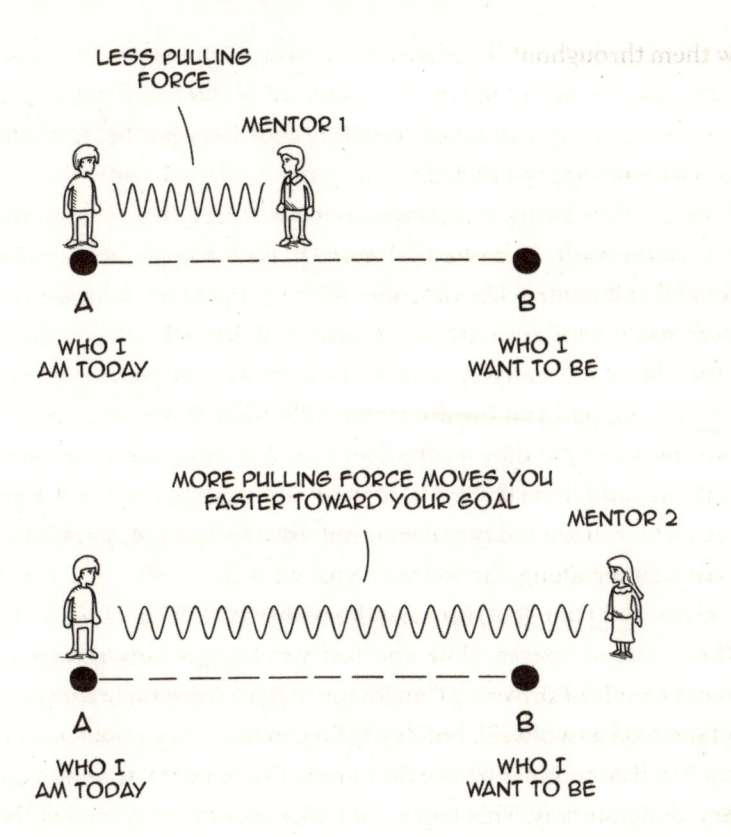

MENTOR 1

A — WHO I AM TODAY
B — WHO I WANT TO BE

MORE PULLING FORCE MOVES YOU FASTER TOWARD YOUR GOAL

MENTOR 2

A — WHO I AM TODAY
B — WHO I WANT TO BE

will help you slightly improve your cocktail-shaking skills. But spending time with an expert bartender would have a much greater impact. If you want to grow rich, Warren Buffett would make a much better mentor than a recently graduated wealth adviser with a 550 credit score. When someone is just a little ahead of us on the path, that person's gravitational pull on us is weak, and we relationshift slower as a result. But when someone is very far ahead, their magnetism increases and we move faster.

The speed at which we change is also affected by the gravity of our peers. Friends who are moving quickly toward a goal will exert more positive force on our own trajectory. Your friends' "speed" is affected by natural talent, work ethic, and the amount of cumulative transformational gravity in their own community.

Returning to the Beastie Boys, a combination of fast-moving peers and high-caliber mentors were behind their rise to stratospheric fame and fortune. The three bandmates were highly talented and likely would have gone on to experience much success even if the band had fallen apart early on or hadn't gotten the chance to open for Madonna. That's not to say they didn't need people to help them relationshift into the band we know today—just that high-caliber people tend to attract other high-caliber people. So, if they hadn't met each other, they likely would have met others who could enable exponential growth. As for the others, Rick Rubin and Russell Simmons had achieved a bit of success by the time they met the Beastie Boys and had the natural talent to propel them to the highest levels of the music industry. Madonna already had enough momentum to earn her a world tour and of course would become one of the most famous musicians ever. So these weren't just seven random people—they were seven of the fastest-moving people in music at the time. That's the level of gravity you need in your community to achieve maximum levels of positive change.

The best athletes have the best coaches. The most outstanding leaders have great luminaries as mentors. Nobel Prize–winning professors do not achieve such a high level of accomplishment without a strong personal network of other high-achieving and brilliant connections. And those entrepreneurs who seem to rise from nothing to become wealthy beyond understanding likely have a cadre of highly successful peers and mentors who helped them along the way.

However, not everyone wants to become rich and famous. Furthermore, the concept of gravity doesn't apply to all goals. If you aspire to live a quiet life alone in the woods, the only mentor you may need is a copy of *Walden*. One doesn't need to marry a world-class dog trainer to have a healthy and happy relationship with their pup. Or you may want to run a little faster to improve your workouts, which doesn't require an Olympic coach—just a running buddy who is fast enough to keep you pushing harder than you would alone.

In chapter four, I detail specific paths for seeking people with gravity. Each has its own approach toward using relationshift. In some, maximum gravity is critical. In others, it's less necessary. But regardless of how fast you want to transform, you're likely to need the help of people you don't already know well. The higher the caliber of the person you seek to add to your network, the more difficult it will be to get their attention.

Pause to reflect

- Who do you know that possesses a lot of transformational gravity? Consider various dimensions (e.g., wealth, charisma, intelligence, happiness) because a mentor can sometimes have a lot of pull in one area and very little in another.
- Have these high-gravity people affected you, either positively or negatively? How much and in what way?
- Which of your goals could be helped most by gaining access to or making more efficient use of your access to high-gravity individuals?

Getting People to Help You

This section outlines four strategies you can use to earn the trust and time of anyone, from a successful business mentor; to a music promoter with access to top local gigs; to the third-greatest WWE fighter of all time, Dwayne "The Rock" Johnson.[1] These strategies are shared tribal affiliation, helpfulness, persistence, and readiness.

Shared Tribal Affiliation

Humans can be surprisingly giving and loving. Yet our species also seems to revel in selfishness and hate. Understanding the circumstances that foster generosity or apathy is one of the keys to understanding how to gain people's help—no matter how high caliber they are.

For most of my life, I assumed getting someone's attention was a numbers game. If I had to ask a hundred people to get one yes, I would need to ask two hundred to get a second yes, and three hundred for a third. Exhausting, yet reliable. As this was the only method I'd discovered that seemed to work, I used it extensively. When beginning my writing career, I queried more than six hundred literary agents before I found one who wanted

---

1. As rated by Kerry Miller of Bleacher Report.

to represent me. After losing everything when my construction company failed, I applied for two thousand positions over nearly a year before finally landing a job. As an amateur salesperson, I often approached hundreds of prospects for every one that said yes.

But if we drill deeper into these examples, we discover that the truth is quite different from what I had assumed. My experience with seeking a literary agent can be divided into two scenarios. In the first, I queried six hundred agents and received six hundred negative responses. A few years later, I queried a single agent and got a yes. With my lengthy job search, I submitted résumés to company after company and received nothing but silence in return. Then I changed my approach and got the next job I applied for. The difference stems from our species's deepest instincts.

Humans developed an intense instinct to help those in our tribe. For millions of years, we depended on shared well-being to survive. If other members of our tribe were well fed, we benefited. Famished people aren't very good at defending their village when the enemy is at the gates. Healthy parents are more likely to produce more vigorous offspring, providing other members of the tribe with mates who are themselves more likely to reproduce successfully. We love to help people in our tribe because it's a way to help ourselves.

Likewise, we are disinclined to help those who are not members of our tribe. We subconsciously perceive outsiders to be a threat. When resources are scarce, we are likely to feel that there isn't enough for everyone. We then prioritize our tribe's well-being over others' due to our desire to ensure our survival.

So the key to getting people to help you is quite simple. You must become a member of their tribe.

● ● ●

In my first attempt to find a literary agent, I reached out to hundreds of people online, sending copy-and-paste emails with no personal connection. I reached out to agents who were not in my tribe, and I was making no effort to find my way into theirs. But when I tried again several years later, I reached out to one particular agent who was a friend of a friend. Because of this mutual connection, my success rate went from 0 percent to 100 percent. As a result of that connection, you are reading this book.

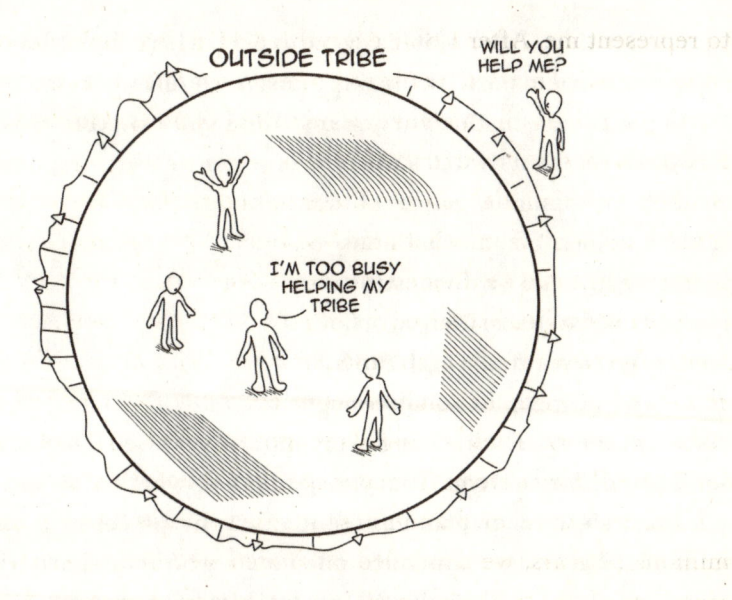

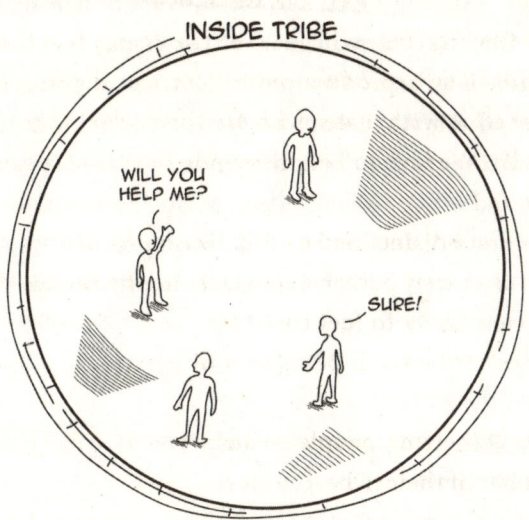

The same is true with my job-hunting experience. When I started looking, I primarily applied to opportunities online with no personal connection. Then I met a recruiter with a background similar to mine. We both had attended the same college and had had businesses fail. I shifted my focus from applying to dozens of jobs per day online to building a relationship with him. This recruiter coached me through revising my résumé for a particular opportunity. Because of our shared history and my investments in our relationship, the recruiter saw me as part of his tribe and was more willing to recommend me to the hiring manager. A few weeks later, I got a job.

In the twenty-first century, many tribes still exist. But these tribes are very different from the ones we lived in while we were first developing our instincts as humans. Some of our modern tribes contain millions of people with common ancestry and shared belief systems. Long ago, however, tribes were limited in size to fifty or a hundred people—small enough that everyone in the tribe knew everyone else very well. They all relied upon one another for survival. Today, regardless of whether we are a part of a cultural, religious, or political tribe, everyone perceives a subconscious form of tribal connection with individuals who may share something in common with us: a similar belief system, history, or heritage. For instance, one reason the Church of Jesus Christ of Latter-day Saints is so wealthy is their sense of tribe is strong. Mormons feel a sense of pride and duty to help each other succeed. Alumni groups are famous for being rich with opportunities for their members. Family and friends are likewise common sources of employment and other opportunities. Many famous actors, models, and artists got their first break from an inside connection.

> "You have to find a tribe."
>
> RuPaul

This sense of shared citizenship can come from countless aspects of life. Examples include the following:

- attending the same yoga class
- supporting the same political candidate
- shopping at the same grocery store
- enjoying the same tastes in art, fashion, or entertainment
- working at the same company
- riding the same bus to work each day
- attending the same festival
- rooting for the same sports team
- participating in the same hobbies
- vacationing at the same resort
- listening to the same podcast

Quite simply, if you want to get someone to help you, find a way to get them to perceive you as part of one of their subconscious tribes. Once you're on the inside, the closer you are to them, the more they are likely to want to help you, just as our ancestors evolved to want to help other tribe members for everyone's mutual survival.

The practice of getting one to perceive you to be in a similar tribe is sometimes referred to as *building rapport*. Anyone who has made a career in sales understands the importance of building customer rapport. Successful salespeople look for clues of commonality when they start customer interactions. They might see someone wearing a Supersonics jersey and bemoan how Oklahoma City stole the team from Seattle. If they notice their customer is carrying a cup from 7-Eleven, they may joke about getting a free Slurpee every July 11. By bringing up shared interests—whether real or fictional—the salesperson is trying to make the customer feel part of a common tribe. And because tribal affiliation is a means of quickly and easily building trust, the customer may become more open to purchasing. When done well, creating a sense of shared affinity dramatically increases the chance of a sale.

We can use these principles to build relationships in diverse contexts. If you want to meet someone, find a way to insert yourself into their path. Stop by the café in their building's lobby about the time they show up for work. And when you find yourself waiting for your drinks together, start a conversation about your coffee preferences, the art on the wall, or the local news. Just play it cool—I'm not going to bail you out of jail if you get arrested for stalking.

If done correctly, this approach can, and should, be both natural and authentic. Taking the initiative in your quest to credibly join the tribe of a desired relationship can take many forms. For instance, you could discover which gym they attend and join it. In time you may find yourself chatting after attending the same yoga class. In other contexts, you can pay attention to the clothes they wear, their office decorations, or their model of car, and use this information to decipher their hobbies and interests. Many people today share their entire lives on social media. Follow their accounts. When you discover an authentic area of intersectionality, send a message they might find interesting or relevant.

Even if you don't have a specific person in mind, you can use this approach to insert yourself into the paths of people who may have a lot of gravity in one particular aspect of life you wish to improve in. The best example I can think of is volunteering at an organization where your ideal connection is also likely to volunteer, such as a group of business executives devoted to helping their communities (rotary clubs, PTAs, local government organizations, etc.).

It's impossible to describe every single way to apply this principle because each circumstance requires a unique approach. Just be creative and persistent. With time, you have a shot at building a relationship with anyone—certainly a much better chance than if you do nothing.

You may have to work hard to meet people who have many demands for their time and attention. But as we discussed earlier, less in-demand people are just as helpful for many paths. With such people, simply reaching out can suffice. If necessary, an introduction from a shared connection is a great way to distinguish yourself. But one of the best ways to stand out is through the second method for getting people to help you: being helpful to them first.

Helpfulness

Tully's Coffee on Main Street in Bellevue, Washington, was once one of the best places to network in the Seattle area. Though many of its sister stores performed poorly, Tully's on Main was always busy. The tables were always occupied by animated businesspeople, shaking hands and making deals. If you were looking for work, your chances of finding your future boss were high if you hung around long enough. Tully's on Main earned its reputation as a mecca for connecting, in large part, because of Jeff Rogers.

Jeff is quick to smile, kindhearted, and genuinely cares about everyone he meets. If you're new to town and need to meet people—no matter what for—few people will do more to help you than Jeff. When he meets new connections, he has a rule: no business. He doesn't want to talk shop until he gets to know you personally. The first meeting is for topics like family, spirituality, travel, or, for suffering Seattle baseball fans, the Mariners. But while Jeff is asking questions unrelated to business, his mind is churning. He's thinking of ways to help the person across from him. The primary way he does this is by making connections.

Jeff teaches a sales system that involves attending three meetings each workday before noon. At the end of each day's discussions, he opens his computer and makes three introductions for each of the people he met that morning. The connections should be as valuable as possible for both parties. He helps people he meets by introducing them to people who can likely help them in some practical way based on the content of their nonbusiness conversations. Perhaps an attorney to set up a last will and testament for someone who mentions they've meant to get that task checked off their to-do list. He might connect you to the best florist in town if he hears your anniversary is coming up, or an executive coach if you expressed an interest in growing your leadership skills.

Introductions are one of the most popular ways networkers help each other, but there are many others. In the back of a book called *Networking Like a Pro*, written by Ivan Misner (the founder of worldwide networking system BNI) along with David Alexander and Brian Hilliard, is a scorecard for determining whether you'll be successful in networking. On the card are examples of networking actions, such as helping someone get a speaking gig or providing a business opportunity referral. The authors built this system on the idea that helpfulness correlates with success.

> "Show goodness onto the world and the world will show goodness onto you."
>
> Joshua Teya

The kind of help Jeff provides is not just for networkers, salespeople, and job seekers. You can use these principles to build a relationship with anyone, no matter how high caliber. If you could solve a time-sensitive and critical need for the president of the United States, you could be meeting with her on Air Force One within hours. And as reciprocal offers of help go, "I can unilaterally pardon you of any crime" is hard to beat.

Helpfulness causes you to rise above everyone else clamoring for a person's attention. The more powerful, wealthy, or famous someone is, the more they are used to hangers-on, users, fame seekers, and any number of others who want to take more than give. When you provide value with no strings attached, you stand out. Of course, this principle works just as well for people who don't run major nations. No matter how busy someone is, their attention is valuable. You must compete against everything else they can do with their time and everyone else who is already in their life. Finding a way to help them gives you a significant advantage toward this end.

The difficulty of this approach is figuring out how to be helpful. The easiest way is to ask. "If I could wave a magic wand and make one of your problems vanish, what would that be?" You could consult their friends or colleagues for ideas. You can appeal to their ego by asking them for advice or offering to feature them in a medium to which you have access, such as speaking opportunities, panels, guest lecturers, op-eds, or contributing to a published work.

If you aren't in charge of such things, create your own. I once founded a blog and paid for advertising to increase its readership primarily for the purpose of inviting guest contributors who I wanted to meet. I've invited interesting people I wanted to meet to guest lecture at university courses I taught. And I've created e-books and single-issue magazines that were collections of interviews or essays by people with whom I wished to connect. None of these were published in a traditional sense. Rather, they were used as tools by the contributing authors to increase their own credibility. Even when I didn't personally possess the level of public awareness that my contributors did, I created value by bringing them all together and doing the work of publishing the content.

Offering someone an income opportunity is about as helpful as helpfulness gets. If you have the means or the power to make such decisions for your employer, you can offer to hire the desired connection as a consultant, coach, or adviser. If they run a nonprofit, you can make a donation or volunteer. If they run an organization that relies on advertising, you could purchase ads. These are, without a doubt, the easiest ways to make a connection.

In some contexts, it's helpful to pursue people with whom you're not directly competitive. For example, a graphic designer could learn from other specialists with a similar business model such as photographers, attorneys, or architects by trading their skills for specialists' time. Or you can introduce people who may benefit from their services. As an added benefit, these other specialists could refer business back to you. If geography is a natural boundary for your line of work, you could build relationships with people in other states or provinces.

Finally, you can offer your services for free or at a discount. If you've ever strolled the aisles of Costco, you know the power of samples. Our lizard brains can't help but be attracted to free mini corn dogs. Items we might typically never consider purchasing become irresistible. And once we've tried them, we are far more likely to put them in our cart.

When I used to sell organic meat at farmers markets, I'd hire friendly college students to hand out samples. I taught them not just to wait around for someone to walk over but to go *to* the customers. Few people will turn down a stick of Sweet and Spicy Jerky when offered freely and with a smile. I never failed to sell out of my famous sausages and pork belly when we had samples to give away. Of course, this was all my way of meeting local chefs who would frequent the markets looking for their menus' next trendy item. Samples not only helped me sell out each Saturday but also helped get my products into some of the best restaurants in town, which meant larger, ongoing orders.[2] Whether you are a freelancer, programmer, or mechanic, giving samples of your work is an effective way to meet people.

As you continue to find ways to help someone, you may have the opportunity to become a more significant part of their life. You could begin working for them. They might become a regular contributor to your blog or even agree to sit on your board of directors. Relationshift works in subtle ways. By simply spending time with people, we slowly become more like them. Any way to get more time with someone helps us toward that goal. If you continue to add value to a person's life, they will continue to want you to be part of it.

---

2. Farming was one of my shorter careers, yet it earned me one of my most embarrassing titles: *The Sausage Baron of Springfield*.

Persistence

The right adjustments combined with perseverance can make almost anything possible. If you have a few million years, something as soft as water can create the Grand Canyon. With enough time, you can become a millionaire by investing what you save from skipping your daily morning Danish. Similarly, persistence in the application of relationshift can make a massive difference in your life outcome.

The slowness of results is one reason many people fail to make the best possible use of the concepts of relationshift. This is a lifelong process. And it's a lot more fun to dream about what kind of life we want to achieve or who we want to become than it is to do the work of getting there. Like how it's more fun to dream of owning a vacation home than to save for it. The problem with results taking so long to show up is that it makes it far too easy to put relationship development on the back burner because of the daily fires that ignite in our lives. It's hard for us to do something we hope will yield benefits years from now when we have so much to do today—whether solving a critical need or merely providing the satisfaction of checking off a to-do that may or may not be necessary.

> "Nothing in this world can take the place of persistence. Talent will not: nothing is more common than unsuccessful men with talent. Genius will not; unrewarded genius is almost a proverb. Education will not: the world is full of educated derelicts. Persistence and determination alone are omnipotent."
>
> **Ascribed to Calvin Coolidge**

Yet persistence is the key to many of life's best outcomes. We must invest time and energy to form and maintain connections with ideal members of our inner circle without immediate signs of progress. We must trust that investing in relationships is the best move we can make.

Practicing persistence requires you to remember the difference between hard and impossible. It's difficult to get time with certain people, yet still achievable. It's hard to figure out whom you need most in your relationship mix, but it isn't futile. Rejection hurts, but it doesn't have to be any more disheartening than you allow it to be. You may feel stuck in a river of molasses, but that doesn't mean progress is not happening. Someday, you may look back and see how one relationship led to a promotion. Or another, to a new way of seeing the world. And still another, to achieving a goal you long believed impossible. Years of investing in a relationship could lead to a call, a big break, an offer you never expected but always hoped was possible. It all starts with the simple activity of spending time with people who are further along the journey.

It's difficult to predict which relationships will lead to which outcomes. You must simply trust the process. Persistence comes down to this: you will never achieve your dreams without it. Only those who have chance on their side get what they want without the necessary work. And luck is never a plan.

Readiness

Perhaps the most important strategy for getting help from the kinds of people who are the best possible fit for your relationshift goals is maintaining readiness. Progress toward our desired destination is often slow. Some nights we may fall asleep feeling as though we have lost ground. But however we feel day to day about our progress, we must stay alert. Opportunities to connect with ideal people can come and go quickly. If the right opportunity presents itself—someone with a Draymond Green–size plus/minus—we must be aware enough to recognize it.

When this happens, we must do everything we can to exploit the moment. We must engage all we've learned about building meaningful and lasting relationships. If we can help the person, we should work twice as hard and provide double the value they are expecting. We should prepare for every meeting, triple-check our emails before sending, and always be ahead of schedule. All of this should be invisible to the person we hope to add to our inner circle. Let them notice nothing but the excellence of our work, the clarity of our mind, and the ease of our company.

We must go to these great lengths because a single relationship can transform our lives. The right connection can save us years, perhaps decades, of trudging through life in the muck. Consider what you would do to save yourself decades of work, costly lessons, failures, and wandering in the desert. This is what readiness can do for you.

Yet readiness requires we address a problematic contradiction that exists between contentment and striving. Chances are you have many more reasons for gratitude than you might realize at any given moment. Contentment is an essential step for one to experience sustained happiness. But satisfaction with our situation is an antecedent to complacency. In fact, contentment and complacency are synonyms. Why strive if we're happy with what we have and who we are?

The key to balancing these opposing ideas is always to leave space for something new in your life. It is tempting to fill every last corner of our existence. But then, when something great comes along, we're too busy or too full to recognize it. We can't be ready to pour something new into our life if we're full to the brim.

> "The important thing is this: to be able at any moment to sacrifice what we are for what we could become."
>
> **Charles Du Bos**

Develop the discipline to rid yourself of a portion equal to whatever you wish to add, always maintaining free space for whatever might be next. Never add anything to your life that is not better than what you already have. And what you let go of should be what is least in line with who you want to become. In this way, you will, over time, replace whatever fills you now with whatever is increasingly better. All the while, you can freely enjoy contentment with your present moment without becoming complacent.

We have access to far more opportunities than we could ever exploit or even imagine. We just don't notice most of it passing us by because we're too busy, too stressed out, and too stuffed. By being aware of what you require to get from where you are to where you want to be, you can practice being ready to pounce when opportunities arise that will help you immensely along the way. Relationshift works best when you learn to make the most of what you already have. Just be ready to take action when someone amazing passes. You never know how long they'll be around before moving on.

FOUR STRATEGIES FOR GETTING PEOPLE TO HELP YOU

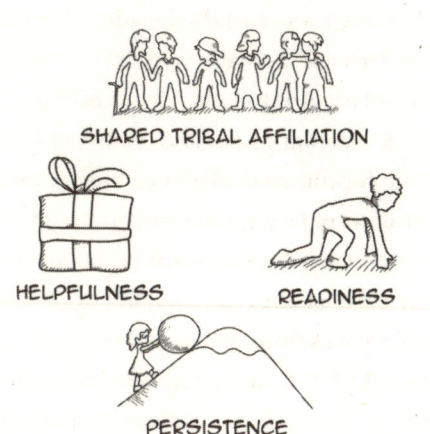

SHARED TRIBAL AFFILIATION

HELPFULNESS

READINESS

PERSISTENCE

Accounting for Luck

A common mistake many people make is taking advice from people who haven't proven they know what they're talking about. For example: getting input on finding happiness in a long-term romantic relationship from someone who has been in a string of short-term relationships or is miserable in their marriage. Another example is taking too seriously the opinions of those with no background in graphic design or marketing when considering the design of your new business logo.

One essential factor in choosing your inner circle is to examine the evidence of their journey. If you want to gain more wealth, take advice primarily from people who are wealthier than you. If you want to accumulate wealth as ethically as possible, take advice only from people who have earned a great deal of wealth honorably. If you want to be more content, don't listen to people who merely talk about living with gratitude for what they have. Find those who regularly show great contentment regardless of life's daily ups and downs. If you want your love life to be one of those "happily ever after" stories, take romantic advice only from people with happy long-term partnerships.

One of the trickiest aspects of determining if someone has what it takes to help you is accounting for luck. Let's say, for example, you are fifty years old and considering early retirement even though you don't quite have enough money to do so comfortably. Rio, your best friend, is ten years older and has been happily retired for the last decade. She quit working without having as much in the bank as financial experts recommend. At a glance, Rio seems like the perfect mentor to help with this choice. However, it's possible she simply got lucky. Perhaps the stock market performed exceedingly well over the previous decade so that she could live well without proper financial planning. Or Rio may have a working partner whose income helps make ends meet. Or she may have written a book twenty years earlier that became a sleeper hit, earning her royalties that enhanced her lifestyle more than would be possible with a relatively small nest egg.

Or consider marriage. Your mentor of interest may have learned from experience the secret to happy long-term romance is to stick with your spouse no matter what—that love is a choice. But perhaps they married someone who turned out over the decades to be an excellent match. It's a lot easier to find happiness sticking with someone when you get along quite well.

Another difficulty with choosing mentors is that we must account for different worldviews. In Rio's example, she may enjoy living more inexpensively than you do. With the marriage example, someone who says they are happy in a long-term relationship may not be very romantic. Perhaps all they want is a companion to watch TV with at the end of the day. Nothing wrong with that unless you are looking for a passionate relationship that doesn't lose steam as the years go by. If so, taking advice from someone who doesn't care about such things may not lead you to the best decision for your own love life.

You need to find people who have the specific knowledge to help you get from where you are to where you want to be. This usually requires them to have walked a similar journey. They were once where you are, they went through similar circumstances, and they learned what was necessary to achieve a goal similar to yours. Not all who are rich know how to teach other people to become rich. Many inherited their wealth and have no clue how to build it from scratch. This person can likely help you more than someone who has no money at all because they may have learned quite a bit from wealth advisers and well-to-do friends, just not as much as someone who started in the same place as you and built from there.

Do your best to decipher the information you receive from others in light of their background and worldview. This will help you find people who are far more capable of helping you get from your point A to your desired point B. You won't be right every time, and you don't need to be. Relationshift isn't a tidy process. But then again, what of high worth is?

Pause to reflect

- What tribes do you currently belong to that include high-gravity individuals (HGIs) as members? Remember that HGIs can be peers or protégés, too.
- What tribes could you join to increase your access to HGIs? What steps could you take to join those tribes?
- What ways can you become more helpful to the kinds of people who could help you grow?
- What can you remove from your life so you can be more ready to capitalize on an opportunity to build a relationship with an HGI?

• • •

Social Capital

If you stroll down Forty-Seventh Street in New York City—America's epicenter of diamond trading—you are likely to notice men wearing black suits and hats and long beards. Yiddish, Russian, and Hebrew are far more common than English among these traders in the many jewel markets that fill the neighborhood. A significant portion of the $60 billion global diamond trade flows through the shops of the Orthodox Jews in New York's Diamond District. Researchers have long wondered why this segment of the market has remained in such unified hands.

The diamond business is a difficult one, partly because gems are so easy to steal. Not only are the assets of this industry small and difficult to track, but diamond merchants rely heavily on credit. Most can't afford to pay for the gems before selling them. Sales swing wildly depending on the time of year, with business peaking from December through February for Christmas and Valentine's Day. This puts enormous pressure on retailers' cash flow, who wouldn't be able to stay in business without credit. In most industries, extending credit for thirty days is a risky proposition. And yet Diamond District merchants routinely negotiate terms lasting as much as a year or more. How is such extraordinary trust possible in an industry ripe for dishonesty and theft? A construct known as *social capital* is the key, a term used to analyze and describe the value of one's relationships. In short, the more social capital one possesses, the more potential one has for positive relationshift. Therefore, understanding how to get more social capital is key to making the most of relationshift.

Since ancient times, the Jewish people have been persecuted, expelled, and denied their full civil, economic, and property rights—in some cases as pretext for pogroms or genocide. Jewish communities have thus learned to form bonds of shared trust for survival, preservation of identity, access to spiritual and intellectual traditions, and opportunities for careers and commerce. They learned to make the most of whatever options were available.

Orthodox Jews have preserved their niche in the diamond industry because of the high levels of social capital they share. They have the same beliefs, they attend the same synagogues, and they grew up playing on the streets in front of each other's homes. It's a lot easier to ask for credit from the guy who, as a child, made forts out of sheets and couch cushions in your mom's living room. Merchants base their social contracts on shared values, trust, and the expectation that mutual connections will enforce any disputes. Social capital makes it possible to run a highly lucrative industry on the honor system.

Researchers have been studying the concept of social capital since the 1950s. They mostly have focused on how social capital benefits people professionally, such as finding a new job or getting a raise. Many studies have examined how organizations can benefit from their employees' social capital. Researchers have proven that social capital can increase our ability to recognize and gain access to opportunities. Other benefits discovered include the ability to increase sales, solidify power, boost personal compensation, improve marketing results, and spread innovations. And these are only the benefits proven by social science research to date.

Social capital applies to many of the nonbusiness contexts discussed in this book. This construct is a subcomponent of evolutionary capital (which we will discuss in chapter five), falling primarily under the category of influence. The study of social capital includes exploring different network structures and how relationship strength affects information flow. This knowledge can help us understand the social systems to which we belong and how to make the most of them. It can aid in identifying people who are our most valuable connections. And it can teach us how strong or weak we should make our relationships to maximize the limits of time against our specific needs.

As you read through the following two sections on social capital, think about the networks you belong to and the relationships you have. How are your networks like or unlike the various structures presented, and how does that affect your ability to move within and make use of those networks? What about the strength of your relationships? Do you tend to foster strong ties with a few people or weak connections to a larger number? As you become more aware of these factors, you can better position yourself to maximize the value of any network you belong to, and you can build stronger, more valuable networks around you over time.

Network Structure

New York's Diamond District is an example of what researchers call a *closed network*. Sometimes this type of system is also called a *clique*. The more closed a structure is, the more likely it is for everyone in the network to have a relationship with everyone else. Outsiders have a difficult time breaking into such a social system. This is what allows diamond merchants to extend almost unlimited credit safely to retailers. In a closed network, trust is high. If there is a problem between any two members, others in the network will facilitate a solution that maintains the trust between members. And each member is disincentivized to cheat because no one wants to lose the faith of everyone else in the tribe. On the other hand, limiting the number of members reduces access to new ideas and opportunities.

Other examples of closed networks include military companies whose members fought together in a war, criminal gangs, popular school cliques, and families who place a premium on bloodline. These structures are depicted in fictional stories such as *Band of Brothers*, *The Godfather*, *Mean Girls*, and *Game of Thrones*. In the fourth episode of *Band of Brothers*, "Replacements," several new soldiers arrive to take the place of those who have died. The new soldiers are eager to impress the veterans but are bitterly rejected no matter how great their effort. It's not until the replacements fight alongside the veterans that the company accepts them.

Some kinds of networks enjoy the benefits of a closed structure while maintaining a level of openness. Examples include associations, Greek-letter organizations, and athletic clubs. Union members may band together to negotiate a better healthcare benefits package and often feel camaraderie, but all that is required to join is to pay the union dues. Locker rooms, private clubs, and cigar lounges are popular places to seal a business deal, yet all that is required to join is being able to pay the initiation fee.

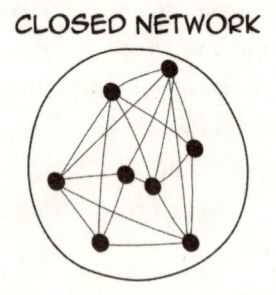

Fraternities and sororities simulate closed networks as depicted by *Band of Brothers* when they require new members to undergo extreme initiations. Running down the street naked, drinking till you black out, or cutting your hand to shed blood are all real examples of initiations into Greek life. College is hell. But in reality, all that's necessary is having parents who can afford the tuition. In each of these examples, the members feel a sense of belonging that increases trust.

The opposite of a closed network is an *open network*. Members of open systems come and go without resistance. Trust is lower among members, but access to new ideas is greater. Examples of open networks include political movements, college classrooms, dating apps, and shared-interest conventions. Because of the natural churn within open social structures, the

RELATIONSHIP WITH PEOPLE IN OTHER NETWORKS

OPEN NETWORK

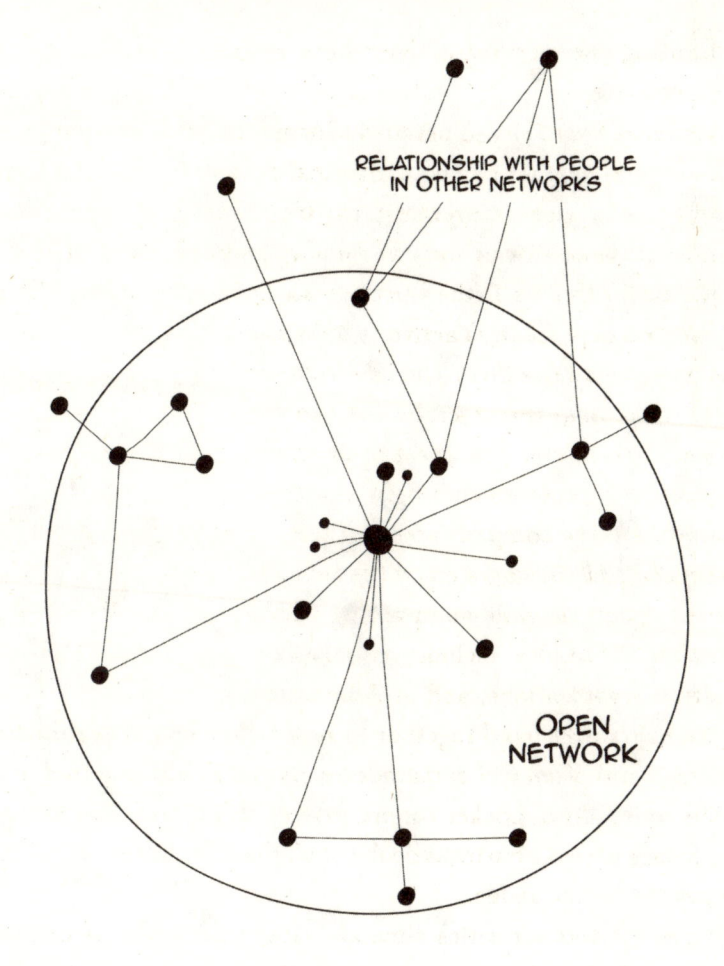

members enjoy access to a much more diverse group of people who are more likely to have broad-ranging experiences, worldviews, and sets of information.

Open networks are ideal for creativity, innovation, meeting new people, and fostering grassroots movements. However, not all relationships within an open network are weak, just as not all connections in a closed network are strong. One can develop strong relationships with members of an open community by investing the appropriate amount of time and energy.

The third category of connections is known as a *bridge network*. A person who builds a bridge network connects with other well-connected people.

BRIDGE CONNECTION

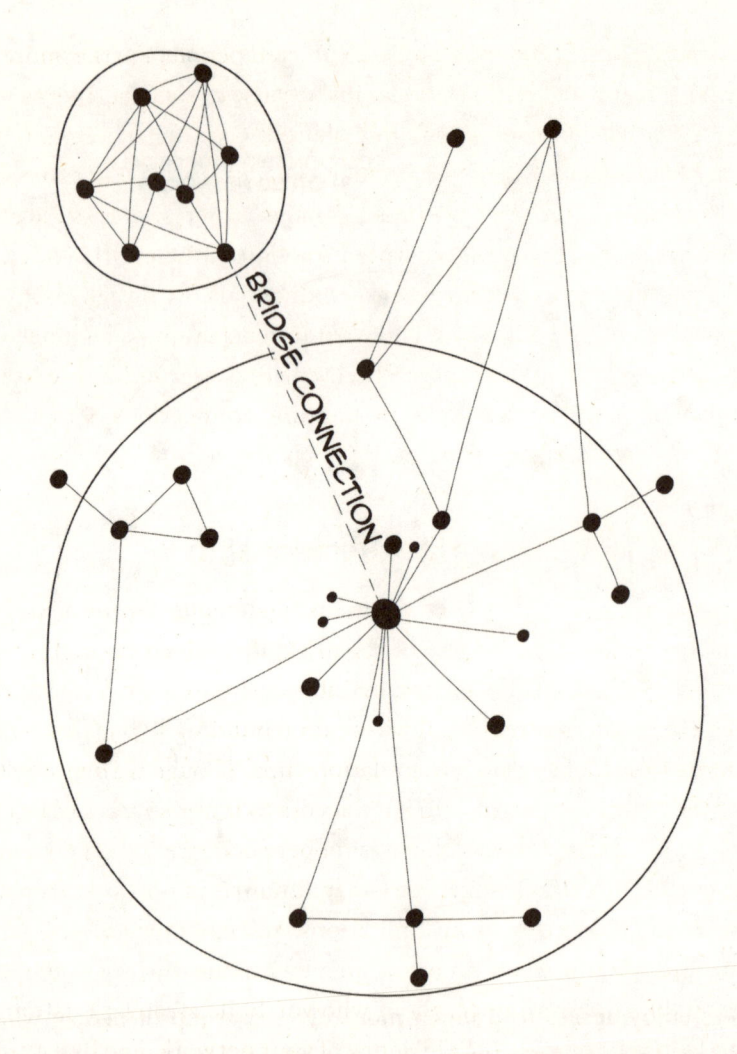

It's called a bridge network because it allows a single intermediary access to many different social systems, either open or closed. These networks would be unconnected if not for the person who maintains connections with other individuals at the centers of their respective networks—kind of a superhero whose secret power is networking. Bridge networks can increase one's social capital far beyond what is possible within standard open or closed systems.

Anyone can build a bridge network, but common examples include attorneys, wealth managers, agents, and life coaches. People in these roles tend to know a lot of influential, well-connected people. Furthermore, they tend to have highly trusting relationships because of their business's nature and the sensitivity of the information shared. Gaining access to a dozen famous athletes is a task that could take decades. But if one can connect with the agent who represents a dozen famous athletes, one can access all twelve through the intermediary with a fraction of the effort. The same is valid for gaining access to very wealthy individuals. By design, many gatekeepers will stand in your way if you want to reach a single high-net-worth person. But a wealth adviser spends their entire career building close relationships with many such people. By building connections with the right advisers, one can gain access to multiple rich people.

Strength of Relationship

Often referred to in academic literature as *tie strength*, this dimension is a major factor in the gain and use of social capital. Given time's finiteness, the number of relationships we can maintain is limited. Stronger relationships tend to require more time. If we focus on building strong ties, we must spend more time focusing on fewer relationships. Though we may rely heavily on these relationships, we will have access to fewer sources of information and favor. Understanding the tension between strength of connection and the number of relationships one can maintain is important to maximizing relationshift because of your limitations. You can only connect with so many people, and the more time you spend with one, the less you have for another. So becoming strategic about who you build stronger relationships with can help you improve the efficiency of your network, and by extension, build a more valuable network that can speed you toward your goals.

Inversely, creating and maintaining many weaker relationships gives us access to copious information sources. However, each tie cannot be relied upon to provide the same level of value as a strong relationship would.

Seven dimensions contribute to the strength of one's relationships:

1. the amount of time spent together
2. the intensity of emotions among actors
3. the degree to which separate parties use each other's services
4. the type and richness of experiences

5. the level of mutual trust
6. the level of individual maturity
7. the frequency of requests within the relationship

Counterintuitively, making requests can build relationship strength by providing more opportunities to give and take on both sides of the connection. If we wish to increase trust, we can do so by investing in any of these dimensions.

Given the limitations of time, we can do only so much to connect with others. This constricts our number of possible ties. Some people have a

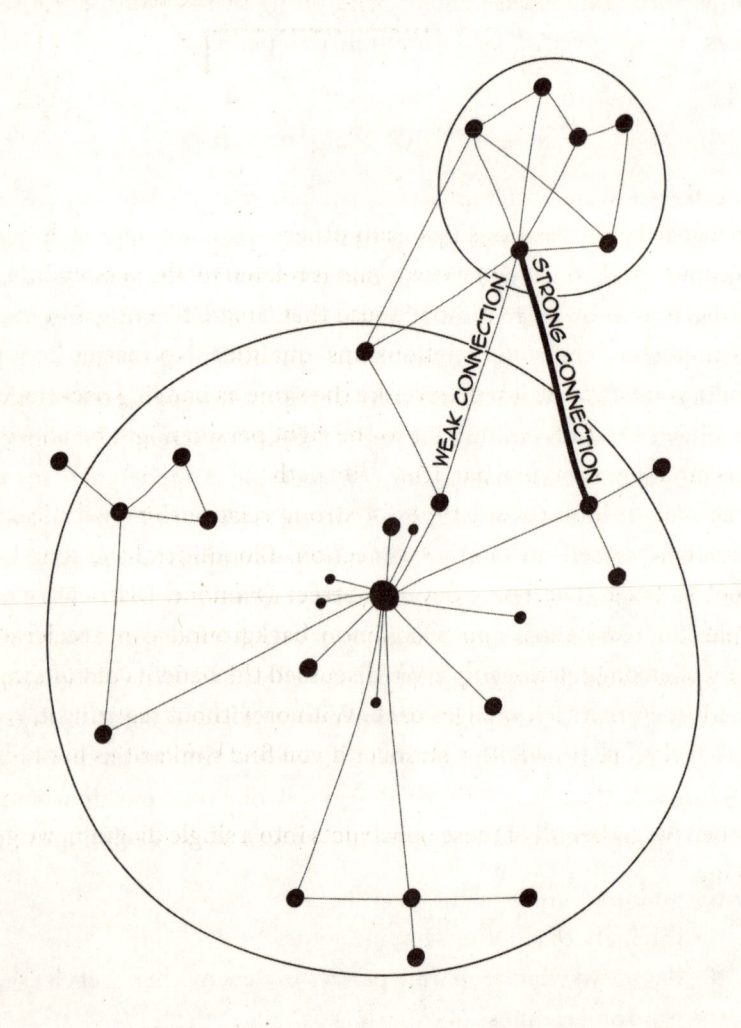

THE 7 DIMENSIONS OF RELATIONSHIP STRENGTH

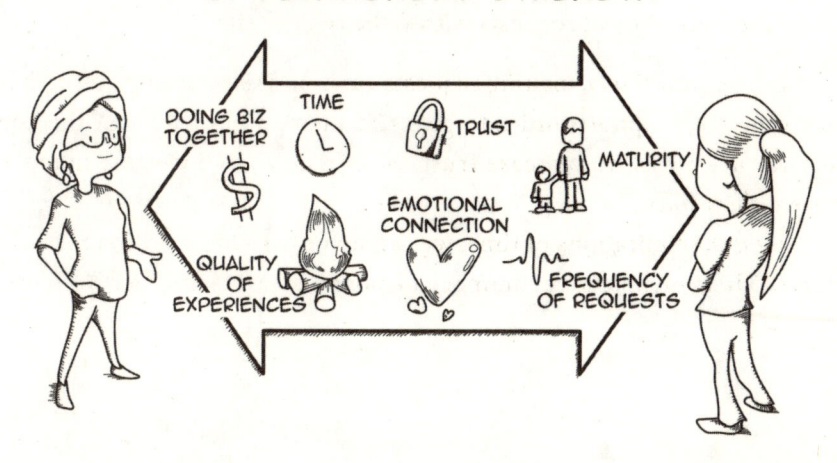

DOING BIZ TOGETHER · TIME · TRUST · MATURITY · QUALITY OF EXPERIENCES · EMOTIONAL CONNECTION · FREQUENCY OF REQUESTS

higher capacity for relationships than others. How we approach building social capital and how much we can gain is related to our personality, available time, and knowledge of how to use that time efficiently. But quantity is less important than our relationships' qualities. No matter how many Beliebers you befriend, it will never be the same as hanging backstage with Justin Bieber himself. A single tie to the right person might be all we need to go as far as we want in a particular life path.

One can maintain some types of strong relationships with less time, such as those based on family connection. Bloodlines have long been a shortcut to trust. The Forty-Seventh Street Diamond District is another example. Shared beliefs and a common background can accelerate the building of strong relationships. We discussed the benefits of building rapport with customers a few pages back. With or without realizing it, you are likely to feel more trust with a stranger if you find similarities between you and them.

When we gather all of these constructs into a single diagram, we get the following:

NETWORK STRUCTURE

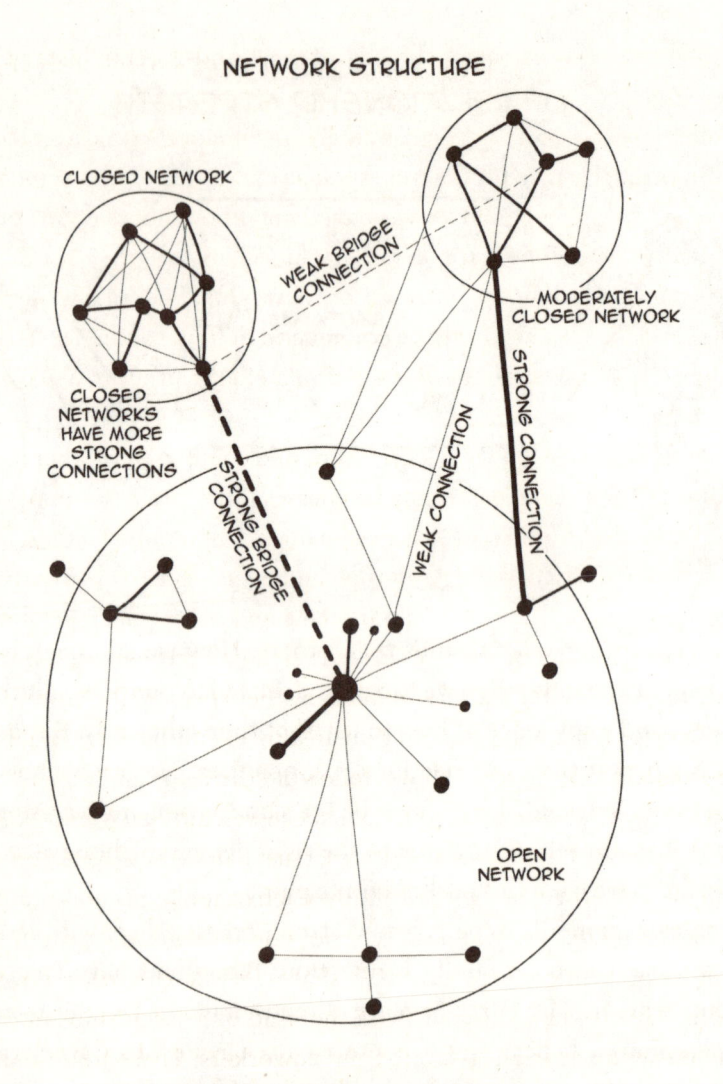

Closed Network

Closed networks have more strong connections

Weak Bridge Connection

Moderately Closed Network

Strong Bridge Connection

Weak Connection

Strong Connection

Open Network

Unilateral Relationships

On November 11, 2017, a twenty-two-year-old with moppy blond hair and nerdy aviator glasses stood with his back to the crowd that filled the indoor ice rink at the Dubai Mall. He smiled for his selfie video, sporting a letterman jacket embroidered with his personal brand—available on his website for just $79.99 (limited quantity, act fast!). Many of the eleven thousand kids who were gleefully lined up for a chance to get their picture taken with the celebrity had waited all day for him to arrive. He shouted that they had just broken a world record for the largest meet-and-greet in history. Everyone screamed.

The celebrity was Logan Paul, a vlogger—someone who chronicles their daily life through video on the web, such as on YouTube. Had he been born a few years earlier, he might never have been known outside his personal circle. Paul is not a movie star, a famous musician, or a member of a royal family. He was born on the outskirts of Cleveland and had few advantages or connections growing up, yet he was able to build an audience in the tens of millions, earning tens of millions of dollars in the process, using only his camera phone.

Vloggers are also known as influencers, and commercial brands pay them for access to their audiences. Many businesses today prefer to sponsor influencers like Paul over A-list celebrities who might be far more famous, because vloggers have enormous power over their audiences—not to mention they can be a lot cheaper. With actors and musicians and other public personalities, the audience sees only a carefully curated version of the person. They may be famous, but we don't feel like we really know them personally. The difference comes down to trust. Vloggers can gain an almost cultlike following because viewers walk in the vloggers' shoes, following their ups and downs, the ins and outs of their relationships, and their successes and struggles.

As the case of Logan Paul illustrates, trust can be built between people regardless of whether they actually know each other. In my doctoral dissertation on the topic, I called these types of connections *unilateral*. In these one-way relationships, only one side shares, while the other gives trust in return. This is very different from the kind of relationships most of us experience with our friends, family, and coworkers. These traditional relationships are *bilateral*. When an author, vlogger, Instagrammer, or musician shares personal information, such as an emotional reaction to losing a child or excitement about studying iguanas, the receivers can come to feel they know the person in much the same way that they feel they know people in their bilateral relationships, such as hairstylists, coworkers, and friends. It's not uncommon to hear people chatting at a café about their favorite reality TV stars, bloggers, or news personalities as if they were personal friends.

In the same way, politicians and military leaders gain trust when their followers perceive shared experiences. Trust for President George W. Bush skyrocketed in the aftermath of the September 11 terrorist attacks because, in part, Americans felt they had a common experience with him. In the same way, generals gain high levels of trust from their soldiers when personally leading them into battle. The final factor of building trust, demonstrated reliability, occurs when a leader delivers as promised year after year—whether they bring profit for shareholders or a good working environment for employees.

In all of these cases, followers feel increased levels of trust for people they have never met. The magic of this phenomenon for those who wish to build influence is that they are no longer bound by the same limits of traditional relationships.

Chances are you and your best friend have invested about the same amount of time in your relationship. Same goes for you and your romantic partner, you and your sibling, and you and your accountant. But a vlogger like Logan Paul can share one video with millions in the same amount of time it would take to share it with one person. Because public figures like him possess such a high volume of trust from so many, their worldview is passed on in higher volume than the worldview of someone who relies only on bilateral relationships.

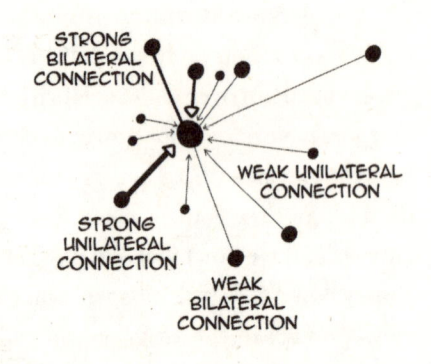

Unilateral relationships are responsible for a large part of how we see the world. When we come to trust someone whom we know only through their work—books, videos, mass events—we will be influenced by this person in much the same way that we would by our best friend, parents, or boss. Using this principle, we can turn a library card into access to the most remarkable minds throughout history.

In some ways, unilateral relationships are superior to knowing remarkable people personally. We can digest their best and brightest ideas, gathered over the course of their life, distilled, edited, and compellingly arranged for quick and easy assimilation. Not to mention a lot of the most influential people are fairly insufferable—save yourself the grief of their company by sticking with their published works.

When we add unilateral and bilateral relationships to our illustration of social capital, we complete our map of social networks. Understanding network structure and how various levels of tie strength affect our access to information can help us form a more helpful personal tribe, and thereby increase our potential for positive relationshift through access to high-gravity individuals. Our next topic centers around the most impactful types of relationship within this inner circle. But before we continue, let's resume my own story to examine how the principles of this section played out in my real-life scenario.

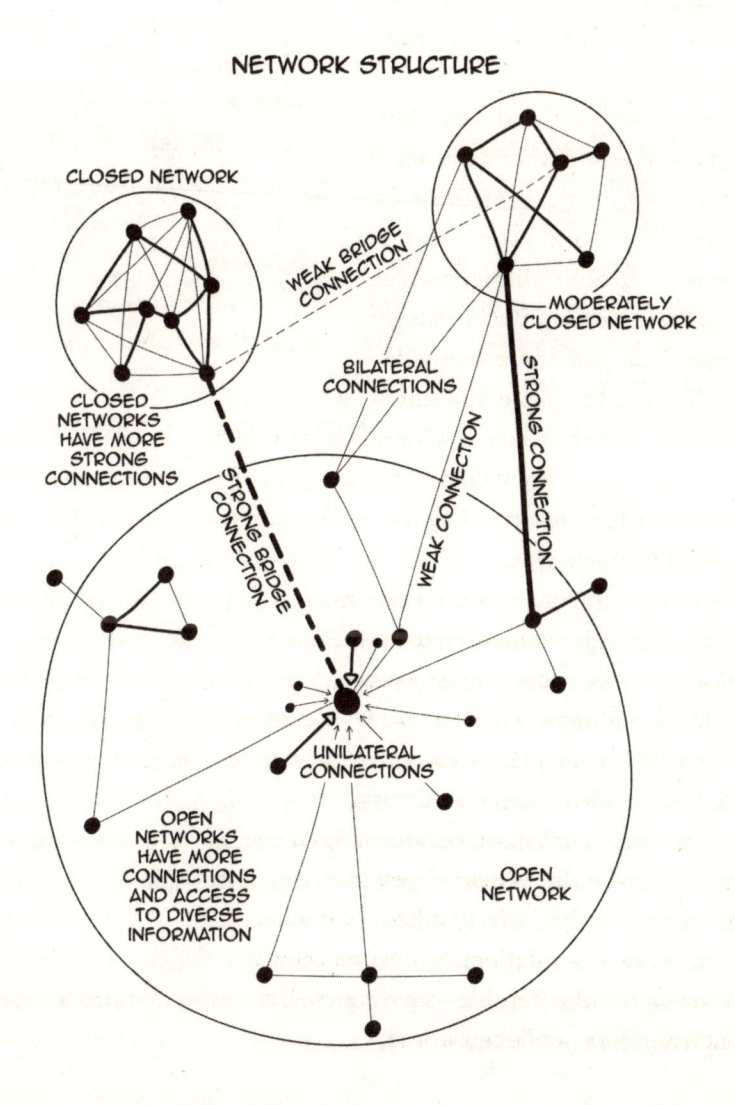

NETWORK STRUCTURE

Pause to reflect

- Do you tend to build strong or weak relationships? Do you feel your approach is serving you well? Would it benefit you to have more strong or weak connections to balance your social capital portfolio, or do you prefer to focus on one relationship strength?
- Are you currently maxed out on your ability to connect with people? If yes, how could you change your approach to make room for more connections to help you achieve your goals?
- Think of one or more people with whom you'd like to build a stronger relationship. Which of the seven dimensions of relationship strength could you use to achieve this goal, and how?
- Do you currently have any bridging connections to people with vastly different friend groups or professional networks? What kinds of bridging connections would be helpful for your goals? What can you do differently to build more such relationships and increase your social capital?
- How would you benefit from building a collection of unilateral relationships where you share information with people you don't personally know, and they trust you in return? What steps could you take to increase your number of unilateral relationships?

. . .

A few years before my divorce and worldview transformation, my career path began to change. After I lost my construction business in 2008, I tried several ways to make money. One of my worst ideas was to become a songwriter in Nashville. After a year of pursuing this dream, I landed a few of my songs on albums and even got a little radio play. But the royalties I generated from these songs didn't have enough zeros even to pay my rent. So I started a social network to connect musicians to industry executives called Zoxsy.com. I received investments from angels and venture capitalists to kick-start the company. This startup failed to scale quickly enough, and I had to move on.

Between freelancing and part-time work for friends, I did the best I could. One of the more glamorous gigs I cooked up was installing Christmas lights for wealthy homeowners. To find customers, I taped flyers to people's doors. At the time, I had a BA in business administration. Perhaps if I got a master's degree, I could work my way up from part-time elf to a mid-level manager at a company with a sexy business model, like making toilet paper. I was ready to start over—poorer, humbler, but also hopefully wiser. So I enrolled in an online program through Texas A&M.

One year later, with my shiny new MBA in hand, I figured I would be back on my feet in no time. You might recall me mentioning I once applied to many, many jobs and didn't get a single interview. This was that time. Even with two degrees and a decade of business experience, nobody wanted me. It took all the positivity I could muster to keep from giving up.

I was in my late twenties, married, with three children, and here I was living with my in-laws. I remember sitting alone at the kitchen table one day, surrounded by unpaid bills, wondering what I would do with my life. I found myself wishing I could have made it as a songwriter in Nashville. The truth was, I had done pretty well for a songwriter with no experience and— let's be honest—limited talent. I couldn't figure out why it felt easier to get a song on the radio than to get an interview with Walmart.

After thinking it over a while, I began to see that my minor success in songwriting had a lot to do with the people I recorded with. One of my producers knew several music-publishing executives. When my songs were good enough, she made some introductions. One connection led to another until I met a publisher who signed me. In turn, he introduced my music to artists who were looking for songs to cut on their next album. A couple of those artists chose my songs and, as far as I know, got them on the radio because they knew the local DJ who played them.

Whether one's big break is playing onstage with Madonna, getting a job, or just earning a few bucks for local radio airtime, relationships are the critical ingredient in getting us from where we are to where we want to be. Before realizing it was my connections that helped me succeed, I thought networking was for schmoozers. But the truth is, everyone networks. We all just call it by different names. Making friends. Sharing ideas. Giving recommendations. Setting up a friend on a blind date. Talking about our dreams. Helping someone solve a problem. It's all just people connecting with people.

As I thought this over, I wondered if I could get a job using the same principles that helped me with songwriting. I started reaching out to recruiters. I focused my energy on a much smaller number of people. I took them out to coffee if they were local. I joked around and found common ground. I sought ways to help them, which, as it turns out, is quite simple with recruiters. They get paid for placing employees, so all you need to do to help a recruiter is to be coachable and get hired.

Within a few weeks, I had my first interview. I drove from Eugene, Oregon, to Seattle, stayed in a hotel room I'm pretty sure could be rented by the hour, interviewed all day, and got an offer. Ironically, my MBA didn't even come up.

The job was commission-based sales of software that enabled churches to track donations, childcare, small groups, and attendance. To get business, we mostly relied on inquiries from interested pastors. I quickly realized the website leads we received each day were mostly from small churches. The more highly profitable opportunities were challenging to find. Those responsible for making big decisions at megachurches are busy and have many salespeople trying to get their attention. Usually, you have to know someone on the inside to have a chance. This seemed the perfect opportunity to test out my newfound love for networking.

I started a video blog about church technology and invited pastors who I wanted to meet to be guest contributors. To my surprise, almost everyone I asked said yes, because I was offering to help my guests gain exposure for their podcasts, social media accounts, and email lists—my guests tended to have sizable followings themselves. So when they promoted the videos, my blog audience quickly grew. This gave me access to even more influential pastors. Soon, I had connected to many of the most successful pastors around the United States and Canada.

Because sales to large churches paid a much higher commission, I earned more than the other five salespeople combined. Being so well connected, and due to the blog's success, unsolicited job offers and freelance opportunities started coming my way. Within a year of getting the job, I quit and founded a marketing agency.

A few years later, my agency had grown to ten employees serving dozens of clients, including a company run by networking aficionado Jeff Rogers. We met one day at Tully's Coffee on Main. He told me he was starting a digital marketing division and would no longer require my services. I said,

"I have a better idea. Why don't you buy my agency, and I'll run it for you?" A few meetings later, we'd struck a deal.

In the interest of brevity, I've left out the countless days working past midnight, the stress about bills that comes with managing a growing small business, and much more. My point is not to simplify how difficult it is to succeed but to illustrate the power of working through relationships versus my previous approach to success. My life transformed in multiple ways when I focused on building meaningful connections with people who could help me achieve my goals. By the time I sold my business, I had become such a believer in the power of relationships that I decided to return to school and earn a doctorate on the subject.

Most people earn a PhD because they want to teach or conduct research. I wasn't interested in writing academic papers, and professing was an occupation I'd never given much thought to, primarily because I had never previously enjoyed school. As I moved through the doctoral program, I had the opportunity to help my peers with their research. I began to realize how much I enjoyed being a part of someone's growth and learning. So I added becoming a professor to my growing list of ambitions, though I didn't know how to go about it or how difficult it can be to get such a role.

A few years after I graduated, got divorced, and entirely transformed my worldview, Jeff Rogers popped back into my life when he called me one day with a request. A professional coach he had recently met, Kristiina Hiukka, was looking for help promoting her brand. I agreed and began working with her as an independent consultant. Kristiina introduced me to Berry Zimmerman, who ran a peer group for leaders called Biz Enrich. Berry created the organization so executives could trade information, help each other grow, and enjoy the camaraderie of people with similar problems and opportunities. In Berry's group, I met Doug Hall, who became a good friend and occasional business partner. Doug introduced me to Frank Coker, who also became a client, business partner, and friend. One day, while having a beer with Frank, I mentioned my interest in teaching. As it turns out, Frank was an adjunct professor at the University of Washington and knew a program manager, Scott Barker, who was looking to staff a course on user experience. Frank made the intro to Scott, and one year later, I was standing in front of my first class as a newly minted professor.

A whole string of people were involved in achieving this goal, just like my experience with songwriting, and just like the Beastie Boys' rise to fame. Interestingly, in both of my experiences, talent and expertise had far less to do with a positive outcome than my relationships. Consider my equation for getting the opportunity to teach at the University of Washington:

Jeff Rogers + Kristiina Hiukka + Berry Zimmerman + Doug Hall + Frank Coker + Scott Barker = professor gig.

Networking is the activity of gaining connections. It's not fast or straightforward, and it's rarely predictable—just look at the string of relationships I needed to get my foot in the door at the University of Washington. I could never have planned that. But I also would never have gained the opportunity if I had not been investing in relationships for years prior. I certainly never would have gotten the job based on my teaching experience, of which I had none.

Now, every time I hear someone lament their lack of qualifications for a job they want, I tell them how relationships matter so much more. Unfortunately, few take this advice to heart. Their worldview is often too established by what their influences have been telling them for decades.

The term *networking* is often limited to the context of building ties to people who can help one get a new job or sell business services. Yet, in a broader sense, networking is a form of relationshift.

Regardless of what we call it, building relationships has proven to be the biggest key to achieving my goals. If you look at positive events in your life, I'm willing to bet you will see a string of people that helped you along the way. For better or worse, we can't separate the course of our life from the people in it. And, of course, some relationships affect us more than others.

Understanding the various roles people fill within our inner circle is essential to making the most of relationshift. Let's look at these next.

CHAPTER 3

Key Relationships

"The meeting of two personalities is like the contact of two chemical substances: if there is any reaction, both are transformed."

Carl Gustav Jung

Long before he became the abolitionist hero we know today, Frederick Douglass didn't want to grow up. As he approached the age of seven, he prayed ever more fervently that he could remain a child forever. Frederick's birthday came anyway.

This was a tragic day in any slave's life. It was the age when Frederick was considered old enough to be taken from his grandmother and sent to Wye Plantation in another part of rural Maryland's Talbot County. This mysterious place seemed to be made mostly of campfire stories told to scare children. And now it was to be his home. He was told he would spend the rest of his days in the service of a man who might as well have been the county's king.

Frederick knew little of what it meant to be a slave at this age, except that Big Master was judge, jury, and executioner for the thousand or more slaves who belonged to him. Frederick was taught to avoid eye contact with a white man—the scars on his back served as a reminder. And, just as he knew that one shouldn't take God's name in vain, Frederick heard that slaves should never speak Big Master's name above a whisper. About the only other thing Frederick understood about being a slave was that the masters and overseers had fathered many of the Black children with whom he'd grown up.

Slaves rarely knew their fathers. Frederick's first flicker of life was likely the result of rape. But he preferred to imagine that his parents were in love and happy somewhere. Slaves weren't allowed to marry, but occasionally Frederick heard stories of slaves' enjoying some version of life that resembled the freedom of their masters.

When the fateful day arrived, Frederick was taken from his grandmother and moved across the county to begin his life as a working slave. The moment he arrived, an older boy and girl threw their arms around him. They introduced themselves as his brother and sister. But it was all too much to process for a scared child of just seven years. He crawled into bed and lay faceup, staring at the rough-hewn floorboards of the room above. All he could think about was his grandmother; he wondered if he would ever see her again. Occasionally dust sifted down, accompanied by the light pounding of footsteps. Minutes stretched to hours until it seemed the night would never end.

Frederick began his new life the next morning before dawn. It wasn't long before he fell into the routine of chores. The other slaves helped him learn how to avoid the beatings that were common on Wye Plantation. He felt a sense of family but couldn't stop wondering if he would ever meet his mother or father.

From his bed one night, Frederick stared into the great expanse of black outside the window. He thought he saw movement, sat up, and squinted his eyes. A woman appeared in the distance, moving toward him as she slipped in and out of shadows under the giant red oaks scattered across the plantation. Her clothes hung loosely, thin protection against the February wind that swayed the creaking oaks' branches.

He pressed his face against the window until it fogged up from his breath. His brother and sister, dressed in their nightgowns, appeared beside him. Frederick pointed in the direction of where he'd seen the woman, saying, "Someone is out there."

The three of them craned their necks, rubbing the glass, but the woman was gone—disappeared into the shadows. They jumped when a soft knock came at the door. Frederick's brother unbolted the door. It swung open, and the woman appeared before them.

"Mamma!" the two children said and squealed with delight.

Though barely a flame rose from the dying embers, its light flickered in her eyes as she searched the room. Her gaze settled on Frederick.

"Are you just going to stand there?" she said. "Or are you going to give your mother a kiss?"

By any measure, Frederick Douglass lived an inspired life. At the age of twenty, he made a daring escape from slavery by posing as a free Black sailor. Douglass became one of the most influential men of the nineteenth century as a famous abolitionist, publisher, orator, and author. In addition to playing a significant role in ending slavery and establishing African Americans' right to vote, he also became a prominent voice in women's suffrage. In 1877, he became the first Black man to serve as a US marshal. His autobiographies are considered classics of American literature.

> "I prefer to be true to myself, even at the hazard of incurring the ridicule of others, rather than to be false, and to incur my own abhorrence."
>
> Frederick Douglass

Though he gained his freedom and achieved tremendous good, Frederick never learned his father's identity.[1] As for his mother, her nighttime visit was the only time they saw each other. She faced great danger had her

---

1. His father is rumored to be Aaron Anthony, his master.

absence been noticed—a lashing at minimum, a noose more likely. Frederick's mother left a few hours after appearing suddenly in the night and died shortly thereafter.

Despite the short time they spent together, she was a primary inspiration in Frederick's life. Visiting her son that night exemplified strength, self-value, and defiance against a brutally unjust system. Frederick learned that his mother could read, though literacy was a skill punishable by death for slaves. Through her example, he saw that it was admirable to live life according to one's values in the face of great danger. He learned from his mother that standing up for what is right is worth risking one's life. Few relationships are as impactful as the bond between mother and child, even when their time together is tragically short.

• • •

Like the connection between Frederick and his mother, certain types of relationship affect us more than any other. This inner circle includes those who have the most power to affect our worldview and change our life direction. Even if you don't like these people, even if you don't trust them, they exert a powerful gravitational pull on you. We'll explore these critical relationships using a matrix that resembles the introduction to *The Brady Bunch*, with you at the center.

As we move through these eight relationships, consider who now occupies each role. Some positions will have more than one person; others, none. Most people have a few gaps. In addition to those already occupying your inner circle, think about who you might add to help you change into the person you want to become. You don't need specific names—a vague idea of the traits you are looking for is enough. By being aware of any gaps you might want to fill, you will be more ready to jump at the opportunity to meet someone when it arises.

Supervisors

The relationship that affects your career and wealth more than any other is likely the one you have with your boss. After you start working full-time, your supervisor is someone you will probably spend more time with than any other mentor. Ideally, they should show you, step-by-step, how to get from where you are to where they are.

Managers are different from other mentors. Most mentors are unpaid, so to get time with them, you must rely on their goodwill. To receive the attention of a professor, you must pay tuition. Professional coaching is accessible but often expensive. And many people don't have parents who are able or willing to provide advice about success. But a supervisor is likely to know how to get ahead in your career and to give you a lot of attention because they have a vested interest in your success.

The best managers see your achievements as their own. They hire rising stars, often regardless of experience, and help them live up to ever greater levels of potential. Pete Carroll, coach of the Seattle Seahawks, exemplifies this trait. He has performed so well as a mentor, and has inspired his team to perform so well under his staff's direction, that his assistant coaches get recruited to coach competing teams.

In contrast, ineffective managers feel threatened by your success. They are insecure about their value. By either negligence or design, they will hold you back to feel superior. Other managers simply aren't able to help you achieve your goals. Or, as you grow, you may pass your boss. If your manager stagnates while you grow, you will gain less from the connection over time. And if your boss is not helping you grow, consider brushing up your resume and moving on.

Fortunately, work relationships are less personal than many other inner-circle roles. You can make strategic decisions about choosing the best boss for your future without feeling as if you're dumping a family member or best friend. Yet employees are often too loyal to businesses or nonprofits that would think little of cutting them loose if the need arose. An employee-company relationship is, in the end, an exchange of time for cash. As long as both sides feel the trade is fair, neither should owe the other more.

That said, loyalty to a person is an excellent value, especially with someone who has done much to help you. I don't recommend casting such a manager aside without speaking to them first. If they are worthy of your allegiance, they should be willing to help you fairly evaluate new and better opportunities without letting self-interest color their advice—as Pete Carroll does with his assistant coaches.

While it's great if your boss possesses traits that match your non-professional life goals—say, being a wonderful grandparent or possessing long golden locks—the key characteristics you are looking for in a supervisor are related to career and income.

> "A manager is a guide. He takes a group of people and says, 'With you I can make us a success; I can show you the way.'"
>
> Arsène Wenger

Your ideal manager is far ahead of you in these areas—the further ahead they are, the faster you will grow. But as we discussed previously in the section about accounting for luck, you will do well to consider factors of serendipity that may have contributed to your supervisor's success when evaluating their fit in your inner circle.

This is tricky. Few people want to believe their achievements resulted from forces outside their awesomeness—especially those whose success is mostly the result of chance. Not to mention, wealthy, powerful, and well-known people tend to be followed around by drooling fanboys, enablers, and yes-women whose lips are permanently puckered for any opportunity to kiss ass. You must learn how to cut through that hot mess. Many experts who study such matters profess that being in the right place at the right time is more likely to be the reason for success than intelligence. And don't underestimate how much more difficult it is to make ideas work on peanuts and Top Ramen than multimillion-dollar trust funds.

In light of this, you should try to find a boss who was once where you are and fought her way to the top without a lot of difficult-to-re-create circumstances. If you can't, even a superstar boss who is luckier than a leprechaun may be able to help you in extraordinary ways through her connections and knowledge of how people think at the top.

Sometimes, to get access to an ideal manager, you have to accept an opportunity that would otherwise be below you. Maybe you have to take a pay cut. Or perhaps you will have to do some tasks you feel are beneath your level of experience and knowledge.[2] While these situations are not ideal, remember that you will likely reach your goals much faster by focusing on who you work for rather than pay or tasks. Sacrificing in the short term is likely to offer a huge payoff as you learn invaluable lessons from a high-caliber boss and gain access to their golden Rolodex.

Finally, make the most of your relationship with your supervisor—an essential consideration with all your mentors. Sometimes people who know more than us tell us things that don't make sense. This is usually because we don't have the experience to comprehend what they're saying in the way they mean it. But too often, we dismiss advice we don't understand as out of touch, unhelpful, or unrelated to our current situation. Perhaps you've had a boss who tells the same parables and stories again and again. You may have rolled your eyes when they weren't looking and joked about them behind their back. But consider instead that they kept repeating themselves because you weren't getting the lesson they were trying to communicate. If your boss is worthy of your admiration, lean toward giving their input the benefit of the doubt, even when you don't get it. Instead of dismissing or making fun of them, try asking them to help you understand what they're trying to say.

Similarly, listen to your manager more than you talk. Don't try to impress with your words—that's what underperformers do. Instead, impress with your work. Supervisors don't need to hear about how wonderful you are; they want to *see* how wonderful you are. So stop talking and start learning. When you're with your boss, soak in every bit of information you can. Keep a journal of notes and lessons you've learned. And always have questions ready.

---

2. Up to a point. There are stories of Hollywood producers who ask interns to stand all day in front of a window so the producers can work in the shade. If you find yourself acting as a piece of human furniture, reassess.

Especially be on the lookout for lessons that your boss doesn't verbalize. Much of what you can learn from someone comes from observing and reading between the lines. Many people don't know how to teach what they do best. Sometimes, they don't even entertain the possibility that other people don't see the world the way they do. It's easy for them because they're great at it. So it can be hard for them to break down a lesson in a way you will instantly get. Teaching is a different skill than being good at something. It can be a humbling experience for someone to realize they must learn the craft of teaching, regardless of how good they are at whatever it is they do. Don't assume your boss cares enough about mentoring to master the art of it.

> "Be observing constantly. Stay open minded. Be eager to learn and improve."
>
> John Wooden

Help your manager help you. Watch how they interact with other people. Observe your boss doing what they do best. And if they are an ideal match, do whatever is necessary to stay close by their side.

Pause to reflect

- If you are in a role that is on track with your career ambitions, is your current supervisor the ideal person to help you grow toward your professional goals? If they are, how can you make better use of your access to them to accelerate your growth? If they aren't ideal, what changes can you make to get a job (either in your company or at another) working for someone who can better help you go where you want with your career?
- If you are not in a role helping you get closer to your career goals, what can you do to find such a role? What criteria will you use to evaluate the qualities of your would-be boss to help you maximize your professional development?
- Regardless of your answers above, is it possible to take on side gigs or volunteer work to increase your access to high-gravity individuals who can help supplement your relationshift (or lack thereof) at work?

Parents

For most of us, parents are the most powerful shaping force in our lives. And though our parents' influence often fades over time, most children retain a strong connection with their mother and father long into adulthood. This category of your inner circle can include grandparents and other elders in your extended family if you have the possibility of a close relationship with any of them. (In this section, I'll use "parents" to represent all of these relationships for brevity.) Those who have a positive relationship with any of these connections enjoy access to mentoring, and sometimes resources, whenever they wish to pick up the phone.

To the extent our parents aren't available or don't have the attributes and knowledge we wish to adopt, we miss the opportunity to benefit from this role within our inner circle. This is not a relationshift death sentence; it merely means we should seek to fill that gap with other mentors and parent-like figures who are more available and have the experience or a worldview that is more in line with our goals. And remember, even the absence of a parent can be a significant influence, as it was with Frederick Douglass.

You can sometimes use your parents' absence, lack of helpfulness, or negative feelings toward you as an advantage. If your parents are less successful, happy, or content than you would like to be, use this as motivation—if you become the person you want to be, you may be able to help them find their way forward as well. If your mother or father is no longer living, honor their memory by enjoying your life—if they were here, they would probably want you to be as happy as you can be. If you are in a negative situation with one or both parents, show them you are content and doing well pursuing your dreams—perhaps this will draw them to you in a way that could bring healing.

In some cases, you may be able to benefit more from your parental relationship than you currently are. For any life goal in which they match your direction, seek your parents' advice often. Explain your goals. Ask for introductions to people who can help you. If they have the financial means, seek ways to partner with them in your investments or big purchases, like a home or college education.

Many people mistakenly feel that getting help from one's parents is cheating. This makes no sense. If everything we accomplish is affected by the people around us, we needlessly limit ourselves and make life harder by disqualifying relations from helping us. If we accept an introduction from a professor, manager, or friend, we should do the same with our mother's or father's connections.

Of course, the family we are born into is entirely luck—no less than being dealt your first hand of cards at a poker game. You can't change the cards you're dealt. You can only make a strategy for winning with the cards you're holding. Parents who can help you in any aspect of your dreams are ideal members of your inner circle. Make the most of these relationships, and feel no shame in taking advantage of the benefits they can provide.

Pause to reflect

- If you don't have parents or don't look up to your parents, who are others that can or do fill this role for you in the most positive way possible? If this applies to you, think of your surrogate parents as you reflect on the following questions.
- What do you admire most about your parents regarding traits you wish to embody?
- Are there any parent-inherited aspects of how you think or operate that are holding you back from living your best life?
- How can you maximize your parents' positive impact on you while minimizing any negative influence they have had or continue to have over you?
- If you are a parent or fill this role for others, how can you increase your positive impact on those who might look up to you?

Mentors

Some of the best mentors, advisers, and guides can be unilateral connections like authors, YouTubers, politicians, and great thinkers of the past. With these you can simply consume as much content as you like, picking what helps you and excluding what doesn't. However, unilateral mentoring comes with several difficulties. You can't ask questions to get input on how to apply lessons to your specific situation. You can't verify that you understand what they're trying to teach you, and you may not know when you're misinterpreting someone's advice. And they can't hold you accountable. Despite these challenges, unilateral guides are sometimes the best we have. Make the most of these resources and simultaneously seek to add bilateral guides to your inner circle whenever possible.

Most everyone has a few potential bilateral mentors built into their inner circles, such as bosses, parents, and extended family, which we've discussed in the previous two sections. Other examples of bilateral mentors include teachers, spiritual leaders, life coaches, psychiatrists, physical therapists, subject matter experts, and friends. In the introduction I mentioned how I curate traits from individuals who excel in areas of life I wish to improve in. These may be managers, friends, children, or anyone else, but if I'm hoping they will relationshift me forward in any aspect of life, they would be considered a mentor in that area. Each role may require a different approach. For advisers unrelated by blood or shared success, you will have to invest more in the relationship.

Mental health therapy is a type of mentor that merits a few paragraphs' discussion. It's a travesty that society has painted seeing a counselor as a sign of weakness. This is like a drowning person being criticized for using a life preserver. No one judges a patient for seeing a doctor for a broken leg. Likewise, we shouldn't judge people for seeing a doctor for a broken heart—or anything else. So don't let insecure people keep you from getting valuable input on your problems from a highly educated professional. It takes strength to ask for help.

Counselors are a gift. Very few areas of life exist where you can whine, be petty, talk on and on without ever listening in return, and share your darkest secrets without fear of judgment or causing annoyance. I believe every living person should have a counselor. You don't need to meet every week. Just have someone you can call when the need arises. If I'm going through a lot—a breakup, stress at work, my cat clawing up my furniture—I might meet twice a month or more. If life is steady, I may not see a therapist for a year. I write down whatever is bothering me in a note I keep on my phone. When the list gets long enough, I set an appointment.

> "A mentor is someone who sees more talent and ability within you, than you see in yourself, and helps bring it out of you."
>
> Bob Proctor

If you've attempted therapy and found it didn't do much for you, I recommend trying again. Just as I wouldn't suggest giving up on reading because you tried it once and the book was boring. It can take a few rounds to find someone who is a match. I put off seeing a counselor for years because of one bad experience. Don't make this same mistake. Try people of a different gender, background, or philosophical approach. I also don't feel the need to stay with one person my entire life. Sometimes it feels as if my psychologist and I have simply run out of topics. If you feel stuck with someone and fear breaking up, simply say, "I'm going to be busy for a while. Let's not set another appointment. I'll reach out when I'm ready." Then you can set an appointment if you want or find another therapist. They won't take it personally. Clients come and go; that's part of the business.

As with counselors, the simplest way to gain an adviser is to pay for their time. We do this when we enroll in a university, hire a coach, meet with a doctor, or consult with a subject matter expert. Countless coaches are available for everything from posture to fashion to vocal confidence. If you can't afford to hire one, you might be able to work out a trade for your time. As for paid services like massage therapists, dentists,[3] and physical therapists, I find that the average search engine or review site works just fine. Just be willing to try a couple of people if you don't feel a good fit with the first person you see.

Pastors, rabbis, nuns, and monks are often willing to spend time with people and give advice without expecting anything in return, but their advice is usually limited to spiritual matters. Also, their input may be colored by their worldview in ways that may not match your desired direction. Like if you're looking for the best way to get more paying subscribers on OnlyFans. They will likely have plenty of advice, but just not the kind you're specifically seeking.

Beyond these examples, possibilities for finding mentors are everywhere. We previously discussed several strategies for getting the attention of people we want to meet. You must add enough value to the relationship that they will want to spend time with you in return—whether that's by paying them, offering your expertise to them for free or at a discount, helping them in some other way, or merely by being a member of their tribe.

As with managers, you should attempt to account for how lucky the mentor has been when evaluating how closely they match your life goals. You also need to watch for marketing spin. Everyone is prone to overinflate their value. But paid coaches and those who benefit from your followership have a vested interest in gaining your trust. Gurus often offer free advice as a path to selling you books and expensive workshops. Even paid seminars can be disguised pitches for even more costly seminars where the "very best secrets" will be revealed. They might use guilt-based messaging like, "If you believed in your potential, if you really wanted success, you would be willing to invest in yourself." Many people have dumped large sums of money into such scams and received little in return.

This isn't just a concern with paid coaching. Spiritual leaders are sometimes incentivized to gain your trust as well, whether it's to feel good about their growing church or because more people mean more tithes, volunteers, and, for some, book sales. Studies prove that church

---

3. I'm interested to know how my dentist would respond if, the next time I get my teeth cleaned, I refer to her as my Tooth Mentor.

attendance correlates directly with pastor salary. But as with paid coaches, this doesn't mean everyone is out to take advantage of you. It's like Jesus said: "Be wise about who you trust. Some people are wolves. Religious leaders included."[4]

With most advising relationships, don't try to set up a regular meeting. These are often canceled, and it's a lot to ask for one person to put the other in their calendars every week or even every month. Instead, compile a list of topics you wish to talk about and reach out when you have enough to fill a coffee date. Better yet, call them with a specific question, and promise it's only going to take a few minutes. Or set up a time to talk while they're taking a walk or going for a long drive. High-caliber people love to multitask.

If you're going out for a meal or coffee, do not ask to split the check. Pay with a smile. Grab the bill from their hands if you have to. Say, "No, I insist." Even if money is tight, better to skip a luxury or two so you can afford to show this person your appreciation. They may insist back. At that point, let them pay, but be clear and concise with your thanks. You want to be sure they know you value their contribution.

Much advice about good mentors is similar to what we discussed previously regarding picking your manager. Listen more than you talk. Come with questions. Understand they may not know how to teach you the stuff they're best at, so you might have to read between the lines a little. Ask if you can shadow them occasionally and watch for habits or ways of thinking that they haven't articulated in your meetings. And if they offer advice that makes no sense, give them the benefit of the doubt. If you've vetted them for factors such as luck or knowing how to move forward in your specific situation, trust their advice even when it seems confusing. They should know some things you don't—you would hope. Your lack of knowledge could be preventing you from comprehending their true meaning. So don't be quick to dismiss their input. Instead, ask them to help you understand. A good mentor would love nothing more than to do just that.

---

4. Paraphrased from Matthew 10:16.

Pause to reflect

- Who are your mentors, both now and throughout your life? How have they impacted you, either positively or negatively?
- Where do you have room to improve your mentoring by gaining or increasing your exposure to high-gravity individuals that align well with your desired life direction?
- Do you make the most of your access to the mentors you already have? How can you get more from and give more to these relationships?

Romantic Partners

A romantic partner's advice frequently has more sway over us than anyone else's input, for better or worse. Their influence affects all our life goals—financial success, living healthfully, finding contentment, expanding our worldview, or learning a new skill. For those who don't have a romantic partner, friends and other relationships can take their place. Any one of these is unlikely to have the same level of influence over your life course. But through a portfolio of relationships, you can create an inner circle that replicates the value of an ideal partner. See also the last paragraph in this section for some advice on thoughtfully picking an inner-circle-worthy partner, if this is a goal of yours.)

Intentionality is less of a factor with romantic partners than with other inner-circle roles. We tend to spend so much time with our partners that we can't help but influence each other. Of more pressing concern is how to approach a relationship with someone who you feel is holding you back from your goals. If this is the case for you, it's likely the most challenging application of relationshift to navigate in your life. But do not ignore the effect your partner has on you—their influence makes too big a difference.

Consider the example of trying to increase your positivity. A negative partner will sap your energy when you need all you can get. Changing our mindset or habits is hard enough without also having to spend a good portion of our drive on overcoming the negativity of the person with whom we live. If you are in this situation, you will become increasingly frustrated as you watch what you pour into them dissipate the moment you stop.

> "Choose your life's mate carefully. From this one decision will come 90 percent of all your happiness or misery."
>
> H. Jackson Brown Jr.

Inversely, a positive partner will propel you forward as you do the same for them. The best possible partnership is when both sides have their own drive source. As they pour into each other, the energy of both partners grows exponentially.

Unfortunately, it's common for people to find themselves in relationships that are holding them back. If you feel this way about your partner, maybe you met when you were a different person and your goals have changed. Or your partner has changed. Or you just didn't know what you wanted when you met. You may have to face the difficult decision to modify or end the relationship before you can grow into the person you want to be. Of course, one should never take this choice lightly. Talk openly with your partner about how you feel your life

WHEN YOU POUR YOURSELF INTO SOMEONE YOU HAVE LESS ENERGY FOR YOURSELF

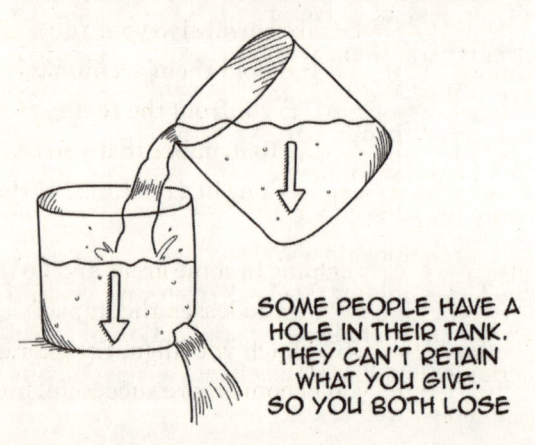

SOME PEOPLE HAVE A HOLE IN THEIR TANK. THEY CAN'T RETAIN WHAT YOU GIVE. SO YOU BOTH LOSE

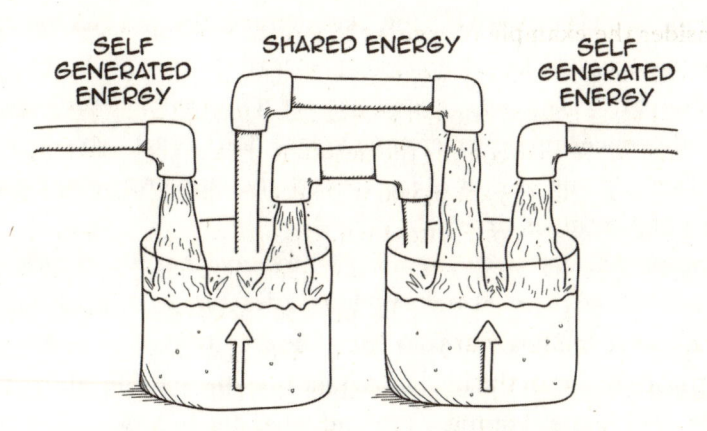

WHEN TWO PEOPLE GENERATE THEIR OWN ENERGY AND SHARE WITH EACH OTHER, BOTH GROW EXPONENTIALLY

goals do not align. They may feel the same, and you will be able to reduce your influence on each other without much pain.

Or they might disagree. They may go to great lengths to convince you to stay, even if you no longer want to. They might try to make you feel guilty or convince you they are the only person who will ever love you. They might threaten to lie about you publicly or post desperate pleas on Instagram for you to give them one more chance. Conversely, you might fear being alone or not finding someone who matches better. There are many reasons to ignore a poor match with a romantic partner, some of them admirable like loyalty, love, and shared children. In those cases, you may find couples therapy helpful. You could set clear boundaries to protect yourself from any areas of the relationship that are harmful to you. You could request that your partner commit to growth and hold them accountable to show progress. But in the end, you may have to confront the reality that your partner may not be the right person for you. Remember that you only have one life to live. Do not waste it by staying too long in a relationship that isn't making you happy.

For many, their partner is helping in some areas and holding them back in others. If this is your situation, try to lessen the impact of their negative influence while enjoying ways in which you align. For example, your partner may be great for helping you become more successful but enabling you to continue habits you wish to quit, like smoking. You can talk openly with your partner and seek their support in places where your goals don't match. In this example, you could ask your partner not to smoke around you. But be realistic concerning mismatching areas—don't expect your partner to align with every one of your life goals entirely. That's why you have other members of your inner circle.

If you are single, you're in a great place to make the most of these principles. In addition to physical and emotional attraction, you should add alignment with your life goals to your list of desired traits in a partner. Don't settle. You're better off having no partner than having one who is holding you back. No matter who you are and what you're looking for, remember there are thousands, if not millions, of potential partners who would match you well. You just have to keep looking until you find them. Given the importance of this relationship, you will benefit greatly from investing in finding and keeping a partner who is a great match.

Pause to reflect

If you have no interest in having a romantic partner, feel free to skip to the next section. If you don't have a partner, but would like to, consider these questions hypothetically as an exercise in evaluating what aspects of an ideal match you would like to have or avoid.

- What life goals does your partner support the most?
- What aspects of your relationship can you be more intentional about to increase the impact your partner has on you in these areas?
- Are there any goals your partner holds you back from actualizing?
- How can you minimize their negative impact on you in these areas without breaking up or harming the relationship?
- Have you discussed your concerns with your partner? Are there ways to introduce this topic without causing pain to you or your partner?
- How can you be a better partner to support their life ambitions more?

Peers

Peers are highly influential because we spend the bulk of our time with them. People in this category of relationship are in a similar place on one or more of our desired life paths. For athletes, this would be two people with similar physical abilities. For activists, a comparable commitment to the cause. For intellectuals, an equivalent IQ and shared subject interests. For most professions, a parallel level of success in corresponding lines of work. In addition to being in the same place now, well-matched friends or colleagues are also moving toward the same goals within any given life path.

We receive different kinds of support from a friend than we do from mentors because peers are, by definition, not ahead of us in life. We may consider someone a friend who is ahead of us in a particular path, but for relationshift, we call that person a mentor because they are further along in that specific area of life. Though we don't often intentionally seek to gain anything from a friend other than companionship, we naturally support and motivate one another. Peers act as a positive force in helping both sides reach their shared destination. They can expand our possibilities, like how Draymond Green improves his teammates whenever he's on the court. We learn together and from one another. If one falls behind, the other can get her back on track. If one gets a big break, she can pull the other up to her new level.

> "Accept that some relationships are seasonal. Learn what they came to teach and let go when it's time for them to leave."
>
> **Unknown**

The way we evaluate a peer for fit is similar to how we approach a mentor—except with a peer, we must project where we think they are going and how far. This isn't as hard as it might sound. If we step back from a relationship and consider a person dispassionately, we can make a pretty good guess about where they are going in life. A person's life trend is like a meteor zipping through space. Without forces pushing a person one way or another, they will likely continue in more or less the same direction at the same velocity. We can chart this path: imagine you could draw a line from where they started to where they are now, and then continue the line along the same trajectory into the future.

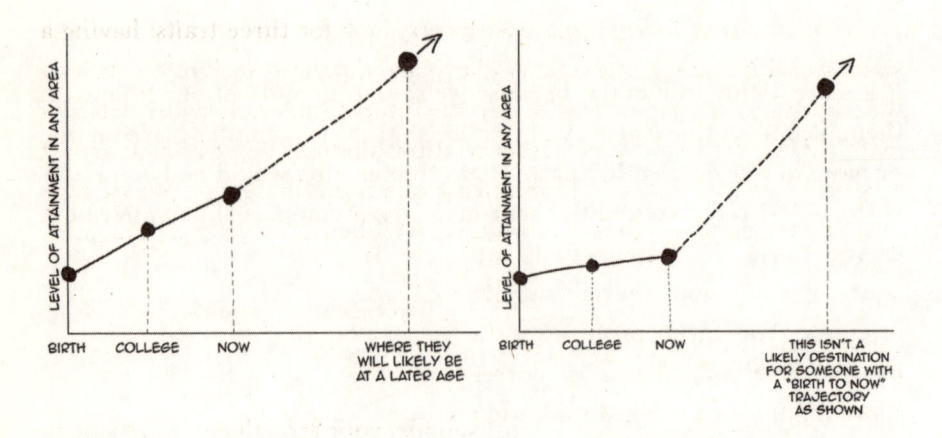

To help you with this analysis, consider where someone invests their energy. A high achiever at twenty-five years old will probably have achieved a lot by retirement. Someone who is committed to learning at the age of thirty will undoubtedly know a lot by the age of fifty. And a college student who invests deeply in her friendships will probably have many friends later in life.

In contrast, if you have to pester your roommate to help you with the business you agreed to start together, you are probably going to have to plead for their contribution as long as you are partners. Don't waste your energy trying to get someone out of bed. Better to leave them where they want to be and find another peer who shares your dreams and your drive to make them a reality.

> "I would rather walk with a friend in the dark, than alone in the light."
>
> Helen Keller

When looking for well-matched peers, look for three traits: having a similar background, being in a similar place now, and seeking to grow in the same ways as you both move into the future. Some colleagues will be a match in more than one area. Other relationships may be for a single aspect of your journey. But try to find at least one friend for every one of your desired life paths, whether your physical well-being, career, spiritual journey, or the like.

Pause to reflect

- Which of your friends most support your growth goals, regardless of how close you are with them?
- How can you consciously attempt to improve yourself more through these relationships?
- Do you have peers who could pull you further or faster than they currently are? How can you make more of these connections?
- Are any of your peers holding you back or pulling you away from your goals? How can you minimize their negative impact on you without ending the relationship?
- Can you think of anyone who would be ideal to most help you grow in the ways you desire? If not, what kinds of traits would embody an excellent match in this way? How can you find people who embody those traits?

Protégés

The final category of your inner circle is for people who are not as far along as you are in any one particular desired life direction, like students, children, and employees. This group can also include friends, partners, and family, even those who might be older than you but are behind on one or more paths. Some people in your life may be a mentor in one desired life path, a peer in another, and a protégé in a third. Their position respective to you on any given path establishes their role in your inner circle.

Protégé relationships are a positive force for growth in multiple ways. First, they provide you the opportunity to give back. Expecting mentors' help without investing in others shows an ungratefulness that breaks the giving circle. People are great at sniffing out users and are less likely to want to help anyone they perceive is only out for themselves. Second, spending time with a protégé is a chance for you to recite the lessons you've learned.

Nothing improves mastery of a subject better than teaching it to a student. And third, protégés are a great source of positive pressure that pushes you forward. They help you measure your progress. As protégés grow, they drive you to stay ahead; otherwise, you may find yourself left behind.

Finding suitable matches for this category of your inner circle is similar to the process for peers. Your goal is to find people going in the same direction as you but who are just not as far along. Ideally, your protégés will end up far ahead of where you currently are in whatever area of life you're attempting to improve. For example, if you want to become a great painter, find students who have a good chance of achieving this same goal. If you wish to live a vibrant, adventurous life into your seventies and eighties, hang out with younger friends who want the same. Try to separate those who think they want something from those who are likely to put in the work to get it done. As with peers, investing energy in those who have a problem for every solution is a significant drain.

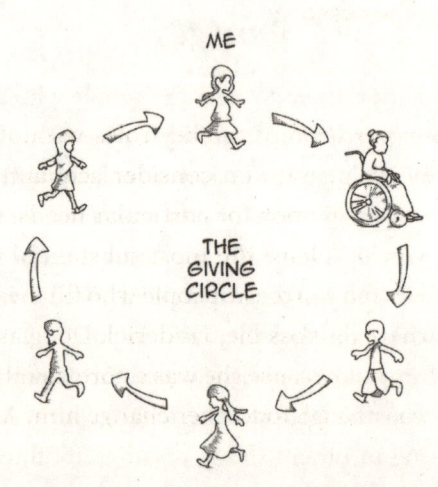

> "What I've found about it is that there are some folks you can talk to until you're blue in the face—they're never going to get it and they're never going to change. But every once in a while, you'll run into someone who is eager to listen, eager to learn, and willing to try new things. Those are the people we need to reach. We have a responsibility as parents, older people, teachers, people in the neighborhood to recognize that."
>
> Tyler Perry

Pause to reflect

- Who thinks of you as a mentor?
- Are there ways to increase their positive impact toward supporting your personal growth goals?
- How can you increase the positive impact you have on their life?
- Can you think of anyone who isn't as far along as you now in any particular area of personal growth but who seems likely to go far? How can you foster a mentoring relationship with them to propel both of you toward more significant positive change?
- Do you have any other key relationships that aren't included in the categories listed in this chapter? How do they affect you, either positively or negatively? How can you increase the positive while minimizing the negative?

• • •

That wraps up our exploration of the key roles within one's inner circle. You may have dozens of people you consider acquaintances, people you see from time to time or call upon for particular needs. But it is the people who are closest to you that have the most substantial effect on your life direction. Pay special attention to the people who fill these roles and seek to add ideal matches wherever possible. Frederick Douglass only spent three hours with his mother, but because she was a core member of his inner circle, this short time was enough to forever change him. As Frederick moved through life, mentors, peers, and protégés played a part in who he became and contributed to his impressive list of accomplishments.

We can't do anything alone. Those closest to you have helped you become the person you are today. And who will you become tomorrow? That depends on the people you allow to occupy your inner circle from this day forward.

CHAPTER 4

Specific Paths

"Every great athlete, artist and aspiring being has a great team to help them flourish and succeed—personally and professionally. Even the so-called 'solo star' has a strong supporting cast helping them shine, thrive and take flight."

Rasheed Ogunlaru

Depending on which aspect of yourself or your life you want to change, your approach to using relationshift to accelerate toward your goal will vary. For example, growing in fame, wealth, or happiness all require different applications of relationshift's principles. This section offers specific advice and considerations for ten different paths. Some of the content may repeat a little, as approaches share commonalities across many of these specific examples. Because these paths are so specific, however, I'm assuming many readers will skip straight to the ones they are most interested in. I want to ensure that the discussion for each path is complete without requiring you to read any that don't apply to you. However, reading through each of these paths can also aid in creating your own journey toward success, as countless other paths exist beyond these ten. Because you may find tips in the full list that can help you with any paths for which I didn't write specific recipes, I therefore encourage you to read through them all.

One additional caveat I'd like to offer before we begin: some of these topics are quite serious and could not possibly be properly addressed in the condensed few paragraphs you'll read below. I certainly don't intend to oversimplify the complexities of achieving your goals in any of these paths; rather, I would like to offer some specific input that can help you get a head start on using relationshift to improve one or more aspects of your life. Consider these as merely brief overviews of a few ideas you can use to apply relationshift in those specific contexts.

Becoming a Great Athlete

Becoming a great athlete has never been a goal of mine. My sports career peaked in about eighth grade, when a guy playing football could make up for being scared of getting hit by being fast enough to run away from anyone with a different-colored jersey. But I've had the privilege of knowing several people who have risen to the highest levels of sports, and I've always admired the focus and effort required to do so.

For instance, I had the opportunity to interview Tony Parrish for a series of videos I filmed on leadership. Tony was considered one of the best defensive players in the world when he was selected for the all-pro team in 2003 while playing for the San Francisco 49ers. The point he made that has stuck with me most since that interview many years ago is that your performance on Sunday is determined by your preparation Monday through Saturday. One must have off-the-charts self-discipline to compete at the highest levels of sports. This can only be developed over the course of a lifetime and is influenced by parenting; coaching at a young age; the inspiration of older, more accomplished athletic mentors or idols; and being pushed by other athletes who are on a similar path toward greatness. In this way, all great athletes share two things in common: they have the best coaching and the best peers or teammates.

Depending on your stage of life and socioeconomic status, strategies for gaining access to these kinds of people varies. If you're in school, securing top coaches is more likely to happen by attending the school where they work. You also may gain the best teammates and peers because they will be drawn to work with the same talented coaches. You would be hard pressed to find a high school American football player who wouldn't do anything to play for Nick Saban at the University of Alabama. Saban's teams have won national championships six times in the twelve years between 2009 and 2020—a display of dominance unrivaled by any of the other 129 teams. And if you land a spot on one of Saban's teams, your chances of making it to the NFL spike. However, it's not just the coaching that makes these teams so good. A positive reinforcement cycle enables the team's extraordinary performance, as good players are attracted to work with the top coaches and push each other to perform even better. This, in turn, allows Alabama to continue to attract and pay top coaches.

If you have the money, you can simply hire great people to work with. Or if you show enough raw talent, you can attract their attention with your own excellence. As discussed in the Saban example, top coaches want to work with the most talented athletes. If you're at a later stage in life, you could consider reducing your expenses to the point where you can hire a great coach. You may need to use some networking skills to get in touch with them, depending on how in demand their services are.

You will also want to be careful not to spend too much time with any peers who pull you away from your goal. This is always true with relationshift, but even more so when you really want to go after an audacious goal like getting into a major college sports program or even playing professional sports. If these are your goals, you really don't have any time or energy to spare. You can be sure that millions of others want the same and many are willing to do whatever it takes to get there. So if you have some friends who love to party, you might not be able to hang out with them much if you find yourself tempted to drink yourself under a table or partake in the harder variety of drugs when others around you are—there's little room for these kinds of shenanigans for those who want to have their bodies in perfect shape.

Pursuing a Fitness Goal

I'm embarrassed to admit that I didn't know what calories were until I was twenty-two. I didn't realize I had been gaining weight for years until a colleague of mine patted me on the stomach one day and asked, "Getting enough to eat?" This is a pointed example of relationshift, if perhaps a cruel one. But it had the intended effect.

I was a buyer at a manufacturing company and had been enjoying the perks of the job, which included getting taken out to lots of lunches, happy hours, and dinners. One of my favorite spots was the Roadhouse Grill. I would often order the pork chops along with a bacon and ranch salad (to make it healthy) and, of course, a generous helping of bread slathered in sweet butter. Throw in two to three pints of beer for good measure, and I was coming in at more than 3,000 calories just in a single meal. My six-foot-two frame had gone from a svelte 150 pounds when I was a teenager to 215 pounds just a few years later.

Once I realized that eating 3,000 calories for lunch was going to kill me before my thirtieth birthday, I tapered off and managed to range between 200 and 215 for the next eight years, until I moved to Seattle. This was my first time living in a more urban area, and I remember feeling like everyone I worked with or saw on the street looked extremely fit. I had come from a smaller town where having a bit of extra weight was much more normal. In both cases, I was experiencing relationshift in action. Now, living among thinner people, I began to see my weight more when I looked in the mirror. I became more serious about getting into shape. I cut back my eating and drinking. I started running. I hated both at first, but over time I grew to enjoy healthier foods and more exercise. I found some friends to run with and before long, I was getting in a 10K multiple times a week. I dropped from 215 pounds to 170 and have hovered near there ever since. Interestingly, when I go back to the small town where I spent my twenties, sometimes people I know still question if I'm getting enough to eat—but now, they are being serious. Relationshift is always at work, pulling us in either one direction or the other.

Getting into better physical shape is a similar path to becoming the best athlete one can be, but far less intense. You don't need the best coach in the world to lose twenty pounds or run your first 5K, but you would definitely benefit from having a good one. Likewise, you don't need to cut off any friends who tempt you to drink, but you should definitely have a few friends who motivate you toward your goal. And if you do struggle with bad habits around food, drinking, or drugs, you will do yourself a big favor by limiting your exposure to these temptations when they come from people you know. Using the principles of relationshift to get into shape or lose weight involves limiting negative shift and maximizing positive shift related to three factors that affect your body and how you see it: what you put into your body, how you use your body, and how you see your body.

What You Put into Your Body

Simply stated, we survive by transforming the stuff we put in our stomach into energy and new cells. For this purpose, our body can make more efficient use of certain inputs, such as fresh fish, than it can with other inputs, such as an entire bag of Frito-Lays. If we put too much stuff in our stomach, especially the stuff our body isn't as efficient processing, we will be prone to gain weight, feel more tired, and otherwise grow less healthy. We can also destroy our cells if we consume too much of certain things like drugs and alcohol. If we don't give our body enough of the good stuff it needs, we will lose energy and even healthy cells such as muscle and brain tissue.

To maximize this aspect of getting into better shape with relationshift, we must hang around people who foster a healthier approach to what we put in our bodies. At the same time, we must limit our exposure to people with whom we tend to indulge. How much we limit our exposure to negative temptation is based on how seriously we want to get into better shape. This isn't a moral judgment. It's a necessary acknowledgment of our own agency in relation to our decisions. And while one can avoid, say, using cocaine, even while their friends are partaking, relationshift shows us that it's simply harder to avoid when in close proximity to those who are partaking. Relationshift doesn't force us to do anything—but the pressure we experience as a result of adjacency to people behaving and thinking certain ways simply draws us toward that position. In the same way, having a roommate who loves fresh veggies and the clearheadedness of sobriety will create a positive pressure to enjoy more veggies and fewer intoxicants.

Many aspects of relationshift lend themselves to the shortcut of simply hiring a professional to help you. Nutritionists can help you understand what diet is best for you, your body type, and your goals. You can also find many thought leaders online who will give away quite a bit of their advice, knowing that a certain percentage of their followers will sign up for paid programs. Just beware of these options, because anyone who is selling something has an inherent conflict of interest. Not to say that they're all just out to get your money, but it's possible that some might be. Dieting in particular is prone to fads because it's hard to sell something we've all heard a million times, and far easier just to market a diet idea that a moderately famous doctor or celebrity just "discovered."

Also, beware of the attractiveness of diet plans that promise better results with less effort. This is highly marketable. We all want to do less and get more. But these plans rarely work out as promised. In the end, it's usually the boring, tried-and-true methods that get the best results. People just don't want to do them because they're slow and hard. As it turns out, getting into shape is hard work. And if substance dependency is standing in your way, both free and paid counseling are readily available.

How You Use Your Body

Besides what you put into your body, your goal of getting into better shape is, of course, greatly affected by how you use your body. Assuming you have good inputs at the right volume for your body size, energy use, and goals, you're going to want to build good habits around how you use your body to achieve your goal of getting into shape. The people around you can greatly affect this process. If your partner wants to drink mimosas and watch movies in bed every weekend, you're likely to join them. If they like to get up early and go for a long hike, you're also likely to join them. In either case, you're not forced to participate in their preferred activities. You're just going to feel a pressure to do so that requires your own compensating force to overcome. This compensating force must come from somewhere inside you, and because of that, it is limited. The more often you have to say no to friends who want to be lazy, the more depleted this inner energy becomes and the harder it will be to resist.

The good news: this works exactly the same in reverse. The more often you are asked if you want to go for a hike, the harder it becomes to say no. You can use this to your advantage by aligning the people you hang around with your goal of getting into shape.

As with hiring nutritionists or counselors to help with what we put into our bodies, it's not difficult to find coaches who will help us move our bodies more effectively. While this comes at a cost, it can be highly effective—if for no other reason than that we take what we pay for more seriously. However, paid coaching isn't an option for many, but that's okay, because there are lots of ways to find other people with similar goals—and the internet offers nearly unlimited content. The risk with this is that wading through what is helpful and what isn't can be difficult. And as with anything offered for free, it may simply be a funnel for some thought leader to profit from selling you something that may not be helpful. This is where having a trusted friend or two who has waded through these waters can come in handy. The best possible match is someone with a similar body type and background who has successfully walked far along this path. Trying to keep up with someone who was born with the natural body type that makes running or lifting weights easier may push you, but could also be frustrating.

How You See Your Body

The last factor to consider when using relationshift to improve your fitness or health is the matter of how you see yourself, something I've learned a lot about from my fitness coach, Titus Kahoutek. We don't fully understand what it means to be ourselves. Are we our consciousness? Is our body us, or is it just a vehicle for our thoughts and memories? I lean more toward the latter because the cells in our body replace themselves over time. So, if we are always changing, how can that be who we are?

Whether you believe God created our bodies, or that they are the result of evolution or any other theory, we are absolute miracles. Titus has taught me to think of my body as the most amazing avatar in our known universe. Not only are they the home of our consciousness for as long as we are alive, we also can mold and shape them for many different purposes and outcomes. To our knowledge, no other thing in this universe, whether alive or not, is so adaptable or can be used for so many different purposes and in so many different ways. We can grow stronger, faster, or more agile; improve our balance; even increase our ability to hold our breath underwater. And that barely scratches the surface.

I like to see my body as this incredible avatar because it increases my respect for it. If someone could construct a vehicle that we could invest with our consciousness that was even half as capable and miraculous as what we were born with, one could charge billions of dollars for such a thing. And how careful would you or I be with an avatar that cost billions? We might be tempted to not take it out of the packaging for fear of harming it. Yet we often disrespect the body we were born with, talk badly about it, and put it into harm's way without much of a second thought.

Sadly, because of cultural pressures, many people have body dysmorphia. They look in the mirror and see themselves quite differently from how their loved ones do. This is a tragic outcome of negative relationshift and can lead to self-harm and even death. If you struggle to see yourself accurately, it's imperative to seek the help of positive influences—whether professional or personal. Paid counseling, which is often covered by insurance, is a great option for anyone who has this available. Spending time with people who help you see yourself more accurately is important. But eliminating any negative influences is imperative. This isn't an area of relationshift to take lightly. If one or more people close to you are reinforcing inaccurate and negative views of how you see yourself, do whatever is necessary to remove this influence. You may not need to cut the person off completely, but closely weigh the cost of having them in your life. It's possible being firm with them and demanding that they desist reinforcing these negative beliefs could be enough. To navigate such situations, I recommend getting the input of other people in your life whom you trust. Beyond people you know personally, you may also want to get off social media or eliminate other sources of negative body image, such as magazines or exposure to unhelpful marketing messages, to reduce any unilateral influences that are making you feel worse about yourself.

Finding a Job

I briefly mentioned my job hunting experience previously. Allow me to raise it again to introduce the specific path of finding a job. When I lost one of my businesses in 2008—after a long run of ups and downs with self-employment—I decided to try getting a job at a corporate gig. Every day, I drove to the same coffee shop, where I spent hours searching company websites, job boards, and LinkedIn for anything and everything remotely related to my background. I revised my résumé and cover letter countless times in an attempt to match keywords and specific requirements cited in the job listings. Averaging six to eight online applications a day, I continued this for more than ten months until I had applied for about two thousand positions without landing a single interview. This is an excellent example of perhaps the worst way to find a job one can imagine. As I mentioned, when I changed my approach, I landed an interview and a job offer on my first try. The difference was networking.

Networking

The higher paid or more in demand a position is, the more networking becomes essential to your success. Most often, the response I get when I urge people to network is some variation of, "I'd rather choke on a stack of 'Hello My Name Is _____' stickers." Everyone seems to know networking is critical to success for job seeking, but no one likes to do it. So, most people go back to hoping the algorithm gods smile upon their many online submissions and serve their résumé up to the right recruiter at the right time. As with many aspects of relationshift, networking is neither a straightforward nor simple process. Yet, in the end, it works better than most other strategies. So, no matter how inefficient networking is, it's better than the alternative—as I learned after months of futility. Here are two steps you can take.

Make a List

1. Create a list of everyone you know, even casually, and where they work. Include everyone at your current job. And if any have recently made a job change, include where they worked previously.
2. Add everyone on this list to LinkedIn. (See below.)
3. If anyone you know works for any company that you might like to work for, set up a time to meet with them. This can be over coffee,

happy hour drinks, or a game of Parcheesi. Let them know ahead of time that you're looking for work and are interested in getting some tips for applying to their company.
4. Anticipate picking up the tab. If you go out for any kind of paid activity like drinks, be sure to cover the bill as a gesture of thanks for their input.
5. Prepare yourself by knowing what you're looking for from this person. You're most likely looking for multiple kinds of help:
    - They can review your résumé to see if it's consistent with the tone, word use, and culture of the company. Every organization has a unique way of talking—the more your résumé and cover letter reflect this, the more you will feel like a natural fit from the first impression. The importance of this step can't be overstated. I've heard hiring managers say they would throw out any résumé that mentioned specific words because they had such a strong preconceived notion of what kind of person would use that word. It's not fair, and I doubt it's an effective way of evaluating applicants, but this practice is commonplace.
    - Many employees get a deeper level of access to job opportunities at their company—they have in-house ways of looking for cross-department openings or can find out who the recruiter or manager is. Depending on your relationship with this person, they may be able to offer you some of this access.
    - Most companies have systems in place for employees to recommend candidates for job openings, even offering a bounty for connecting the company to a quality hire. Using these referral tools is the best way possible for you to get your résumé to the top of the pile—essential when you're competing with all those online submissions, especially when you don't meet all the stated qualifications for a job. Many people don't realize that you don't need to meet every requirement if you know someone on the inside who can sell you to the recruiter. Most managers would prefer a candidate who doesn't quite fit the position but who came through a networked connection over someone who appears perfect but came through an online submission.

6. Contact every person you know who works at a company that might have a position for you.

Use LinkedIn

Next, connect on LinkedIn with everyone on your list. This will allow you to research their employment situation. Search your connections' connections; LinkedIn calls these secondary or tertiary connections. When you factor these in, you likely have a network of many thousands of people. For these connections, you can mostly follow the process just outlined, but with LinkedIn, you may have to first ask your friend for an introduction to anyone who shows up as a third-level connection to you (or is unconnected). This may seem like too big an ask, but most people will oblige if you ask sincerely. We all know how hard it can be to find a job. Once connected, don't be afraid to send a personal message introducing yourself.

Working with Recruiters

Besides reaching out to your connections and people they know, you can also build relationships directly with recruiters. Rather than sending them your résumé without any other contact, find a recruiter who is well positioned in the space where you wish to find a job and foster a relationship with them. Call them on the premise of trying to understand best what they are looking for in candidates. Let them coach you on how you present yourself, both in your résumé and in interviews with the target organization. They get paid when you get placed, so this is a unique example of when the person you most need to meet has a vested interest in your success. Remember that recruiters are people who thrive on human connection, just like you. They will be far more likely to help you get what you want if you invest in the relationship and listen to their mentoring.

Get Comfortable Acting Differently

Remember that people generally are perfectly okay with you acting differently when you're searching for a job than they might expect in other circumstances. For example, it's often considered annoying to hear friends talking confidently about their talents, accomplishments, or income history. However, when job hunting, humility isn't the best path. So, although asking a friend to coffee explicitly to seek their help may cause some to fear they may come across as "users," when you do this properly, many people will help you even more than in other circumstances if they know it's to help you get a job.

Becoming Famous

So you want to be a star. Nothing wrong with that! This particular path requires a more aggressive relationshift approach, which is one of the reasons I split all of the following specific paths up to address individually.

I've long been interested in the energy that surrounds famous people. I've mentioned writing and publishing music in Nashville. One day, I was having dinner in a hotel restaurant near Music Row when I noticed a guy sitting alone at the bar. The waiters and bartenders chatted him up, as you might expect to happen with any regular customer. But something was definitely different about this person's energy. He had a quiet confidence—the kind of persona one might develop when, after being given so much attention, they must take measures to avoid getting more. I felt certain he was famous, but I didn't recognize him. So I asked the waiter, when he brought me my second Negroni. The waiter shrugged and said, "He's just a regular." I squinted at him but didn't argue.

When the waiter brought my bill, I reasoned with him: "I'm not going to bother that guy. I don't even know who he is. I'm just curious if he's famous and have to know if I'm right."

The waiter hesitated, then confessed, "It's Mark Bryan, from Hootie and the Blowfish."

My song publisher explained to me once that you can tell if someone is going to be a star, even before they are, within seconds of meeting. She said you should be able to feel the energy they bring when they step into the elevator with you. Whether someone developed this energy naturally through the course of their life, or whether they're faking it till they make it, projecting extreme confidence helps signal to music publishers that one has what it takes to command the attention of thousands of fans from the stage.

Developing this energy is just one aspect of becoming famous. I wouldn't say it's impossible to become famous without it, but it certainly doesn't hurt. Along with many other important factors that contribute to someone's fame, one way to develop this energy is through relationshift.

Fame is a lot like being popular in high school, except one is attempting to be admired by millions worldwide instead of a few dozen students in tenth-grade chemistry class. A few well-timed jokes at the expense of a substitute teacher are enough to earn a big chunk of the attention available in the relatively small world of most teenagers, but in the wider world, you're going to have to be literally one in a million to be considered famous. Because of this, few paths rely more on vastly increasing gravity (page 40) than seeking fame. To some, the following tactics will be a turn-off. But if you want to reach the highest pinnacles of achievement on the most difficult of possible paths, you're going to need to do whatever it takes. At least in this area of your life, you're going to have to be willing to be a bit cold in how you approach your relationships.

Do Whatever It Takes to Hang Around Famous People (to a Point)

The concept of gravity means that the further people are ahead of you on the path you wish to walk, the faster they will accelerate your growth. If you want to go really far in life, like becoming one in a million in anything, you're going to need some people who are *really* far ahead of you on the path. This is one reason why it's so important to live in London, Los Angeles, or New York City if you want to become a famous actor or musician—they're where the highest concentration of famous people live, and where you'll have a much better chance of hanging around them if you live in closer proximity.

So, if you're really serious about becoming famous, you likely will have to make some big sacrifices. One example, which would also help you build a relationship with someone much more famous than yourself, is to sacrifice some of your time by volunteering to help them in some meaningful way. Write emails, send DMs on social media, stand outside their office with a sign if you must. It's actually not as impossible to reach famous people as you may imagine. If you stick with it and keep trying long enough, you have a good chance of success. Just always make sure to be sincere in whatever you say and however you approach them. Powerful people are used to lots of creative gimmicks to get their attention. Sincere eagerness will make you stand out, plus it's an antidote to the fakeness that can creep in if you become too calculated in how you approach relationshift.

Another way to get near famous people is to take a low-level job where you'll work with them. Network your way into a grip's role on a movie set. Become the errand runner for a music recording studio. Load concert equipment in and out. In time, and if you're smart, you can leverage these low-level roles into those that are closer and closer to the talent, giving you more opportunities to meet your target audience.

You can also network to hop closer and closer to a famous person. Assuming no one in your network personally knows anyone famous, you can ask friends of friends (secondary connections) or friends of friends of friends (tertiary connections) to help you gain access. This is a long process, because to do it properly, you have to add value at each step in order for people who are less and less related to you to be motivated to help. The best way to do that is to find ways to be thought of as included in your target connection's tribe or community. Then, once you build a relationship with that person, you have to do the same for the next, until you get close enough to a famous person for a direct intro.

Surround Yourself with the Most Talented Peers You Can Find

Make every effort to include people in your life who are pursuing the same goals and who are equally or more likely than you to become famous. If you know the story of Matt Damon and Ben Affleck, you know that they supported each other in the earliest stages of their acting careers long before they won an Academy Award for writing *Good Will Hunting*. They met for business lunches in high school to talk about their plans to make it big in acting. They even had a shared checking account so that if one of them was getting more gigs for a while, the other would be supported during their dry spell. If you fancy yourself the next Matt Damon, you would do very well to room with the next Ben Affleck while you chase your dreams together.

This tactic can be one of the colder aspects of relationshift because it requires you to choose who you spend your time with based not just on whether you enjoy their company, but also on whether you think they are talented. That's not to say you can't have friends who aren't pursuing the same path, or those who, in your opinion, are not likely to go as far as you. However, every minute you spend with people who aren't pulling you toward your goals is a minute you don't get to spend with those who could. This is one of the more difficult aspects about attempting to become a big success: you may be forced to make some tough decisions for the sake of your dreams. I recommend, however, that you keep some close friends around who you've known a long time and have nothing to do with your career. You need people to ground you, and you need to have meaningful connections that aren't about success in order to balance out the more cut-throat aspects of becoming famous.

Want It, but Don't Need It

One of the most important aspects of achieving something really extraordinary is wanting it, but not needing it. It's okay to want anything you can imagine, but if you need it so badly that you won't be happy without it, you are setting yourself up to live a less happy life. Achieving something extraordinary is, by definition, rare. Many people want the same thing, and not everyone is going to get it. By needing it, you're tying your happiness to what is largely outside of your control to achieve. We're not talking about something that is difficult but that nearly anyone with the right work ethic can accomplish, like running a marathon. You also can ruin the process of reaching your goal by being too focused on the outcome, which may or may not even happen. Instead, learn to find your joy in the journey toward a big, audacious outcome, and your happiness will be assured—either you will get it and be happy, or you will not get it and you will have enjoyed trying.

Becoming a Successful Artist

What I lacked in ambition for sports, I more than made up in my drive to succeed as an artist. I've put serious effort into acting, filmmaking, graphic design, illustration, performing music, composing and songwriting, photography, poetry, fiction, and, of course, nonfiction. With most of these efforts, I had big dreams but lacked the talent and focus to take them very far. Despite this, and depending on my goals as an artist, I might consider myself successful in any of them. The definition of what makes one successful in the arts varies depending on who you ask. And depending on how you define it, your path will vary.

If your goal is to become a famous artist, I suggest you take the aforementioned path toward becoming famous. This was often my goal when I was younger, one I no longer care to pursue. The thought of being recognized every time I leave the house sounds like an enormous pain in the ass—not to mention being a target for scammers, users, and attention seekers.[1] But fame isn't the only benchmark for artistic success, and it's not even a very good one. It excludes three far more attainable goals that make better measuring sticks: enjoying the artistic process, gaining critical acclaim, and getting paid.

Enjoy Yourself

You can begin enjoying your art today without anything other than your own desire to create. Because of this, I think this is the best place to start for any artist, no matter your ultimate goals. Making enjoyment of the process your primary goal is a great way to attain the other benchmarks of artistic success, too, because if you're enjoying the process, you're far more likely to keep investing in it. Your lack of insecurity around gaining others' approval makes you more attractive and frees you to create with greater originality—rather than creating for money or praise, you can create for yourself. You also make better art when you're having fun. When I was recording, I remember how important it was to the studio musicians I worked with that we all laugh and goof off together. They taught me that listeners can hear the difference between an artist who is having fun while recording and one who is in a bad mood.

As you continue to create, enjoying each step of the journey, you repeatedly put yourself in a position to win critical acclaim and paying fans. If you're not enjoying the process, you are much more likely to quit before these outcomes become reality. To consider relationshift's role, finding

---

1. Author Tim Ferris offers eleven excellent reasons to avoid the goal of becoming famous in a blog that I highly recommend.

friends that you enjoy creating with is an essential step toward enjoying your art, regardless of whether anyone likes it or is willing to pay you for it. They're going to push you to create more frequently and stick with it longer—both essential inspirations if you're going to have any hope of achieving any other artistic goal.

Critical Acclaim

To the extent that you want to achieve critical acclaim for your art, you should surround yourself with the most talented peers you can find. This is most easily done by living in a major artistic hub like New York City, Nashville, London, or Los Angeles. Depending on the type of art you're interested in, you'll need to go where others like you can be found: art shows, conferences, and networking parties. You could consider attending a school or workshop, but not for the reason most people do. I've always believed the best asset a scholastic setting can provide is connections to talented peers and mentors. Of course, all of this can be expensive. You may need to accept a high cost of living as a trade-off for access to inspiration and opportunity. However, I know of several friends who found a way to live inexpensively in Manhattan or on Music Row to invest in what matters to them most. Alternatively, you could also teach a class to meet talented protégés to collaborate with. Many research articles started as a class assignment in a doctoral program. After the class is complete, professors often extend an offer to coauthor the paper and submit to a journal together.

Getting Paid

The final, more attainable goal of artistic success is simply getting paid to be an artist. This is the classic definition of being a professional artist. It's also not as difficult as you might think, if you are willing to pursue a version of your artistic expression that consumers are most often willing to pay for. Most artistic pursuits have a well-worn path of profitability, though these tend to be less sexy than most people are hoping for when they think of being a professional artist. Examples include wedding or portrait photography; teaching piano; or corporate gigs like blog writing, graphic design, filming interviews, or recording voice-overs for commercial clients.

For instance, if your goal is financial success from your writing, there are easy and hard ways to achieve this. Selling your poetry at a farmers market is the hard way. Ghostwriting for executives at big corporations is a much easier path. Simply being aware of and accepting a more profitable version of your artistic expression is the first task. You can find your way into these roles in much the same way as you would find any other job. I refer you to the section on finding a job for more on this.

Growing Rich and Investing Smarter

I have a friend—we'll call him Earl—who is the son of a wealthy investor. Their family isn't *Succession* rich. More like local gentry. They own avocado fields in Southern California after Earl's dad converted a nice career in financial advisement into enough dirt that each of his kids don't appear to need a job. Earl, who is in his mid-thirties, lives with his wife and newborn baby in downtown Seattle in a nice but not extravagant condo. They drive a mid-price SUV, hardly ever eat out, and rarely splurge on nice things.

Contrast this with another friend of mine—we'll call her Uma—who recently cashed in stock options at Apple. Uma, who is about the same age as Earl, drives a brand-new Maserati, lives with her girlfriend in a newly remodeled three-story row house in San Francisco, and listens to her extensive vinyl collection on a $50,000 sound system that is so hi-fi it somehow makes you feel as if you are inside the record. Uma is an upwardly mobile, high-income member of the new-money tech class. Earl's life, on the other hand, is powered by generational wealth.

Each of these scenarios is, of course, affected by relationshift and the people we surround ourselves with. Earl was raised by his parents to think differently about money than most of us. What rich people know that most of us don't is that making money and keeping it are two very different things. If you want to become wealthy and stay that way, first you have to focus on keeping what you have. This is why people from old-money families tend to be more frugal than those more recently rich who have high incomes and low net worth. New-money folk tend to be surrounded by others in the same category. They aren't as likely to have parents who can mentor them on wealth matters. They're making so much money that they often imagine they will continue to do so. They see their friends cashing in stocks, enjoying large steady paychecks, and living large, so they are more likely to do these things, too.

It may seem surprising, but many high-income individuals have little or no wealth. They make piles of money and spend it just as fast. They assume their incomes will keep rising, so why bother with savings? This is the mentality I had in my twenties when my businesses were doing well. If the cash was flowing in quickly, I made sure it was flowing out quickly as well. Some I spent on expanding my business, often inadvisably so because I lacked good business mentoring. Other times, perhaps in response to being raised poor, I wasted it on eating out, clothing, travel, and other temporary pleasures. Ironically, the more expensive the clothing, the faster it often goes out of fashion, which causes pressure to keep buying more. And no matter how fine the foods and liquors are that we enjoy, they go down the toilet just the same as macaroni and cheese. Before long, I'd lose a client or exceed my business income with over-expansion or poorly considered investments and find myself selling the jewelry and worrying about how I would cover payroll week to week. This cycle is a surefire way to get gray hair in your thirties and die of a heart attack far before your time.

A third scenario exists, one that most people experience: having neither high income nor wealth. It's certainly much more difficult to build wealth with a low income, but not impossible. "Low" is relative. At its most simplistic, one must spend less than they make to build wealth. This can be done with $30,000 a year or $1 million. Couch surfing, buying used clothing, and eating inexpensively at home, or living in a very low-cost area and selling your time to people in high-cost areas, are two ways to wring savings out of a relatively low income. But these tactics are far more achievable if you have the right people around you. Depending on your circumstances and goals, you will want to think about relationshift differently.

Low Income/Low Wealth

If you find yourself in this category, don't be hard on yourself. You're in good company—this describes most people throughout all of human history. To build wealth, whether for retirement or because you want to retire well before the traditional age, you must achieve two objectives: saving money and investing it wisely. Each goal may require different people to help you achieve it.

One of the best ways to ensure that you invest regularly is to have an amount you won't miss pulled directly from your checking account every paycheck to be deposited into your chosen investments. My friend Earl would tell you to buy a small amount of Bitcoin every day to avoid the stress of the ups and downs in a volatile asset (this is called dollar-cost averaging). Regardless of your specific approach, build discipline around the idea that you invest that money, and you will never pull it out for anything—even emergencies. However, to do this effectively with a lower income, you will also need to have separate savings for surprises that are sure to arise, such as flat tires, cavities, job loss, and the like.

Now you may be thinking, *how am I supposed to save for an emergency fund and long-term investments on my income?* Unfortunately, there is no easy answer. Building wealth with a low income is incredibly difficult but not impossible. It requires creative thinking, discipline, and having the right people around you. You may want to consider spending more time in the sections of this book that talk about getting a different job to help yourself along with this goal, as it's obviously easier when your income increases. Just don't make the mistake of thinking increasing your income is the only way forward, or a path that assures you of building wealth. I promise you that plenty of people in this world make a lot more money than you do, yet live paycheck to paycheck with credit card debt to boot.

Saving

Saving money often comes down to having the right peers. You need people around you who don't tempt you to spend more. If you have a partner, they need to be on board with your goals and willing to sacrifice short-term pleasures for long-term gains. You also may want to find a community of people who think differently about living—those who might be willing to live in a low-cost part of the world like Thailand and contract to expensive places like Europe and North America. Or you may wish to go someplace like Singapore to teach English while living in provided housing and saving every dollar you can. There are lots of creative ways to earn more than you spend;

you just need to find other people who are doing these things so you can avoid having to come up with all the ideas and inner motivation yourself.

Such people already may exist in your life. Think about the friends and family who are frugal, then spend more time with them. You may need to learn to say no to some of your higher-income friends who like to visit expensive restaurants and travel frequently. Or those who shop every weekend, or make you feel insecure about how you look because of their expensive fashions. Or, to combat the negative feeling of always turning friends down who are inviting you out for drinks and a movie, you can take the initiative of making the plans by inviting them over for a homemade dinner and board games. Most of this stuff isn't advanced and doesn't require a mentor as much as daily motivation to stay on track with your goals while minimizing temptation to spend more than you have allotted.

Investing

By contrast, you're more likely to invest wisely if you have people in your life who are a lot further down the wealth path than you are. Your frugal friends might have some good stock tips, but if they haven't proven their advice with a history of success, you're in greater danger of making poor decisions with their advice than with someone who has a track record of achievement.

One lesson I've learned far too many times is that shortcuts to wealth are about as uncommon as bath-loving cats. This is equally true with diet plans, finding love, achieving greatness, and a good many other aspects of life. There are far too many people in the world seeking the same things for any shortcut to be kept secret for long—especially in today's hyperconnected, information-rich world. If something works, everyone is going to know about it soon. And if you're not careful, you can spend a few decades chasing shortcuts only to find that none of them panned out. Then you will be wishing you had just taken the proven long way, because anyone who invests wisely over multiple decades will have better odds of accumulating wealth.

Fortunately, finding smart investors isn't really that hard. You probably know some people, even as secondary connections, who have some proven success with investing. When looking for the best investing mentor, try to find one who isn't always talking about some secret tip that few know about. Even if they are rich, it can be hard to determine if they got it by luck or skill. People love to give advice. It makes them feel smart and, even better, they don't have to suffer the consequences if their advice doesn't work out. Also, avoid those who prescribe anything that you can determine to be high risk. If you don't have much to invest, and if it came from your hard work and frugal living, you don't want to lose it by gambling. For those who lack the tools and experience to properly assess such risks, be sure to do your homework or seek the advice of third-party experts to avoid costly mistakes.

Because, make no mistake: much of speculative or uninformed investing is no different from betting on sports or playing the slots. While you could get lucky, luck isn't a business plan. And by definition, for each person who wins a game of luck, there are more people who lose. If you wish to improve your chances of increasing personal wealth, focus on savings and a slow, steady approach to increasing your return from that savings. This will feel painfully slow when you are starting out. But over time, you will see your account balances rising until you realize you're earning more from your investments than all of your friends who were chasing "secret" shortcuts and high-risk gambles.

High Income/Low Wealth

If you're in this category, congratulations! Your job of building wealth is much the same as that of low income/low wealth individuals—it's just a lot easier. However, you still face a few unique difficulties.

One is that you are more likely to have other high-income friends and family who will act as a magnetic force pulling you toward spending more. Humility may be required to decline a trip to the Galápagos Islands when all your friends are going, especially when you could easily afford to go as well. They are still going to pressure you to go, not out of spite but because they like your company. Yet you may have to say you can't afford to join them in their lifestyle, even if you technically have the money, because you're trying to save. Or if all your friends look great in the latest expensive fashions, you may need to shop at a lower-cost store in order to accumulate enough cash to keep your investment goals moving forward.

You can help this situation by spending more time with people who make less money than you. Or find a friend or two who has a high income, but a similar goal of investing as much of it as possible. And as mentioned, if you have a partner, they will need to share your goals—no one affects our spending more powerfully than our significant other, especially if you have shared finances. If this is the case, agree to the amount of your discretionary spending and hold each other accountable to that. Once you are reliably saving money each pay period, you can approach investing in much the same way that I described for those with low income.

Starting a Business

Somewhere there is a graveyard filled with the failed businesses I've started. There's the naturally raised pork company, Heritage Farms; the home audio installation company; and the auto brokerage, which landed me driving an old dump truck I'd purchased to strip down and sell for parts down Interstate 5 at forty-five miles per hour, its max speed. I ran a metal fabrication shop from the garage of my suburban home to make parts for RVs. Enough of the aluminum dust from sawing parts got tracked inside our house that we were still finding it years later. I designed and built plastic computer workstations for a semiconductor plant. I created, with a group of angel investors, a social network for musicians to connect with producers. I remodeled homes, installed industrial equipment, created online courses, and sold large rolls of lint-free paper towels that were used to clean up autos after painting. Likely at least a dozen others.

I generated pithy names, nifty websites, and spiffy business cards for at least twenty different businesses. Later I realized that all the time and money I spent on new business ideas was a symptom of my love for dreaming about my future success rather than doing whatever was necessary to achieve it. It's a lot more fun to design a new logo than to attend networking events and follow up with potential customers . . . for me at least.

Most of what I did for work brought in enough money to pay the bills, but none of those companies are around anymore. I attribute my poor results to a severe case of shiny-object syndrome, inexperience, lack of focus on what mattered most to achieving long-term stability, and a sort of laziness that caused me to look for something easier every time whatever

I was doing became boring or too difficult. It's also just plain hard to get a successful business off the ground, especially when you have a wife and three kids to support with no other income in the family to help you get by when business is tight and there's no safety net to catch you when you fall. So, when whatever I was doing started to dry up, I often felt compelled to switch gears and try something else.

It wasn't until I was in my early thirties that the momentum of my life's work began to make business achievable enough to sustain long-term success. If you're in your middle age or beyond, you might have found, as I have, how the good decisions and hard work of your youth have begun to pay off in the form of reputation, experience, and financial strength. These factors go a long way toward accelerating one's success. Once you've established yourself, business is a lot easier when you have customers calling you for what they've heard you can do for them or when you easily recognize the tasks that need your focus based on years of on-the-job learning. As you might guess, relationshift can speed your accumulation of these assets and help you avoid many costly mistakes.

The Right Mentors

One key to making the most of being mentored is that you have to actually listen to their advice. You can have the best mentor in the world, but if you don't do what they tell you, they can't help you grow. I can look back and see lots of times I was given advice I should have taken but instead ignored. At the time, I didn't realize the advice I was getting was as helpful as it was. Sometimes I thought the person was out of touch and didn't know how to succeed in today's world. Or I didn't want to follow their advice because it was boring or too much work; I was certain there was a shortcut that would be more fun if I kept looking. Or I simply didn't understand what they were telling me because I lacked the experience to fit the advice to the context of my situation.

For instance, when I was building my construction company during the housing boom of the mid-2000s, I took on huge amounts of debt to finance the growth. When housing prices were rising at 10 percent to 15 percent a year, I realized the more properties I bought—even if they were financed at 100 percent of the purchase price—the more money I would make just on the increase in equity. I had never seen a bubble before and had no idea that housing prices might drop. However, a friend of mine cautioned me to slow down. He said it's better to finance less of the property so you have a buffer if anything goes wrong.

I rejected this idea as too cautious. I thought, I don't know how long these prices are going to go up at this rate, so I should take every advantage I can. That meant spreading my money as far and wide as possible. I turned out to be wrong about this strategy in epic fashion. Then, when everything came crashing down, I continued to keep my employees on payroll until I ran out of money.

While this may seem admirable, it actually hurt me and my employees more than if I had taken another mentor's advice. She said I should cut my expenses in every way possible to give myself the best chance of riding out the downturn. I could have laid off my team, keeping only the most essential people and potentially maintaining the company through the worst of the economic crises, then rehired whoever wanted their jobs back as we picked up new clients. Those who were laid off could have collected unemployment and those who stayed on would have kept their jobs. Instead, I rejected her advice, wanting to do the right thing for my team, and in the end everyone lost their jobs anyway, including me.

However, another key to making the most of mentoring is realizing that a lot of would-be mentors have bad or unhelpful advice. Using limited funds for potential mentors touting expensive seminars with flashy, yet unproven, influencers may leave you feeling hyped up while offering little actual value beyond what you can self-generate for free—confidence, excitement, drive, vision, and the like. Other mentors may truly be out of touch with modern opportunities and threats, causing you to either miss possibilities or ignore potential negative outcomes that didn't exist when this person was making their way. And still others can have an ivory tower mentality—they've forgotten what it's like to be at the bottom, working one's way up, and can only give advice that works if you've already made it. Some mentors have good advice about some issues, but not others. Unfortunately, you have to sort out what advice to take and what to ignore, often without having the experience necessary to accurately do so.

It's a difficult task, but not impossible. Beyond choosing mentors who have good advice for you and your specific situation, it's also important to consider how much further along the path your mentors are. Starting a business is a path that benefits greatly from hanging around people who are much further than you in the journey. Highly successful business mentors are more likely to relationshift you further and faster with their connections and knowledge of what it takes to reach the higher echelons of success. Refer to the discussions on finding high-caliber mentors in chapter two for more help in selecting the right people.

Supportive Peers

You'll also need a few supportive peers in key relationship roles. If you have a romantic partner, it's important for them to be on board with your business ambitions. No one can give or take more energy from your dreams than the person you sleep with. I was lucky to have my first wife, Anna, who handled the ups and downs of my early career with grace and constant encouragement. Business is also a lot easier when you have partners who complement your skill sets and fill in your weaknesses. If you're a highly creative person, having a partner who loves administration and implementing others' ideas can be a lifesaver. Or if you're great at making something, perhaps having a partner who loves to market or sell would go a long way toward helping your product get into the hands of customers. You can hire for these roles, but that requires money, something often in short supply when just starting out.

One of the best places to meet potential partners and peers is in business school, either at the undergrad or graduate levels. This may come as a surprise from a professor and someone with three degrees, but when it comes to business, I believe the networking opportunities of school outweigh the educational benefits. Of course, one needs to know specific things to be an engineer or a doctor that can only be learned in a formal educational environment, due to the need for widely accepted accreditation. But in business, much of what you need to be successful is actually better learned on the job. So if you're still in school, or if you're thinking of going back to get a degree, make a concentrated effort to identify and build relationships with other students who show great aptitude. Even if you don't partner with these people, their friendship, knowledge, and positive energy can go a long way toward helping you succeed in business.

If you don't want to go back to school or aren't in a place in life where it makes sense for you, you can find good peers with traditional networking. There are lots of people who can move into this role in your life, so if you want to go as far as possible with your business, you'll want to be selective about who you invest in. This can be a bit harsh relationally as you may have to decide that one person or another isn't an ideal match based on how you perceive their potential. To minimize the possibility of forming overly transactional or purely self-serving relationships, commit to forming real bonds with people of any caliber. However, since your time is limited, you will need to make decisions on who you will spend it with. And if you want to go as far as possible, you will want to invest more time with the highest-caliber people possible. This doesn't mean you have to be rude to those you don't judge to meet this standard. Regardless of whether you believe in karma or not, this world is small in many ways and well connected. How you treat people will affect your reputation and future possibilities. Rather than thinking of this in a negative light, such as, "My dreams are too big to spend my time with so-and-so," instead aim to spend your time with those you've identified as the best fit for your vision. Then you can honestly and authentically find yourself with too little time to invest in those who aren't a fit.

Protégés That Push You

Success in business is an area of life that greatly benefits from having the best protégés pushing you forward. Not only do you want a fantastic team to help execute your vision and bring their own ideas to the table; you also want people who push you to increase your own skills and experience. The excellence of your team can create a positive pressure that propels you to grow so, in turn, you can continue to help them develop themselves.

If you have people on your team who aren't a good fit, that are holding the company back, you will benefit from having the fortitude to let them go. This is better for you and them. No one wants to be the weakest link and everyone has different skills and personality. This person who is holding your company back will be a great fit somewhere else where their experience and personality can thrive.

If you want to win, you need to insist on having the best team, and in business that mostly includes protégés. Insist on recruiting the very best you can find and you will be well on your way to success.

Overcoming Addiction

Addictions come in many forms, some colloquial (like a video game "addiction"), some destructive (like substance dependency). Many require serious professional intervention. I am not an expert on overcoming harmful addictions, but many experts are ready and willing to help. If you know you have a problem, I urge you to seek the input of such professionals. For instance, you can talk to your family doctor, a counselor, or psychiatrist, or call one of the hotlines that are often available for free to anyone who desires help.

If you're not sure if you have a problem, be completely honest with one or more people you trust and ask them if you should get professional help. Sometimes we can overestimate our problem out of an abundance of caution. Other times we can be in denial about something that is or could soon seriously affect our life and the lives of our loved ones. If you're embarrassed to talk to your friend or even perhaps your family doctor, make an appointment with a professional counselor. Whether you wait a few sessions to share more deeply or do so immediately, find someone who can receive the full and complete story. Don't under-report your situation out of embarrassment. Professionals have heard it before. Addiction is common, and a true professional will never judge you. Your friends and family, on the other hand, might judge you or respond in some negative way. This could be because of their fear, insecurity, lack of empathy, or lack of understanding. It's okay to discuss such topics with professionals or crisis counselors first before sharing your secrets with those closer to you.

Besides seeking mentoring from those who can help pull you out of whatever you're facing, you'll also want to make sure that the people in your circle aren't tempting you to continue the behavior you're attempting to limit. Whatever addiction you face, being around people who are actively indulging in that same activity is going to make it nearly impossible for you to stop. This is one aspect of relationshift that may require you to completely cut certain people out of your life, depending of course on the severity and harmfulness of the addiction. If you deal with depression or boredom by shopping, you don't need to cut off a friend who loves to shop. Maybe just avoid going to the mall together. In other cases, even with more severe addictions such as drugs or alcohol, you can potentially keep some people in your life who love to partake. Just avoid going with these friends into circumstances where the activity is likely to happen, such as parties. These can be very complicated issues and I recommend you seek help on a level of professionalism and seriousness that matches the potential harmfulness of your addiction. With help, use your growing knowledge of relationshift in a variety of contexts to increase your chances of conquering whatever addictions you might be struggling with.

Improving Your Love Life

When it comes to romantic relationships, dating a lot of people can be an essential component of finding the most rewarding love life. Of course, books, podcasts, and workshops can be a huge benefit to learning about yourself and what makes a relationship successful. Couples counseling can also save your relationship, but I recommend not waiting until things are falling apart to seek professional help. My ex-wife and I saw a very helpful counselor who might have helped save our marriage if we'd started seeing him ten years earlier. Sometimes so much gunk accumulates between two people that the work of cleaning it all out has become too difficult. But nothing quite compares to the personal experience of two people trying, failing, and finally succeeding at making things work.

If you want to improve your sex life, you can read about it in magazines while you check out at the grocery store, or you can jump into bed with a lot of different people. And I don't just mean hooking up. Long-term relationships are also an important part of discovering and maintaining your best sex life—trust and shared history can't be replicated in a one-night stand. This advice doesn't just apply to single people. If you're finding it difficult to maintain romance and the kind of intimacy you desire in your long-term monogamous relationship, there are a number of ways to explore different levels of openness that you might find are just what you need to reinvigorate your long-term partnership—though you will of course want to have a lot of clear and honest communication with your partner first. Try to get the number of someone you're attracted to at a party, even if you don't plan on doing anything with it. Dancing, flirting, kissing, going to a movie or a romantic dinner—all of these are possibilities for people who want to explore openness without going all the way to sex. With any of these approaches to reinvigorating your romantic relationship, I can't stress highly enough that honest and clear communication between partners is essential to taking any step in this direction. There are lots of good books and even dating coaches who know a lot more about these topics that I encourage you to check out. For the purposes of this book, however, I simply encourage you to be open-minded and seek out the input of people who can help you grow into the person you want to be, with or without a partner.

If you're looking for a rewarding long-term partner, this, too, is a goal that benefits from dating lots of people. If we assume that a certain number of people exist in this world with whom you can be happy in a relationship—let's say one in a hundred—then you need to date enough people to raise the chances of finding that person. Now, I have friends who have been dating for more than a decade and can't seem to find who they're looking for. Maybe they fell in love with someone who didn't feel the same in return. Or maybe they just haven't been excited enough about anyone to make it last. If this describes you, I encourage you to seek some input from people who know you well, or review your history with a professional counselor. It's possible that you are hung up on a "type" to whom you are attracted and that you repeat this pattern because you keep going for the same kinds of people who aren't right for you. It's also possible that you've just had bad luck and need to keep trying. But giving up certainly isn't going to get you any closer. There are so many people in the world that there has to be someone out there—lots of someones, for that matter—with whom you can share a happy life.

You also need to meet the right person at the right time in your life, which relates to the fact that you may have some things in yourself to work on before you can be ready to love the person who is right for you in a way that is right for them as well. Perhaps you have a narcissistic streak you'd benefit from stamping out, or insecurities, or an addiction that would put too much strain on your partner. I believe that if you keep working on yourself and keep looking, everyone can find someone.

As a personal example, when a certain well-documented pandemic lockdown began in early 2020, my dating life ground to a halt. I didn't want to meet anyone new because the thought of socially distanced dating sounded about as much fun as having Zoom meetings with my boss. In those first isolated nights, I scrolled through profiles and chatted briefly with lots of other bored, lonely people sitting at home like I was, but my heart wasn't in it. I offered to reach out to a number of matches after lockdown, which at the time I presumed would end in a few weeks.

But one woman was different. I made Anya the same offer to meet when the pandemic ended, but we couldn't help but keep chatting. Every morning, I'd look at my phone in bed and hope to have a message from her. She asked if I wanted to have a FaceTime call, and we did a few days later—my one and only video first date. The first time we met in person, we took a walk through a park, maintaining six feet of distance between us the whole time. Having just moved to town, Anya was living with a friend who was immunocompromised and couldn't afford to endanger his health. I offered her a can of wine I had brought and she asked me to roll it to her across the picnic table where we were sitting.

For a month this went on, somehow both frustrating and exciting as hell, until I noticed an apartment down the street from me was available. I suggested she check it out, hoping she might move to my neighborhood. I helped her move in, and we've been inseparable ever since. A few months later, I helped her move again, but this time to come live with me. And a year later, I asked Anya to marry me. I met someone who was perfect for me, and I for her, and I've never been happier.

The secret is that I'm certain we wouldn't have met (or if we had, we wouldn't have been the match that we are) if not for my few years of rapid-fire post-marriage dating. I grew so much during those years: shedding insecurities; learning about myself and how I could be the best partner possible, different ways of communicating, and how to listen more empathetically and less defensively; changing my look to better reflect who I really was inside; and on and on. All of this experience built up inside me so that when I met this person who was so right for me, I didn't mistake Anya for just someone else I was attracted to; instead, alarm bells were going off in my head telling me that she was worth my full and complete attention. I don't think I would have been so confident about that a few years earlier, and I easily might have missed my chance to be so happy in love.

Developing a New Worldview

As I've chronicled throughout this book, I've gone through some massive swings in my most fundamental beliefs. I didn't set out to change myself, but rather found myself changing as I adapted to the events of my life. In any given dimension of my worldview, I discovered more happiness by changing from A to Z, but I've heard other people tell stories of how they discovered more happiness by changing from Z to A. It's not my goal to tell you how to live your life or which worldview is best suited to you. But I do want to challenge you to consider that your current positions on major, fundamental beliefs may be holding you back in ways you don't realize or may not want to admit.

It's strange to write this because I know there are many aspects of the way I see the world now that may be limiting me. Some of these I'm aware of, like needless insecurities. Others I'm blissfully unaware of. If I could wave a magic wand and transform any aspect of my life that is holding me back, I would love to do so. Of course, that's not possible for any of us. So how do we approach this idea that we are being held back in ways that we are aware of but find difficult to change—and, even more problematically, areas that we don't even realize exist?

Of all the paths I have detailed over the previous pages, this one applies the most universally: all our worldviews could use further development. This is one area of our life where we can experience some of the greatest transformation. Better yet, we don't have to work that hard to find people who can relationshift us in these ways. They are likely already in our life; we just need to identify them and consciously begin to listen more. But most importantly, of all the paths I write about in this section, this is the one we are probably the least likely to identify as an area of our life that we want to develop. That's because of this tricky concept that we don't know what we don't know. Using the A to Z analogy again, how are we to know if we should change from A to Z, Z to A, or L to K? The answer to that question truly depends on the person. Only you can determine this, only you must deal with the consequences of whether you were right or wrong in your decision, and only you get to decide when or if you are satisfied with any change you've made.

Rather than trying to define for you what you should be willing to reconsider about your worldview, I will encourage you to compare who you are today to an imagined, ideal version of yourself: the wisest, happiest, most fulfilled person you could possibly be. This version of you, upon your dying breath, would, of all other possible versions of you, be the most content with your life's outcome. I think all of us can agree this would be an ideal goal, whether you currently believe in using your life to please God, believe in reincarnation and karma, or are a nihilist who believes nothing you do matters.

You can work through aspects of your worldview that are causing you to veer away from this ideal version of yourself (for instance, as mentioned, insecurities) with the help of friends, mentors, counselors, and others. I address some of these in a few of the paths that follow this one. But the areas of our worldview that are holding us back in ways we don't realize, these are the real difficulty. Examples could include bigotry of all kinds, religion, politics, philosophy, societal norms, oversights and personal characteristics such as narcissism or jealousy, the way you see yourself, and artificial limits on your possibilities. And now for the hard part: Which of these apply to you? And how can you know what to work on if you're unable to perceive how these beliefs might be limiting you?

Realizing the extent to which we are imperfect creatures informs the strong possibility that we could all find ways to free ourselves and become closer to an ideal version of ourselves in every one of these categories. It's natural to think that we are more or less correct about our closely held beliefs, but it's more realistic to admit that we are probably a little bit wrong about everything we believe. To deny the possibility that we are wrong about anything over which there is serious disagreement among the world's population is at best naive and at worst the height of arrogance. Thus, the first step toward exploring these possibilities further in our own life is to admit that we could be wrong about anything we believe. This can be a scary thought, so scary in fact that the temptation to ignore it altogether is strong. But the benefit of keeping an open mind in this way is that you give yourself a much better chance of growing into that ideal version of yourself, the version of you who will be most satisfied with your life when you've reached the end of it. Not as I define it, nor anyone else—the ideal version of you as the ideal version of *you* defines it.

Once you've taken this leap, the next step is to start adding people to your life who will challenge one or more aspects of your fundamental beliefs. Find people who are thoughtful about their positions, not those who simply regurgitate talking points they heard from their friends and information sources. The more thoughtful they are and the more curious about the truth, the better. It can be hard to accept this, but there are very intelligent people with logical paths toward and evidence for their beliefs on all sides of issues that are diametrically opposed. This goes for politics, people on the far right, middle, or far left of any given issue; across all religions and among agnostics and atheists; or any other spectrum of belief.

Once you identify people in your life who match these characteristics, who have thoughtful positions in opposition to your own, spend time with them. Listen empathetically. When you state your opinions, be more interested in how they respond rather than trying to convince them of what you believe. If you find yourself afraid to listen open-mindedly in any particular aspect of your worldview, challenge yourself to anyway. If you're afraid to hear others' opinions on some aspect of what you believe, this could reveal an area of your worldview that most needs outside input. And if you listen to a bunch of other views and come to solidify what you already believed, all the better! However, I have rarely experienced this. Whenever I've really listened to what another person who disagrees with me has to say, I tend to find that my own views were perhaps too black and white, too harsh, too self-centered, or lacking understanding, even if in small ways.

As I tell the next story, I ask that you do all you can to set aside your own views on the issues I'm going to discuss. Just for the next few minutes, let go of everything you know about the context. My point is not to convince you of any point of view as correct or incorrect, so regardless of which side you are on, it doesn't matter which side I'm on. However, I must get into some controversial topics in order to tell the story and reach the conclusion, which will illustrate how this all works in real life. It turns out to be a lot more difficult in practice than it is to write on a page.

One of my oldest friends, Kate, moved from Seattle to Dallas a few years ago. We have stayed in touch, but with the physical distance, it's obviously difficult to spend as much time together. Meanwhile we've made new friends and, as a natural result of relationshift, we've begun to drift apart in areas where we were once similar. As I transitioned toward a much less religiously based worldview, she has maintained much of what she believed when we were hanging out frequently. I moved to Capitol Hill, one of the most liberal neighborhoods in a very liberal Seattle. My political views have shifted left. Kate lives in a suburban oasis of Texas conservatism. Her views have shifted right.

During the hyper-polarized COVID crisis, we had very different experiences. I didn't see more than a couple of bare faces over the entire summer of 2020 outside my closest circle of friends. Kate told me life was practically back to normal in many ways, that people were going out without masks, and that she even had stories of businesses refusing customers who wore masks. When the COVID vaccines first rolled out, most people I knew were trying to find ways to get them as soon as they possibly could. Kate and her community were skeptical of the vaccine, and most of them swore they wouldn't get it at all. They didn't see a reason to, in Kate's words, "put something in their bodies that was experimental to prevent a sickness that was little more than the flu." When restaurants and sporting venues in Seattle began to require a vaccine to enter, Kate was furious. She saw this as an assault on freedom and, on a trip to visit friends here, refused to go. I felt it was quite reasonable to require a vaccine and supported any mandate to that end.

We talked from time to time, trying our hardest to stay away from this area of conflict between us, but it was impossible. The issue was too pressing, too ever present to avoid. Yet we kept our discussions civil, and I feel we both tried to be empathetic to the other's point of view.

Around the time I began writing this section, I received a voice message from Kate. She had spoken with another friend who was very pro-vaccine and pro-mandate. They argued about statistics, and offered studies and evidence that both felt proved their point of view. The result of the conversation was that Kate's friend felt they couldn't be close anymore, that this issue was too important to accept that another person they cared about could think differently from themselves. Kate was upset at losing a good friend and sought my support. She wanted to make sure that this wasn't going to happen to us, but was afraid it might. She told me that she had to cancel a trip to San Francisco because everything she wanted to do there required a vaccine and there was no point in going. Other people in Kate's life who were pro-vaccine made her feel like she was getting what was coming to her, that if she was "dumb" enough to not get the vaccine, she shouldn't get to enjoy the activities that those who "accepted science" could.

I found myself listening to this message thinking, *I've had similar thoughts.* While I wouldn't use the word "dumb," I might have had a conversation with like-minded friends that was less than empathetic toward people who couldn't do what they wanted to because they refused to get a vaccine that I and my community felt was safe and effective. I realized I had been presented with the perfect opportunity to test out my beliefs in empathetically listening to those who have a diametrically opposed point of view to mine.

I called Kate and told her that, though I disagreed with her position, I was sad that her view prevented her from doing the things she wanted to do. This wasn't easy for me at first, but as Kate responded, I began to realize that I needed to find room in my heart to extend this empathy to my friend. Regardless of where I might stand on this issue, I had to admit that it was possible to come to a thoughtful, researched point of view that was different from my own. Kate wasn't simply reading a single supportive news source or hanging around people who thought like her. On the contrary, she frequently sought opposing points of view. She looked into the source of her information and read research studies from a variety of sources. She listened to me whenever I gave my point of view on the topic and didn't immediately interrupt me to cite contrasting stats or evidence. She seemed to really want to know the truth, and I respected that regardless of the difference between us.

As we were talking and I felt myself opening up, I had a thought and proposed it to her. I asked Kate if she felt that she could be empathetic in the opposite direction. Could she be sad for people like me who felt that those who were not getting the vaccine were contributing to our unhappiness and preventing us from returning more quickly to a normal life? I wondered out loud if she realized that people in my circle frequently express anger at those who aren't getting the vaccine because they see them as a major factor in the pandemic lasting so long and affecting so many aspects of our lives.

She thought for a moment, and replied that she felt if I could be empathetic to her point of view and the way it was negatively affecting her, that she could do the same for me and mine.

Now, you may be thinking, *well, Kate's point of view is causing her pain, whereas the pain in my situation is the result of other people's point of view.* And maybe you're right. But one of the lessons to consider here is that friendships, and the conflicts that might arise within them, don't have to be even. They simply are what they are. In this moment, I wasn't interested in making Kate understand that my point of view was superior to hers, and she wasn't interested in making me understand that her point of view was superior to mine. We simply cared about each other—two thoughtful, truth-seeking individuals who came to different conclusions.

What was the result of this exchange? I don't find myself feeling any less pro-mandate. I don't think Kate is any more pro-vaccine. Does any of it matter if neither one of us changed our minds? Absolutely. In fact, our minds were both changed, just in a different way than we usually measure. Becoming more open-minded is a valuable change in and of itself, even when we don't come to an entirely new conclusion about a position we hold. Exercising the open-mindedness muscle makes it possible for us to explore other topics with greater honesty and gives us the chance to find other areas of our mindset that could benefit from alternative points of view.

Moreover, practicing empathetic listening is always a positive—the world needs a lot more of this, no matter what form it takes. Closed-off minds are like a castle with tall walls all around. The more resistant to alternative views, the thicker and taller the walls. In the real world, walls are built to defend against danger, to protect against infection, to keep anything uncomfortable out. If an alternative view has no merit, where is the danger? Why must we protect ourselves from something that has no teeth, no potential to change us? The only reason to protect ourselves from ideas that we feel have no merit is fear that we might be wrong. Make no mistake, it's scary as hell to open ourselves to the possibility that we might be wrong about ideas we hold close, especially those we've built our lives upon, those that, if they prove to be incorrect, could cause everything we know to come crashing down around us. I, for one, would rather face these fears, open myself to whatever I'm most afraid of, and give myself the chance of coming out the other side a happier, more fulfilled person with more empathy and understanding.

Other Paths

You may have other paths you wish to travel that I didn't cover, but many other paths are similar to at least one I've described in depth, or a combination of several. Goals like getting the best grades in school and growing smarter; improving your mental health; being happier or more peaceful; healing from depression; healing from trauma and loss; changing the world and helping your community; gaining ambition, vision, or drive; being a better parent; having more friends; becoming more outgoing, adventurous, or fashionable—the way to approach each of these is similar to my approach to one or more of the other ten paths. I encourage you to read through the various paths and pick and choose what works for whatever it is you wish to improve in yourself.

Pause to reflect

- Which of these paths are most similar to your goals?
- Were any of your ambitions not covered specifically? Which of the paths described apply most closely to these goals, and how?
- What are some concrete ways you can you use relationshift to move more intentionally toward your goals, whether they were covered explicitly in this chapter or not?
- Can you think of any aspects of your worldview that would benefit from becoming more open to alternative views? How can you discover and explore those alternatives more?

PART II

Who Do You Want to Become?

"If you cannot see where you are going, ask someone who has been there before."

J Loren Norris

Long ago, in a village nestled at the foot of the Himalayas, Queen Maya Devi and King Suddhodana welcomed the birth of their son, a prince who would someday rule their clan. A soothsayer present at the birth made a shocking prophecy. Though his parents hoped he would become a great warrior king, the soothsayer claimed the prince would renounce royal life. In an attempt to prevent this, the parents showered their son with luxuries. They wanted him to know how wonderful royal life could be.

One day, the monarchs commissioned a gift for their young prince: a chariot of unequaled opulence. The boy enjoyed traveling throughout the kingdom in his beautiful new chariot. After a while, however, the prince became distressed at what he saw. Many of his people were poor and feeble, and others were deathly ill. He carried these concerns with him into adulthood and, years later, when the boy had married and had a child of his own, he came across a corpse that had been abandoned along a roadside. The prince ordered his chariot stopped. Flies buzzed loudly as he climbed down and looked with horror at scavengers fighting over the remains. As the prince reflected on the tragic chasm between his extravagant life and his people's everyday experiences, he noticed a traveler had appeared beside him.

They began to speak about the prince's conflicting feelings. He enjoyed the benefits of wealth and power, but he also felt deeply for those who experienced suffering daily. The traveler confessed to the young ruler that he had long ago surrendered his royal claim to another clan. He recalled how his power and riches had failed to bring him happiness, how he'd found the pleasures of this world had caused more pain than good.

The renouncer's statements resonated with the young ruler. As the traveler continued on his journey, the prince made a decision. He left both his wife and son, his parents and his royal claim, to live in the forest alone.

Eating little to nothing, he was soon at the point of near starvation. One night, he sat beneath a fig tree, exhausted and on the verge of death. He stayed up all night, meditating until dawn. As he watched the sun peek over the horizon, he realized a remarkable transformation had occurred in him. He had achieved what he would later refer to as nirvana—a transcendent state where one experiences neither suffering nor desires. When he returned to civilization, the young prince, once known as Siddhartha, had a new name: the Buddha.

Today, five hundred million Buddhists follow Siddhartha's teachings. This 2,500-year-old story is one of the earliest examples in human history of recognizing and rejecting society's rules of life. Regardless of your religious affiliation, the prince's story has many helpful lessons. As a young man, Siddhartha recognized that the expectations placed on him were subjective, not absolute. He then compared the way of living established by his parents and tribe to his desires and found they didn't align. So he set out to create his own set of life rules and live by them instead. As a result, he found a level of contentment he hadn't realized was possible.

> "Our life is shaped by our mind; we become what we think. Joy follows a pure thought like a shadow that never leaves."
>
> **Buddha**

• • •

In part one of this book, I covered how you became who you are today. We analyzed how the people around us relationshift us by writing in the pages of our books, and how our thoughts assembled into a worldview, which changes our options and how we see them. Then we worked through the strategies necessary to implement conscious relationshift and went into detail on ten specific paths and the various strategies necessary to maximize each.

Part two is dedicated to helping you explore what you may want to change about yourself or your life. This is critical to making the most of relationshift because, just as Buddha found as a young man, some of the areas in which you could experience the greatest breakthroughs may currently be invisible to you. Furthermore, we want to ensure the ways we are relationshifting are not merely helping us get more of what we think we want, but actually moving us toward a more fulfilled, meaningful, and happy existence.

To this end, chapter five will delve into our inherited evolutionary instincts, and how they may sometimes drive us to act in ways that make us less happy or fulfilled. Following this, chapter six reveals what we can do about those outdated instincts, how we can go about choosing the ones with which we want to live in accord, and those we would rather ignore, while also examining how ideas pass between people and generations. We will seek to understand why we sometimes ignore good advice and how we can overcome the issue of being unaware of what we don't know—one of the most powerful inhibitors of personal growth. This will enable us to release the instincts we no longer find helpful and embrace rules of life that propel us toward a more fulfilled and happy existence. Last, once we are equipped with the freedom to choose any path we wish—regardless of what our evolutionary instincts or other people think we should do—we will explore in chapter seven how to live with greater purpose, however you wish to define it. This will help you understand how you want to best use relationshift in your own life.

In short, part one helped you strengthen your grip on the steering wheel of your life. Now, let's discuss which way you should turn.

CHAPTER 5

The Game

"I am free, no matter what rules surround me. If I find them tolerable, I tolerate them; if I find them too obnoxious, I break them. I am free because I know that I alone am morally responsible for everything I do."

Robert A. Heinlein

The meerkats stretched high on their hind legs, scanning the horizon, watching for danger in the tall grass surrounding them. Their instincts told them to be on constant alert, and they were so diligent. I imagined them rising every day, standing guard as if they had to eke out a bit of food here and there as their hard lives might allow, as if they were in constant fear of being eaten alive by some unknown predator lurking just out of view.

But these little creatures I was watching could have been enjoying life a lot more if they knew they were living in a zoo exhibit. Contractors had fabricated the world of painted walls and one-way glass around them so children could watch wildlife at the Woodland Park Zoo. They received meals with such regularity, it was posted on the wall: "Meerkat Feeding Times at 11 a.m., 1 p.m., and 3 p.m."

I felt sympathy for these simple little creatures. They lived in constant fear of starvation and death, when they could be eating their fill and taking long afternoon naps. But then I realized how I was just like them. Most of my fears are no more dangerous than a painted tiger crouching in the shadows of a mural. Most people do not live in constant danger of starvation or murder, so many of our instincts—like those of zoo animals—are not needed for the purposes they evolved to fulfill. Yet, these instincts are still there and operating on overdrive, searching for somewhere to apply their energy.

We have discussed how relationships have played a significant role in shaping you into who you are, and that through relationshift you can change who you are by hanging around certain kinds of people. To take full advantage of relationshift, however, we must also get more familiar with the rules we've been living by and figure out which ones we want to change and *can* change to better suit our purposes. The problem is that many of the rules we erroneously accept as objective reality are making us miserable. Some are holding us back from our dreams. Others are causing us to carry around guilt and regret needlessly. Still others are fostering unloving judgment toward others in our hearts.

We are being relationshifted at all times, whether we know it or not, and whether the way we are being shifted is making us happier or not. So if we are to take control of where we are going in life, toward whatever goal we may have, we must understand the forces that are pushing us now, and why. To do so, we must understand the rules of the game as we have inherited them from our ancestors. We must decipher which are universal—meaning everyone must abide by them—and which we can ignore or bend to our will. Let's unpack where our default ambitions and goals come from so we can begin to sort the universal laws of life from those we can manipulate however we like.

The Goals of the Game

From the very first time one cell split into two, life has bent its energy and ambition toward survival and domination. From cancer cells to blackberry bushes to the yapping little chihuahua next door, all forms of life share this trait with humans. At this instinctual level, every life form strives to expand its species's domain, even if it means killing the host on which it depends for survival. (For instance, harmful bacteria kill people every day because organisms such as these don't have a conscious mind that could enable them to consider whether expansion is desirable. They simply obey their impulses.)

So, despite possessing the world's most extraordinary intellect, we operate with basically the same goals as a single cell of *E. coli*. While we possess the ability to override these instincts and do whatever we want, we don't make use of this ability nearly so often as we might like to believe. Just look at what we have been doing with our own host habitat. Humans have been expanding and killing off anything that stands in their way for the past one hundred thousand years. No species has ever been so successful in the destruction of this world.

> "There was nothing humane about humanity. At the end of the day, they were all animals with only survival instincts."
>
> Sherrilyn Kenyon

But don't beat yourself up over all this too much. At the subconscious level, we are little different from any other species. Without midsize predators like cats and foxes, rodents would cover the earth until they encountered some new restraint, such as a limited food supply. Without reptiles and birds, insects would fill the sky. We're all in this together, every cell in every plant and animal. On an instinctual level, you have been playing this game since the moment of your conception, and you will play it until you die.

Though you likely don't recognize this, you may also be attempting to *win the game* when you go to the gym, swipe left on Tinder, switch jobs to get a raise, watch a comedy show, argue for a better grade, cheat at cards, eat a second helping of rigatoni, or feel anxious for no apparent reason. This is

THE GAME

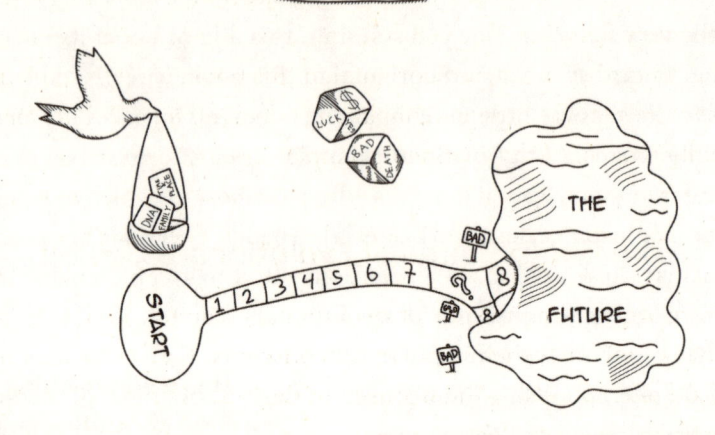

the game of life, and our evolutionary instincts are willing to do almost anything to win.

The goals of the game we evolved to play are simple: survive, multiply, improve. Species are teams that compete against each other for the future of the world. And within each species is a sub-competition to lead the team. The modern world reflects this in many situations like business, university, politics, or junior high spelling bees. We want our team to continue winning, expanding, and growing in power as long as it can. We want our

> "Morals: They're nothing but a coded survival instinct!"
>
> Theodore Sturgeon

team's influence to grow because that validates our success and gives us more clout. We want our fellow teammates to prosper because their achievements help our tribe remain healthy.

To achieve these goals, we are all trying to gain a currency of sorts. I call this *evolutionary capital*, or *e-capital*, because this currency is the driver that satisfies our deepest instincts, those installed in us when we were mere single-cell organisms. This drive for e-capital is the only reason we are alive today. Over the millennia, as we have gained intelligence and abilities, we have dramatically refined the strategies by which we gain more. This pursuit of e-capital is the reason we have warehouses, universities, religions, obnoxiously loud motorcycles, and everything else in our modern world.

The concept of e-capital is original to this book. However, the internal drive it represents is supported by many scholars. See *12 Rules for Life* by Jordan B. Peterson as an excellent example.

The Components of Evolutionary Capital

There are three components of evolutionary capital, and they are the underlying motivators behind our subconscious. Our conscious mind is capable of overruling these subconscious desires, but most of the time, we are generally unaware of how much our evolutionary instincts affect our daily decisions. They act like three different voices whispering in our ears. Let's explore these further.

"To survive is to win."

Zhang Yimou

OUR MOST FUNDAMENTAL SUBCONSCIOUS DRIVERS

SURVIVE   MULTIPLY   IMPROVE

Survive

Before we do anything else, we must survive. This is the first and most demanding of three subaccounts that make up our e-capital. When two or more conflicting drivers are present, we will tend to choose what best assures our survival. The folks who didn't get the "stay alive at all costs" memo didn't stick around long enough to become anyone's ancestors. Another way to look at this is, when faced with multiple options, we choose the path that we subconsciously believe will reward us with the most e-capital. For example, if we badly cut a finger while cooking, we have the option of continuing to prepare the meal or tending to the injury. In the long term, eating is essential to survival, so opportunities that provide food deliver a high level of e-capital. But we recognize bleeding as a more urgent threat to our survival, so fixing this will be perceived as conveying more e-capital at that moment.

> "Nothing defines humans better than their willingness to do irrational things in the pursuit of phenomenally unlikely payoffs. This is the principle behind lotteries, dating, and religion."
>
> Scott Adams

I'M STARVING. SHOULD I...

BROWSE FOR SELF-HELP BOOKS

EAT FOOD

The diagram on the previous page shows this decision as choosing between options based on which provides the most e-capital.

And though we all desire to improve ourselves, you will not find many starving people casually browsing the self-help section at the bookstore. When we are hungry, we temporarily assign more value to any options that immediately help us solve this need.

With obvious choices like these, our brain takes little time to decide. We know the option that will help us gain the most e-capital at that moment. Barring uncommon scenarios where other evolutionary instincts override this driver, such as to protect someone we love, we will make the choice that best assures our immediate survival without a second thought.

> "Hunger, love, pain, fear are some of those inner forces which rule the individual's instinct for self-preservation."
>
> Albert Einstein

Reproduce

For most people today, however, survival is not often in doubt. So the subconscious driver that affects us daily more than any other is the need to *replicate our DNA and ideas.* We want to spread ourselves as far and wide as possible. We devote a lot of our time to gaining e-capital so we can multiply more prolifically. Getting into shape, wearing designer clothing, gaining popularity or fame, or earning a promotion at work are highly desired by many people because we subconsciously feel these traits will, in part, help us attract a higher-caliber mate. We even evaluate the sexual partner we seek on the same criterion: Who will help me spread my DNA most successfully? Furthermore, when we argue with a friend about politics, write a blog about protecting the Great Barrier Reef, or run for city council, we attempt to satisfy the very same impulse. We all believe, for the most part, the most accurate way to see the world is through our own eyes. Logically, it follows that we would want everyone else to see the world the same way as we do. We want our ideas to multiply, which is just another way of leaving our imprint on our shared existence. Most of these drivers are buried deep in our subconscious, yet they explain much of our daily decision making.

> "Evolutionarily speaking, love is all about procreation."
>
> Abhijit Naskar

Improve

The final component of e-capital is our desire to improve our species. Life has a way of seeking positive change. From single-cell organisms to humans, we are all striving to create a better species. We compel ourselves to innovate, invent, and devise the next best thing. We are driven to explore, even when it means we are risking death. (This is an example of when our desire to improve is perceived to provide more e-capital than assuring our survival.)

We can now update the game illustration from page 148 to include these as the default goals.

> "True nobility is being superior to your former self."
>
> Ernest Hemingway

THE GAME

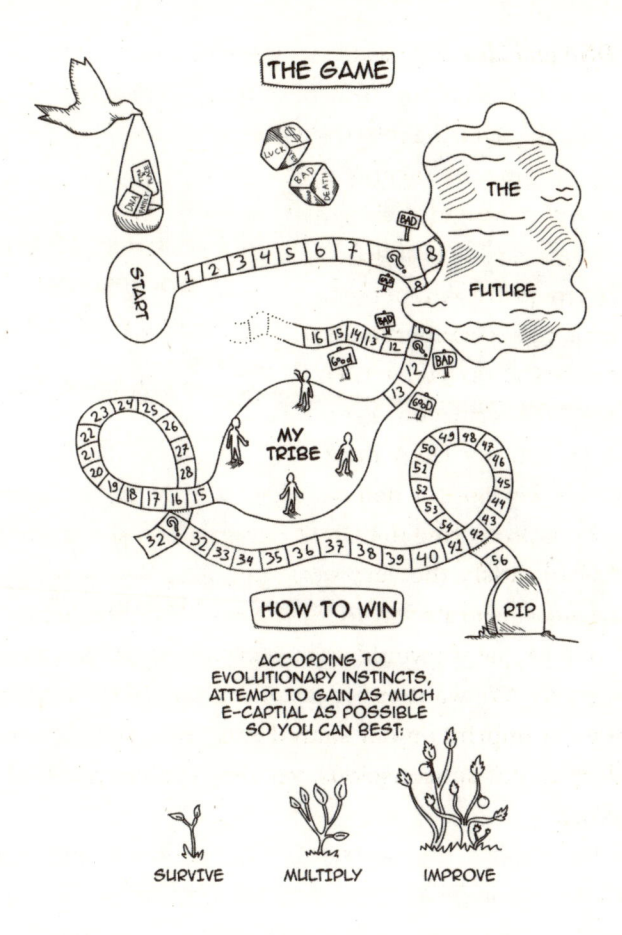

[Board game illustration titled "THE GAME" with spaces numbered from START through 56 winding past "MY TRIBE" toward "THE FUTURE" and ending at "RIP". Labels include LUCK, BAD, FATE dice, GOOD/BAD signs.]

HOW TO WIN

ACCORDING TO EVOLUTIONARY INSTINCTS, ATTEMPT TO GAIN AS MUCH E-CAPITAL AS POSSIBLE SO YOU CAN BEST:

SURVIVE   MULTIPLY   IMPROVE

Six Strategies for Winning the Game

Though all organisms share the same three basic drivers, some of us have developed more sophisticated methods for assuring we come out on top. Humans in particular utilize six main strategies for obtaining e-capital: safety, sex, acceptance, resources, influence, and novelty. They are important to understand vis-à-vis relationshift because we want to use the concepts in this book to better our life, not just win a game our evolutionary instincts tell us to play in a certain way. To visualize these tactics, imagine the voices representing survival, multiplication, and improvement are visiting different rooms in our heads, each expressing a different strategy.

SEX INFLUENCE

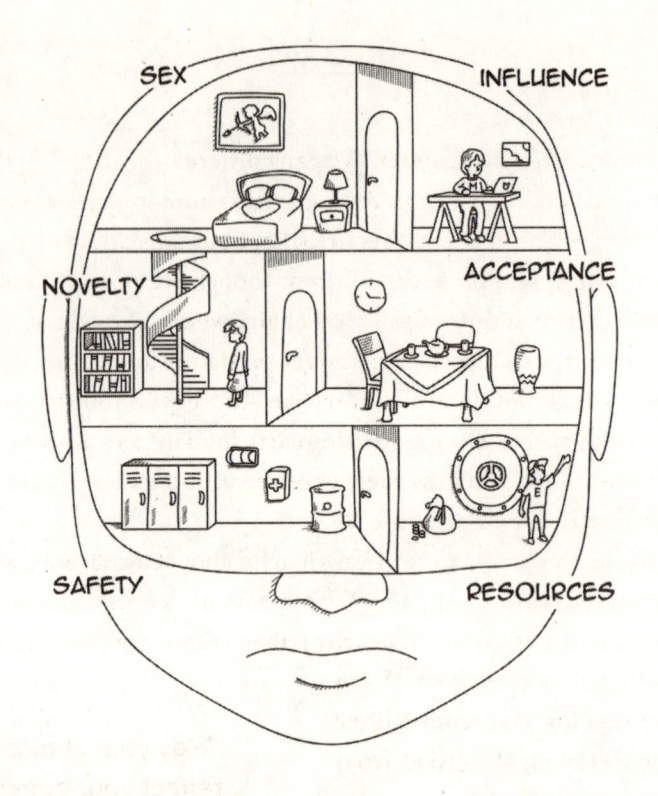

NOVELTY ACCEPTANCE

SAFETY RESOURCES

As we further explore the six strategies we use for gaining e-capital, I'm going to discuss their origin and how they affect us today. Then, in chapter six, I will dive into how we can go about overriding these strategies when we find they are no longer serving our purposes. We may have gotten this far by submitting to these instincts, but if they aren't making us happy in this modern world, why allow them to control us any further? We can make use of our extraordinary conscious minds to overrule these impulses, and in so doing, use relationshift to move toward a life course more to our liking.

> "It is not until you change your identity to match your life blueprint that you will understand why everything in the past never worked."
>
> Shannon L. Alder

Safety

Origin

Sex sells, but fear sells even better. We can't procreate if we are dead. So, we seek safety first. This is why anxiety is perhaps humanity's most dominant force for change. The desire for security kept humans alive for a very long time during our evolution and still does, though we need it far less than ever. Located in the middle of the food chain, we developed a strong sense of fear, always wary of threats from larger predators and competing tribes. The happy-go-lucky humans of yesteryear—those who didn't worry about looking over their shoulder or collecting extra food in case of a long winter—didn't last long enough to pass their carefree attitudes on to their descendants. They lost in the game of life.

Meanwhile, those who were always fearful about eating more when they had the chance, always sharpening their spears in case of a lion attack, and always scouting the activities of nearby tribes—these are the ones who survived, multiplied, and evolved. If you choose the smallest dog from a litter to breed with the smallest dog from another litter, you will, over many generations, produce smaller and smaller dogs. So also do fearful people joining with other scared people produce even more freaked-out children. Over countless generations, our fear instincts have been sharpened and refined. Yet, that wasn't enough for our survival, so we created societal and religious systems that increased and channeled our safety-seeking behaviors.

> "May your choices reflect your hopes, not your fears."
>
> Nelson Mandela

Today

Fear has been so effective in helping us develop as a species that we now no longer have most of the problems that caused us to develop the instinct in the first place. Sure, a little fear comes in handy when we're facing a dark alley in a bad part of town. But far more often, we experience more fear than is necessary for our modern daily lives. We fear rejection by our friends for being different, being fired for not working hard enough, and being dumped by our partner for letting our bodies go. All day long, we fret about fears—that people are ignoring us because they don't like us, that we will be made fun of if we wear certain kinds of clothes, that we will fail if we try something new.

> "There is no illusion greater than fear."
>
> Lao Tzu

These are all examples of a highly developed fear instinct that doesn't make much sense in our modern world. Yet, we indulge these fears because of our supercharged impulses to survive, multiply, and evolve. We crave safety like a drug, and we subconsciously feel we are earning more e-capital when we exercise our fear drive—a remarkable disconnect between our subconscious value system and reality. In fact, the vast majority of fears we experience hinder us more than they help.

Suppose we can change the rules of the game so that we no longer listen so strongly to our fears and instead see the value in taking risks, letting go of worries, and focusing on possibilities. In that case, we will find ourselves letting go of the need to accumulate e-capital that isn't helpful to us in our modern world. This frees us to find more happiness and health, or whatever it is we'd rather have more of than fear.

> "Worrying does not empty tomorrow of its troubles, it empties today of its strength. Stop worrying and let life go on, happily."
>
> Tshepo Koos Maluleke

We seek out fears where there are none. We see danger in the shadows under a dark forest canopy when reality proves to be merely soft moss, perfect for a nap in the filtered sunlight. We fear being fired, but the truth is that getting a new job isn't all that bad. Many times, failing is the perfect way to find our true passion in life. We fear losing someone we love, either by death or divorce, but the reality is that no separation in the future can steal the joy of our present moment. We fear injury or sickness, but we have many medical marvels available to us that no generation before us had. And our bodies can often heal themselves, so our worst fears are often unrealized. Even death, what we fear perhaps most of all, gives meaning to life.

Humans possess a far greater ability than other animals to see the walls around us for what they are and override our instincts to achieve a higher level of life. However, we often fail to access the fullness of our humanity, adopting a more instinctually limited view of the world around us instead. That humanity provides us the ability to let go of the need to control our outcomes. When we do so, we may find we are in no more danger than meerkats living in a zoo.

When we feel dread in our stomachs as danger approaches, we become terrified of fear itself. Indulging two terrors is not the way to overcome one. In our unmeasured response, we are overwhelmed and consumed—imagine trying to defeat a bear with hate. We often respond to fear with loathing—for the fear or ourselves. We scream at it to leave us alone; we beg it to be gone and never to return. Making demands of a bear is not a way to beat it.

Instead of fighting, running, or lying down to die, what if we can instead make friends with the bear,

> "Fear is natural. Failure is normal."
>
> Collins Hasty

with, say, a nice marmalade sandwich. Then we will find we can harness its power and wildness to not just overcome the fear but perhaps achieve more—focus, drive, ambition, strength, safety, creativity, peace, and even a moment of genius. What limits are there on the power and might of a wild bear, befriended and yoked to us? When we harness the bear's strength for our own good, her power multiplies our own. Thus we turn fear into our ally on the path toward achieving whatever we dreaded would fail.[1]

Understanding how our desire for safety interrelates with the laws of relationshift is essential to applying those laws in our daily lives. Because of

---

1. It's worth noting that many fears are based on real danger or justifiable concern. Sadly, those who struggle to get by tend to live in a much darker and more dangerous world than those with means. As a result, many people must live with fears that are not mere manifestations of our evolutionary instincts.

fear, many people do not embrace their ability to grow into the people they wish to be. They fear hurting certain people by cutting them off. They fear change. They fear who they might become. They fear failing in their effort to become who they most desire. Any number of fears can derail us on our path, but we can learn to embrace our fears and use them to our advantage. And critical to the point of this book is this: without the presence of other people and their ideas, you can easily stay ignorant of your fears and how they are holding you back. We need other people to help us identify and overcome our fears, or we face undue suffering by going it alone.

Sex

Origin

Fortunately for you, every one of your ancestors—your parents, grandparents, great-grandparents, and on up the chain through all of human history—survived long enough to procreate successfully. In this game of life we evolved to play, that's the only task we must accomplish to win. You heard it here first: getting laid is winning at life.[2] And thankfully, your ancestors achieved this goal with perfect success. You come from a line of thousands of generations of consecutive sexual winners without a single loser among them.

> "It's amazing what the gene pool will do to perpetuate itself."
>
> Mohsin Hamid

Today

Sex is not a kind strategy for achieving e-capital. We may pretend to be open-minded and loving to all, but when it comes to choosing sexual partners, we allow ourselves to indulge bias, judgment, and prejudice as much as we like. Have you ever rejected the advances of a potential lover? Swiped left on a dating app? Broken up with someone? Do you have any preferences

---

2. As long as getting laid results in a healthy child who survives long enough to procreate.

in dating for sexual orientation, weight, height, intelligence, income, or age? Of course. We all have some preferences in dating that might otherwise be considered inappropriate. While we may shout along with social justice marches and donate to equality-focused nonprofits, we are not nearly so equal opportunity when it comes to adult nap time.

These biases exist for many reasons, not all of which will be explored here. However, one factor that affects how we evaluate partners is that our subconscious is calculating a potential partner's e-capital value based on

HOW WE EVALUATE POTENTIAL PARTNERS BASED ON OUR PREFERENCES FOR SPECIFIC DIMENSIONS OF E-CAPITAL

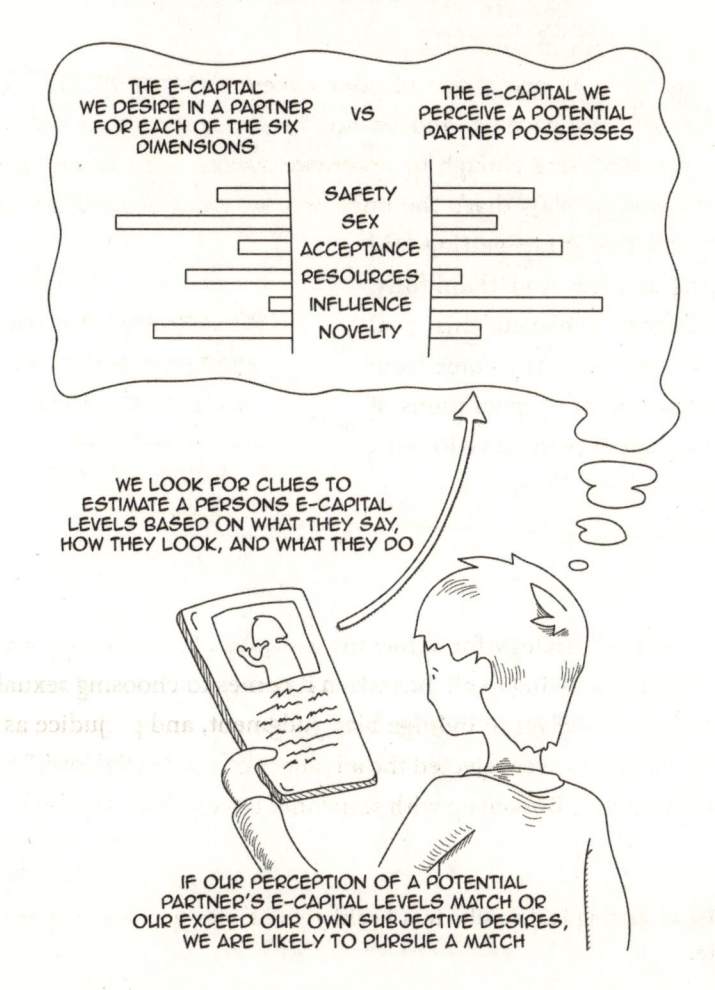

THE E-CAPITAL WE DESIRE IN A PARTNER FOR EACH OF THE SIX DIMENSIONS
VS
THE E-CAPITAL WE PERCEIVE A POTENTIAL PARTNER POSSESSES

SAFETY
SEX
ACCEPTANCE
RESOURCES
INFLUENCE
NOVELTY

WE LOOK FOR CLUES TO ESTIMATE A PERSONS E-CAPITAL LEVELS BASED ON WHAT THEY SAY, HOW THEY LOOK, AND WHAT THEY DO

IF OUR PERCEPTION OF A POTENTIAL PARTNER'S E-CAPITAL LEVELS MATCH OR EXCEED OUR OWN SUBJECTIVE DESIRES, WE ARE LIKELY TO PURSUE A MATCH our subjective ideas of what we want—what will help us satisfy our deepest desires to survive, multiply, and improve. Some value money more than others, some looks, some cultural similarity, and some emotional balance.

The values your subconscious applies are subjective. So while you may not be as judgmental about looks or money, you most certainly are critical when it comes to what matters to you—perhaps kindness, emotional

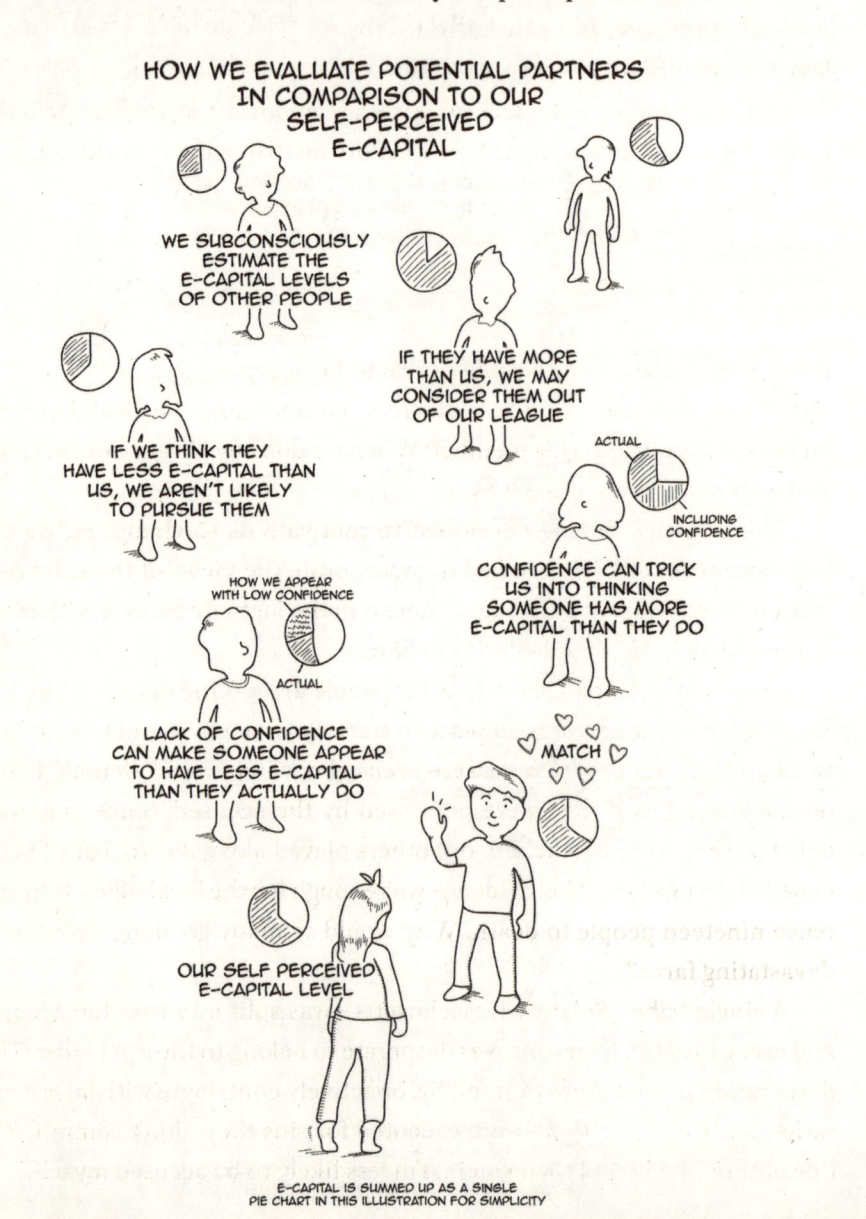

HOW WE EVALUATE POTENTIAL PARTNERS IN COMPARISON TO OUR SELF-PERCEIVED E-CAPITAL

WE SUBCONSCIOUSLY ESTIMATE THE E-CAPITAL LEVELS OF OTHER PEOPLE

IF THEY HAVE MORE THAN US, WE MAY CONSIDER THEM OUT OF OUR LEAGUE

IF WE THINK THEY HAVE LESS E-CAPITAL THAN US, WE AREN'T LIKELY TO PURSUE THEM

ACTUAL
INCLUDING CONFIDENCE

CONFIDENCE CAN TRICK US INTO THINKING SOMEONE HAS MORE E-CAPITAL THAN THEY DO

HOW WE APPEAR WITH LOW CONFIDENCE
ACTUAL

LACK OF CONFIDENCE CAN MAKE SOMEONE APPEAR TO HAVE LESS E-CAPITAL THAN THEY ACTUALLY DO

MATCH

OUR SELF PERCEIVED E-CAPITAL LEVEL

E-CAPITAL IS SUMMED UP AS A SINGLE PIE CHART IN THIS ILLUSTRATION FOR SIMPLICITY stability, or finding a partner who will wear flannel onesies with you on Sunday morning. The traits that attract or repel us can be hard to define when our tummies buzz with butterflies.

Once we become aware of this internal motivation, we can begin to lessen its pull on our conscious decision making, freeing us to focus instead on relationshifting toward areas that matter more to our enlightened selves. More on that in the next chapter.

> "I write about sex because often it feels like the most important thing in the world."
>
> Jeanette Winterston

Acceptance

Origin

Every person alive has a strong desire to be accepted by their tribe. This makes a lot of sense, given how much of our ancestors' survival depended on being a supported tribe member. When we don't feel known or accepted, we feel terrible about ourselves.

This negative feeling developed to motivate us to change so we can feel more accepted. We learned to incorporate the views of the tribe fully into our consciousness, with less interest in the factualness or health of the opinion than in the simple desire to fit in.

Countless examples show how far people are willing to go to fit in. The Salem Witch Trials are a great place to start. Between 1692 and 1693, at least two hundred innocent people were accused of witchcraft. "Victims" flailed on the ground as if they were possessed by the accused. Some may have believed they were bewitched, but others played along due to fear of being expelled themselves. This evidence was enough for the local officials to sentence nineteen people to death. Why would so many go along with such a devastating farce?

A single tribe—Salem, Massachusetts—was split into two: the accused and everyone else. Everyone was desperate to belong to the right tribe. This desperation moved them to stand by, or actively contribute with false accusations, as their neighbors were executed for sins they didn't commit. The line of thinking is, "If I turn you in, I'm less likely to be accused myself."

Today

We might consider the Salem Witch Trials impossible in today's world. Yet cults persist to this day, and many are extremely dangerous. Some have such devoted followers that they engage in self-mutilation or mass suicide. Others foster followers of such devotion that they are willing to murder. For example, devout QAnon follower Matthew Taylor Coleman was indicted in 2021 for killing his two children because he believed "he was saving the world from monsters." Our human mind is virtually identical to that of our ancestors, and we are just as likely today to believe nonsense to fit into a group as were our cave-dwelling forebears.

Perhaps the most remarkable aspect of this phenomenon is the degree to which intelligent humans can succumb to their delusions. This implies that we are all deluded in ways that we don't realize and should be careful to judge others for their fantasies without looking deeply at our own belief systems. Are they based on facts or the testimony of other people? Do they require faith without proof?

> "Man's desire for the approval of his fellows is so strong, his dread of their censure so violent, that he himself has brought his enemy (conscience) within his gates; and it keeps watch over him, vigilant always in the interests of its master to crush any half-formed desire to break away from the herd."
>
> W. Somerset Maugham

When examining your beliefs, keep in mind that evidence isn't always what it seems. We have such a powerful mechanism for deluding ourselves to fit into the tribe that we developed the ability to justify our beliefs in any way possible. Evidence can be interpreted to support nearly any faith or system if we never challenge its most fundamental assumptions. If you need proof of this, google how Stanley Kubrick's *The Shining* is a secret confession that he faked the moon landings. Sadly, the colorful examples of human delusion have no end. Social networks like Facebook and Twitter are the perfect places for conspiracy theorists to find others who support their views, no matter how unsupportable by fact. These networks' algorithms are designed to show you what you want to see because this keeps you scrolling, which mints more advertising revenue.

Self-deception is one way humans have evolved to deal with the negative emotions of not fitting in. But we have also developed the ability to create masks that conceal any rough edges that would prevent our full acceptance into the tribe. At the e-capital level, humans are not all that different from any other animal. What makes us different is our ability to conceal our subconscious desires with a more palatable version of ourselves. This is essential to tribal acceptance because of the societal rules we impose on each other for our species's welfare.

> "A great deal of intelligence can be invested in ignorance when the need for illusion is deep."
>
> Saul Bellow

You can learn a lot about what drives your desire for e-capital by examining creatures with the same instincts but little ability to mask them—for example, dogs and toddlers. Observe any of these and consider what aspect of yourself their behavior reveals. Some dogs seem to want to hump just about anything that moves. If teenagers could not understand the repercussions of their actions, if they had no self-control, if they had no real goals apart from their evolutionary instincts, how much more would a college campus look like a dog park?

> "I'd spent so long trying to fit in, trying to be someone I wasn't, that I had no idea who I was any more."
>
> Dorothy Koomson

This control comes from the more advanced part of our brain that elevates reason over impulse—an ability dogs have in a smaller proportion to humans that in turn leads to more public ball licking. Since we understand our actions' repercussions (sometimes), have self-control (at least more than dogs), and have goals apart from procreation, we disguise our desire for sex. Instead, we present this side of ourselves in a way that is aligned with what is acceptable behavior within our given tribe. Some people are not able to maintain their masks as well as others. They are identified by society and then ridiculed, labeled, locked up, exiled, or killed.

Masks are somewhat inaccurate in this analogy because we imagine them as false and separate constructs—something we put on to fool others. But in reality, the guises we develop become habits as we use them—increasingly part of who we are. We can even begin to feel that we have always been that way. We can confuse our nature at birth with how we have changed to fit our environment because both can feel equally natural. The big difference between masks and DNA is that we can change a mask with focus and energy. We can evaluate whether we like the personas we have developed. We can actively choose to form new guises or strip away whatever walls we have when we wish to be more open. We can develop additional masks to fit more diverse situations or use a small collection of façades more frequently. We might call this being more genuine.

Rather than labeling alternative personas as unfavorable and attempting to avoid them, we should try to use disguises as a positive force in our life. We should seek healthy masks, not fabrications based on who we think people want us to be.

> "A need for approval lies behind all efforts of evangelism. If someone else can be convinced, that will show us that we are on the right path. The attempt to convince someone of anything is a mark of insecurity."
>
> Ravi Ravindra

What is more important is who *we* want ourselves to be. We should seek to recognize which personas are holding us back and which should be modified or developed to aid us on the journey of our choosing.

Resources

Origin

Above almost anything else, humans desire control. It's not hard to understand why the desire for resource control developed so intensely in our ancestors. The more access early humans had to resources, the greater their chances for survival, multiplication, and evolution. In other words, our subconscious perceives that monetary capital provides a great deal of e-capital. Control over resources also granted early humans greater authority over their tribe, much as how the most popular person at a work party is the one with the drink tickets. This allowed our ancestors to more ably pass their ideas and DNA down to future generations.

Today

Humans today are controlled by our desire to gather resources in much the same way as the cave dwellers, farmers, conquistadors, and rulers who preceded us. Many people will do anything to make more money. And no matter how much they gain, it's rarely enough.

We want to control our emotions, how people treat us, who we marry, the number of hours we must work, and how we look. Wealth is powerfully desirable because it provides a bit of this control we seek. Money gives us options. People of means have more choices available for healthcare and living situations. They have more access to healthy food, knowledge, and power. Wealthy people have a larger pool from which to choose their friends, mentors, partners, and hookups. They have the option to defer or offload more responsibilities than the less well-to-do. This lets them take bigger risks with less consequence or possibility of catastrophic failure.

We hate being under the control of other people, and we hate any influences outside our control. We resent our managers and leaders if we smell even a hint of their using their power over us to forward their ambitions. Yet we love those in power when they empower us. We love those who give us more control over our lives through mentoring, support, shared connections, and access to their power. True, many people fear having options because they worry about making the wrong choice. It can be easier to allow others to choose

> "Hoarding can never end, for the heart of man always covets for more, its raging appetites can only be quenched by the heavy sands of the grave."
>
> Bangambiki Habyarimana

for us. Yet, even in this scenario, we want to have the option of going our way or allowing another to decide.

You might be thinking that plenty of people are not motivated by money. It's true that, depending on the person, those mental voices that drive us to survive, multiply, and improve spend different amounts of time in the six rooms of our head. But even those who claim that other values are more desirable are unlikely to pass up the opportunity to pluck a hundred-dollar bill from a rain gutter. Whether minimalist, communist, forest hermit, or poverty devotee, few would turn down the prospect of gaining control over their tribe's resources if they could do so without threatening their other values.

Examples of our insatiable desire for resources are endless. If you ask people why they overeat, they may answer, "I just love food." The truth may be far more complicated. They could be eating to distract themselves from other subconscious feelings of inadequacy, depression, fear of failure, or boredom. People may realize this through psychological therapy or self-reflection. This is the conscious mind examining its unconscious desires and attempting to gain control over the process—easier said than done. It's a lot of work that many people avoid. To circumvent this, the conscious mind generates a reason to defend its subconscious desire to hoard calories. So we simply rest on the position that we overeat because we love food.

> "People's love of sweets and guilty feelings about overindulgence are pretty universal."
>
> Will Cotton

Influence

Origin

We spend a lot of energy trying to spread our ideas to other people through influence. When we give advice, we attempt to improve our tribe's chances of survival and expansion by modifying individuals' behavior within that society. When we ask how people are doing, we are concerned with their welfare inasmuch as it affects the tribe. If something is off, we often take it upon ourselves to be a part of the solution. When we discuss work, school, a project, a passion, or politics, or tell a story from our childhood, we are subconsciously attempting to control and improve the direction of our tribe. We share information with the other tribe members in much the same way that our immune system continuously monitors our bodies, looking for hazards to correct or expel. And we have an insatiable appetite for these kinds of discussions because we have evolved to have strong impulses around ensuring the success of our tribe.

Today

This tribe policing feeds into our e-capital needs by tapping into all three of our core instincts: survive, multiply, and improve. If we have influence, we are essential to the tribe and more likely to be kept safe. We want our ideas to help take our species forward, to change positively. And we want a legacy, one that dovetails with our desire for multiplication. Not only do we want to pass on our DNA in the form of children; we also want our ideas to multiply and expand. We all may think we're trying to influence each other for good, but it's possible our attempts to influence are based on evolutionary instincts that, deep in our subconscious, we feel compelled to pass on, whether or not these lessons are actually helpful for the person we are trying to influence. People who love us most can do the same to us. Again, being aware of this is a great first step, but we will talk more in the next chapter about how to break this often negative cycle of propagating unhelpful ideas.

Novelty

Origins

Something inside our brains pushes us to explore and seek newness. We do this even if we must ignore our other instincts, such as the need for survival or to feel connected to our tribe. It's all about what we think gives us the most e-capital, and each of us has a unique measuring stick. Countless people have risked death, embarrassment, loneliness, or financial ruin to climb mountains, invent new technologies, traverse oceans, strap themselves to rockets, or even try a mysterious berry in the woods. We quickly grow bored. We long for a new job, a new friend, a new crush, a new place, a new sound, a new taste—or if our pet pygmy goat has just chewed up the family couch, a new pet. This is such an integral part of us that scientists included it as one of five major personality traits on a spectrum they call "openness to experience."[3]

This insatiable and often unexplainable drive to explore is central to being human. Long ago, humans traveled hundreds of miles searching for food, clean water, shelter, and safety from wild animals or other tribes. They were also driven to find new places. The idea of going somewhere else has always fascinated us. In a recent study, 76 percent of respondents said they wished they could travel more. It seems most everyone longs for more adventure. This all stems from a single-celled organism's desire to seek more resources for its survival, improvement, and procreation.

> "We need the tonic of wildness... At the same time that we are earnest to explore and learn all things, we require that all things be mysterious and unexplorable, that land and sea be indefinitely wild, unsurveyed and unfathomed by us because unfathomable. We can never have enough of nature."
>
> Henry David Thoreau

Today

Consider what a powerful motivation is necessary to drive someone from the comfort of their home into outer space—an environment so hostile, billions of dollars of technology are required to keep just one person alive. Or deep into the ocean, where we must rely on advanced technologies and strict safety measures to ensure we make it back to the boat alive.

---

3. Besides openness to experience, the other four personality traits social scientists include in what they refer to as the "Big Five" are conscientiousness, extraversion, agreeableness, and neuroticism.

Novelty, as perceived by our subconscious, generates e-capital in all three of our core instinctual categories. Though traveling can be dangerous, it was also our ancestors' method to better assure the survival of their tribe. New hunting grounds could mean more food and less competition from other humans or predators in the area. Novelty also helps us multiply. Adventurousness is an attractive trait that can help us win a mate with greater e-capital. And by moving about geographically, we are more able to spread our ideas and influence. Last, novelty is perhaps the best chance we have for improvement. When we experience new places and ideas, we have the opportunity to grow and change.

The desire to become new ourselves—to switch careers, for example—is how we act out our hopes for a better future. And as we create new technology, we are accelerating our current phase of evolutionary transformation. We are supplanting a multibillion-year evolutionary process with our own shockingly fast form of change. From DNA editing to prosthetic implants, to making use of ever more sophisticated artificial intelligence, to the ever increasing integration of robotics into our daily lives, to combining the near-infinite volume of knowledge available on the internet with our personal subjective experiences—these are all examples of this new state of evolution in motion. Our desire for novelty has brought us to this startling point in history.

· · ·

Before we move on, let's add these six strategies for gaining e-capital to our game illustration. And since we have explored the idea that we can overcome our evolutionary instincts to create our own way of winning this game of life, we'll include the alternative way to win: you decide.

If you are willing to examine yourself in a cold light, you will see many ways in which you are making decisions to gain e-capital, even at the cost of your own goals, happiness, and health. You will see that many of your feelings, motivations, and internal drives are part of an obsolete evolutionary system that resolves to increase human domination at all costs. Once you realize this is your instincts' purpose, you can decide if you want to keep participating. You will then get to decide what you want from life and choose the path that helps you get it, rather than the one that your peers and evolutionary history have selected for you.

THE GAME

[Board game illustration showing a path from START through numbered spaces 1–8, looping through "MY TRIBE" area with spaces 9–41, continuing to space 56 "RIP", with "THE FUTURE" cloud area. Dice labeled LUCK, BAD, and cards shown.]

EACH TURN

DRAW E-CAPITAL CARDS

[Cards labeled: Sex, Influence, Resources, Safety, Acceptance, Novelty]

QUANTITY DETERMINED BY:
1. NATURE
2. NURTURE
3. PAST CHOICES

PLAY UNTIL YOU DIE

THE GAME WILL CONTINUE WITHOUT YOU

HOW TO WIN

ACCORDING TO EVOLUTIONARY INSTINCTS, ATTEMPT TO GAIN AS MUCH E-CAPTIAL AS POSSIBLE SO YOU CAN BEST:

SURVIVE   MULTIPLY   IMPROVE

ALTERNATIVE WAY TO WIN

YOU DECIDE

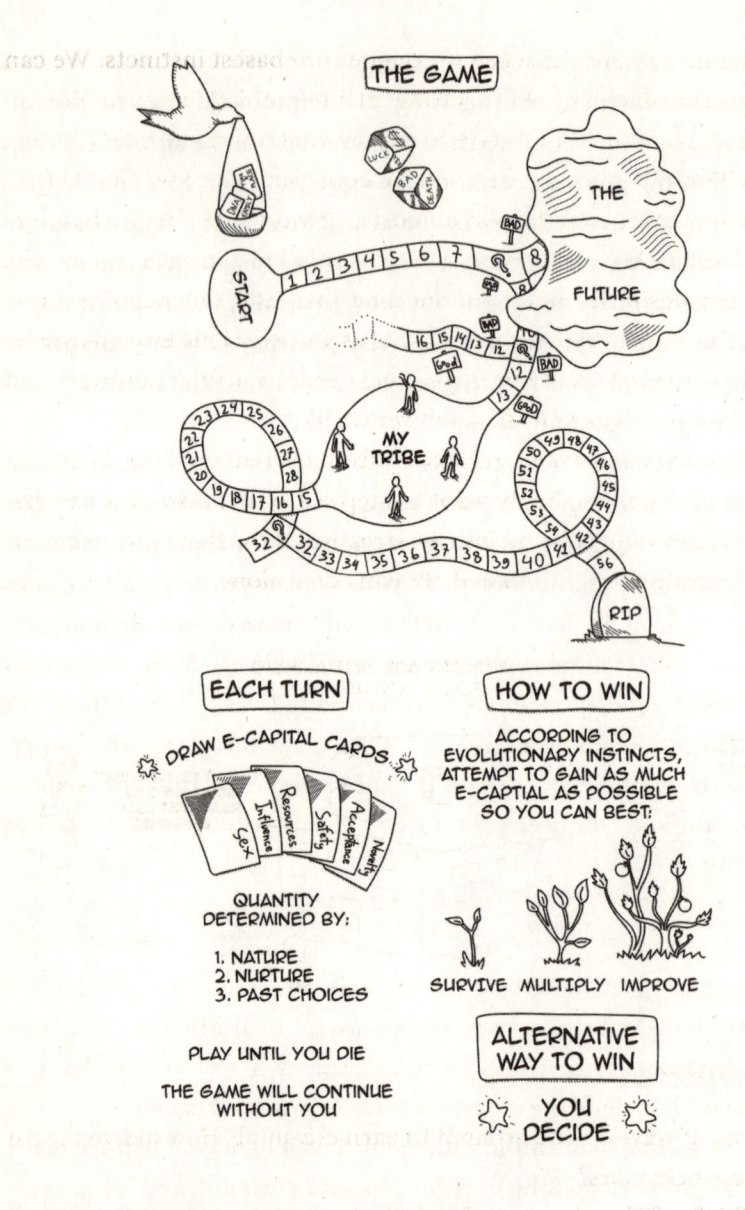

Overcoming our inherited compulsions is no small task. When I was first learning to scuba-dive, I found the simple act of breathing to be far more challenging than expected. Every time I put my head underwater, my evolutionary instincts screamed at me: "Humans can't breathe underwater!" Twice I panicked and rushed to the surface, gasping for air. My fear was unnecessary, of course. Once you get used to it, breathing through a scuba regulator is relatively easy. But defeating these impulses required practice.

In the same way, we can learn to conquer our basest instincts. We can choose to give altruistically while getting little to nothing in return. We can choose a mate or a job or a lifestyle based on whatever factors we like, not those society or our instincts demand we consider. We can stop giving in to fear, accumulating resources at all costs, or worrying about what people think about us. We can develop a healthy relationship with sex, money, fame, and our desire for newness, one that increases our happiness and that of those around us rather than making us and everyone else miserable. We can stop worrying about our instinctual needs to survive, multiply, and evolve at all costs and instead do whatever we like.

If life is a river of various relationshifting currents pulling us in one direction or another, we simply want to step out of the flow of those that push us away from our goals and into the stream of those that move us closer.

And whichever way we proceed, we can't do it alone.

Pause to reflect

- In what ways do you attempt to earn e-capital? How did you learn these behaviors?
- Which of the six strategies (safety, sex, acceptance, resources, influence, or novelty) do you have the healthiest relationship with? Which is the most toxic? What influenced you to use these strategies in the way you do, whether healthy or not?
- Are you subconsciously or consciously attempting to earn e-capital in a way that is sabotaging your deeper craving for happiness, fulfillment, or otherwise making the most of life?

- How can you reframe your thinking and life approach to set yourself up for results that are more in line with your most fundamental desires?
- Who in your life seems to have a healthier relationship with the urge to accumulate e-capital who can relationshift you toward a better approach?
- Does anyone with influence over you reinforce your negative relationship with the collection of e-capital? How can you limit their negative impact?

CHAPTER 6

Viral Ideas

"For millions of years, mankind lived just like the animals. Then something happened which unleashed the power of our imagination. We learned to talk and we learned to listen. Speech has allowed the communication of ideas, enabling human beings to work together to build the impossible. Mankind's greatest achievements have come about by talking."

Stephen Hawking

The first trip I took outside North America was to Myanmar when I was about thirty. The country had long been isolated from much of the world and was transitioning under new leadership to a more open stance with American visitors. A friend was visiting for a month to film leprosy victims for a nonprofit fighting the disease. He needed an extra hand to work the cameras. Though the job paid very little, I jumped at the chance to go on one of my first big adventures. Having never ventured far from the West Coast of the US, I had no idea what was in store.

After almost forty-eight hours of nonstop travel—including three airplanes, an overcrowded bus, armed checkpoints, a ferry, the back of a truck, a moped, and the final few miles by foot—we reached our destination, where the mayor of the town was waiting to have tea with us. Though it was well over one hundred degrees outside and my clothes were soaked with sweat, I politely drank my hot tea and tried to keep my eyes open as our guide spoke with the mayor.

The buildings were built on stilts above a shallow lake, all without doors or windows. I looked out through a gap in one of the walls and noticed people carrying sand in bags on their shoulders as they walked across a dirt bridge that ran across a narrow section in the middle of the lake. It seemed everyone in the village was in the parade. Even young children carried tiny sacks filled with dirt. They walked to the middle of the bridge, dumped the bags out, then returned and got more.

I asked my interpreter what they were doing. She explained that the bridge was made of fill from the nearby riverbank and was continually sinking into the lake. So the villagers regularly had to carry more sand out onto the bridge and build it up to prevent it from disappearing. She said the village had been maintaining the bridge in this manner for generations.

The Henry Thoreau in me thought this village's simple and isolated ways made for a beautiful existence. I found no signs of electricity and certainly no internet. I asked my interpreter why they didn't build a permanent bridge with lumber they might have cut from the village's many trees. The interpreter said it was unlikely that anyone in the town realized an alternative to sand was an option.

This is a vivid example of how ideas can't spread without human interaction. These isolated people didn't have access to the information necessary to innovate a better solution to their bridge problem. The sand method was working just fine, even if it did require a constant investment of time and energy, and would continue to demand this indefinitely. So they kept at it because it worked, and more importantly, because it was all they knew.

Just as the villagers in Myanmar could not fashion a better bridge without access to people with the knowledge to do so, we cannot be made of ideas to which we have never been exposed.

This is also true of ideas that are harmful, such as marketers and those who love pushing us to pursue more e-capital at all costs, even when it's hurting us. Even ideas from loved ones who want the best for us can be detrimental if they don't realize their advice doesn't apply to our situation the way they think it does. For example, advice on how women can close the gender gap from a loving grandmother who worked in big corporations in the 1970s may not apply perfectly to a young woman graduating college in the 2020s. The previous chapter includes many examples of how we can be prone to seek objectives that actually aren't making us any happier. The people we love are sometimes the guiltiest of pushing us to pursue these goals with greater fervor. Many who give well-meaning advice are inadvertently steering you down the wrong path merely because they themselves are not aware of how their own way of seeing the world is built on the same outdated evolutionary instincts that previous generations reinforced in them when they were children.

> "If you have an apple and I have an apple and we exchange these apples then you and I will still each have one apple. But if you have an idea and I have an idea and we exchange these ideas, then each of us will have two ideas."
>
> George Bernard Shaw

This chapter builds upon the previous one by examining what we can do about all these ideas floating around, whether our own analysis of our desire for e-capital or the relationship-shifting influence of the people around us. We must sharpen our ability to decipher which ideas we should accept, which we should ignore, and how we can find those we're not even yet aware of. We can, with practice and persistence, become better at finding gaps in our knowledge—these tend to be the most exciting and the most able to accelerate our journey to places our younger selves would be astonished to know were reachable.

We will start by exploring the analogy that ideas are like viruses. People pass ideas, both helpful and unhelpful, to other people through a form of proximity based on trust. Next, we will discuss a remarkable feature of our brains that works a lot like our immune system, rejecting some ideas while accepting others based on how our brains have been programmed through instincts and previous experiences. We will dive into our worldview, how it was created, and how we can reprogram it to better suit our purpose for living our happiest and most fulfilling lives, free of the outdated evolutionary instincts from chapter five or what anyone else might think we should do. Then we will cover a critical aspect of this book related to knowing who we can trust to relationshift us, and how we know they are the ones to move us toward our goals the fastest and most efficiently. After all, it's not much good to relationshift ourselves if we are moving further away from our goals or just going around in circles getting nowhere. Last, we will tackle one of the most difficult topics of all in today's modern world of rampant misinformation: how to determine what is actually true. This will be a nuanced discussion, one that places factualness on a spectrum from objective to subjective.

In short, chapter six is devoted to giving you the tools necessary to realign your worldview in whatever way sets you up to become whoever you want to be, not whoever everyone else wants you to be.

All Ideas Come from Somewhere

Ideas are like viruses. They pass from person to person. If you are not close to a carrier, you can't catch the virus. Relatedly, the laws of this universe dictate that nothing comes from nothing. In a similar way, novel thoughts do not create themselves, nor do they leap from nothingness into existence. Everything in this universe is formed from smaller pieces. Likewise, ideas consist of preexisting fragments. The human mind cannot produce completely new ideas, regardless of the amount of LSD one ingests. To illustrate, try imagining a new color. Or consider how the aliens in most movies look an awful lot like humans, just with bigger eyes, antennas, or an additional boob[1] or two.[2]

---

1. See *Total Recall* (1990).

2. See *Rick and Morty*, season one, episode two.

Ideas are formed just as humans evolved: by incremental modifications of what already exists. But what about the iPhone? Didn't Steve Jobs cook that up out of thin air? By some measures, nothing quite like it existed before. But in actuality, all of the components of the iPhone were present before Jobs put them together. He just combined many features and technologies in a way that no one had seen before. Or what about the general theory of relativity? Einstein's crowning achievement is an undeniably groundbreaking feat. Yet, he never could have conceived of it without the advancements of countless other theories and ideas that had preceded him. More than two centuries earlier, Newton had devised the concept of gravity. Many researchers observed and recorded flaws in Newton's work in the years between these two scientists' theories. These were some of the breadcrumbs Einstein followed until he had collected enough to put them together in a new way that advanced our understanding of physics.

> "Great new ideas don't emerge from within a single person or function, but at the intersection of functions or people that have never met before."
>
> Clayton M. Christensen

So, yes, every idea you possess came from somewhere outside of you. However, you can combine and rearrange the ideas you've been given in any number of ways. We rig up our new constructs from bits and pieces of old ones, like MacGyver making a hang glider out of a hat stand and some trash bags. But you can't manifest an idea if you don't have all of the pieces needed to construct it.

Suppose we want to be more positive and are unable to find positivity within our existing mind space. In that case, we need to gather the necessary components from other people. We can learn to achieve a high level of success by gathering information directly from very successful, high-gravity people—the essence of maximizing positive relationshift. A slower approach would be to combine mindsets from moderately successful people with the views of philosophers, religious leaders, teachers, or experts in other tangential topic areas. In either case, we are building our knowledge from the contributions of others.

The villagers I encountered in Myanmar could have improved their lake-crossing method without modern engineers' help by combining two ideas they already understood: sand bridges and strong trees. However, it's much easier to adopt the ideas that other people have already developed than to build them from disparate pieces on our own, such as buying an iPhone versus assembling one from scratch.

> "An idea is like a virus. Resilient. Highly contagious. The smallest seed of an idea can grow. It can grow to define... or destroy you."
>
> Ziad K. Abdelnour

But how do we know the idea-fragments we are putting together are the best available for our purpose? Let's assume that at some point in history, the wheel was square. If this was the case, someone had to improve it by rounding off the edges. We can be prone to combine square-wheel ideas with other square wheels. This is not likely to lead anywhere but to a trip to the chiropractor. Likewise, not all ideas are equally helpful for our purposes. To move forward efficiently, we must learn to sort the useful notions from those holding us back. And most difficult of all, we must figure out the knowledge we need that we don't even realize is necessary.

Ideas and Relationships

For most of my life, I was like the villagers with the sand bridge. I didn't realize there were more efficient ways to reach my goals. I had ideas and access to many more, but I didn't know which paths I should follow and which I should ignore. How could I learn what I needed if I couldn't conceptualize what I was missing? Without a doubt, I'm still in this state in new ways I have yet to discover. We all are.

What's more, my goals didn't align with the ideas in my vicinity. I was trying to catch chickenpox by sharing a bed with people sick with the flu. If one is surrounded by people who are not aware of bridge-building methods that last longer than sinking sand, one must invent the design oneself. While this is possible—someone had to invent the first wood bridge, after all—it's a much more difficult path. So challenging, in fact, that for most people, not having access to the right ideas is a recipe for never unlocking their promise.

My dad was a con man and petty drug dealer, and to be honest, he wasn't very good at either. Simple pleasures many people enjoy from time to time, like eating out at Burger King, were luxuries I rarely experienced as a child. So with my father's impoverished state ever on my mind, I wanted to become just about as different from him as possible. Specifically, I decided to become a billionaire. Looking back, I'm embarrassed that I didn't see this as a goal so much as an expectation of my future state. I had no way of understanding just how difficult a path I was expecting to unfold before me and how my poor decisions and lack of mentoring made the task exponentially more difficult.

After getting married and having my first daughter, Anna and I decided to have two more children so they could grow up close in age to one another. By the age of twenty-one—with three daughters, a wife, and an overdrawn checking account—I wasn't off to a great start toward my goal of becoming filthy rich. I didn't have a relationship with a single person above the middle class. My stepdad told me to become a plumber or an electrician like him. "Get yourself a trade," he said often, "and you'll never want for work." It's decent advice, but this foolish kid with an overabundance of ambition wasn't listening.

The only other mentor figure in my life, Clyde, was an underpaid clergyman and handyman with basically the same advice—take up a trade or go into the Lord's work. I enjoyed construction, but it didn't seem likely to finance my ridiculous ambitions. And God certainly didn't pay well enough (the average pastor earns as little as $25,000 per year in the United States)—though I was promised a generous "retirement" package. I was playing the game of life with a collection of limitations I had no way to understand: the hubris of youth, a complete lack of respect for risk, and an inability to stay focused in the presence of shiny objects.

> "Ideas and products and messages and behaviors spread just like viruses do."
>
> Malcolm Gladwell

This is, of course, a simplified view. We can grow rich without knowing wealthy people. We can attain nirvana without living among Buddhist monks. Besides picking up lessons from books, podcasts, seminars, and so forth, we can piece together a workable path toward our goals by collecting pieces from various sources. We could learn hard work from one person, innovation from another, frugality from a third, and sound investing from a fourth. Combined, these "viruses" could create a billionaire. However, the task is made much simpler with direct access to someone who has done precisely what we want to do. Without a guide, it's hard to determine what knowledge we need.

Ideas and Viruses

Let's return to the ideas-as-viruses metaphor. Both share several traits beyond what I discussed at the beginning of this chapter. First, just like ideas, some viruses are helpful and others are unhelpful. For instance, scientists have discovered a kind of virus called a bacteriophage that seeks out and destroys unhealthy bacteria inside the body. To heal from certain infections, doctors can inject lab-manufactured bacteriophages into the bloodstream to help a patient recover. Other viruses, like Pegivirus C, have no known negative symptoms yet have been proven to reduce the harmful effects of HIV on a person's immune system. *The key with ideas, as with viruses, is to know which ones we want to catch to achieve our goal and which to avoid.*

A second way that viruses and ideas are similar is how they spread geographically. The percentage of people with sexually transmitted infections is higher in some areas of the world than others. This makes sense, of course. If more people in a particular city or country have chlamydia, then other people in that area are more likely to catch it. For example, in 2017, seven of every thousand Louisianans had chlamydia—one of the highest rates in the US. But 2,500 miles north in Vermont, only three of every thousand residents had the same infection—less than half the rate.

Comparably strong correlations exist *between beliefs and a person's physical location*. Rural, southern states are more politically conservative and religious than their counterparts to the north. In contrast, cities, regardless of location, lean liberal and less religious. Some posit the reason for the difference in cities is that exposure there to so many ways of living, personal belief systems, socioeconomic statuses, and cultural backgrounds causes one to become infected by more ideas. Amid so many opinions, one is more likely to be open-minded about God's name, character, or existence. And if one is close to social issues like homelessness or the separation of immigrant families, it's more difficult to dismiss the problem as mere laziness because proximity tends to reveal nuance.

Alternatively, others believe that exposure to many different views pulls one away from the truth. If there is one true god, then being influenced by people who think differently could be eternally harmful—get this right, or you could burn in hell forever. Some theorize that proximity to social issues like homelessness or immigration clouds our judgment and makes us soft toward people who need tough love. My aim is not to paint one perspective or another as true or false, but simply to show how prolonged and persistent exposure to ideas causes us to become more sympathetic to them, whatever those ideas may be.

When one lives among any given subset of the population, it's much more challenging to think of them as "those people" because we can see our common humanity with every interaction. And when we don't have much personal exposure to the problems or perspectives of a group, it's a lot easier to believe something like, "*Those people* need to pick themselves up by their bootstraps and get a job." Or, "*Those people* are just selfish and would rather pay fewer taxes than help those in need." *Us* becomes *them* the further we are from someone, either in worldview, cultural background, or socioeconomic status, or because of a geographic distance.

> "Software innovation, like almost every other kind of innovation, requires the ability to collaborate and share ideas with other people."
>
> Bill Gates

As one may expect, and directly in correlation with population density, suburban areas tend to be more conservative than downtown areas, though less so than rural areas. Population density is higher in the suburbs than it is out across the fruited plain, but unlike in urban city centers, people can quickly move from their house to work and through their daily errands while encapsulated by their SUVs and gated communities with little to no exposure to diverse, conflictive ideas.

Another interesting similarity between viruses and ideas is that health epidemics often originate in highly populated areas in much the same way as innovations. With all those people close together, viruses have more opportunity to interact with various other biological phenomena and, in so doing, morph into something new that our bodies don't know how to fight. Though the physical viruses that get the most attention are often unhealthy for humans, like Ebola and H1N1, new idea viruses can be either healthy or unhealthy. And new ideas often originate in places where lots of people are interacting and sharing. This helps explain why five of the most influential companies of our time—Facebook, Google, Microsoft, Amazon, and Apple—are based in just two metros, Seattle and Silicon Valley, which are a mere 750 miles apart. All those nerds stuffed into two cities surrounded by other nerds with knowledge about the internet, technology, and future trends are far more likely to pass ideas around, which fosters an environment ripe for innovation.

> "One of the greatest values of mentors is the ability to see ahead what others cannot see and to help them navigate a course to their destination."
>
> John C. Maxwell

Living in a sleepy city like Eugene, Oregon, where people are more interested in peace-drum circles than becoming billionaires, I had little access to the necessary ideas to achieve my ambitious goals. The only mentors I had at my disposal came in the form of books, but these can be tricky to learn from. It's easy to dismiss the advice of an author.[3] We can too easily assume that their perspective is not transferable to our situation or that they're out only to profit from those foolish enough to keep buying their unworkable ideas. We can also easily ignore the advice of those whom we don't come into contact with—there is no pressure to do what they tell us. We also can't as easily be sure that the advice offered in a book applies to our unique situation, or whether the author is more interested in selling inventory than actually helping people.

Though I read several books on investing, picking successful careers, and starting businesses, I can't say that I followed much of the advice. I

---

3. I realize you're going to dismiss this advice.

remember feeling that I'd tried these ideas, and they didn't work for me. Other times, the path seemed too hard or too long for me to persist. Further complicating matters, with books, seminars, podcasts, and the like, it can be challenging to sort the good ideas from the bad. Some authors really *are* selling snake oil. And many ideas work in some contexts but not others. Without a trusted mentor to guide us step-by-step, we can easily get lost in the seemingly infinite abyss of contradicting or confusing ideas. Or we may attempt to seek shortcuts that lead nowhere.

Following a mentor who knows the way is like having a map with clear instructions for avoiding pitfalls, traps, and roadblocks. Sometimes this can feel like the long way around. We may grow impatient with advice that seems to take too long to show results. But which path is quicker: the so-called shortcuts that get you stuck, waste your time, and take your money, or the seemingly longer route that gets results?

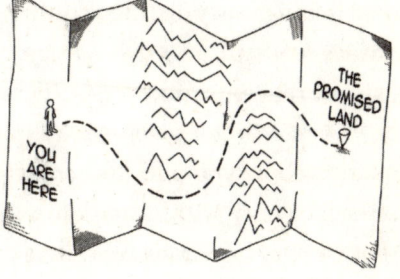

I remember hearing about how most shortcuts lead nowhere. Some of the people in my life would have been able to tell me the truth about these matters. And perhaps they did. So why didn't I listen? I could have found a proven mentor in the form of a book or workshop to guide me through the shortcuts. Unfortunately, this approach is more difficult in practice than in theory.

The truth is that we have access to nearly all of humanity's collective knowledge on the phones we carry. The problem isn't access to wisdom. It's that we have something like a mental immune system that blocks ideas it doesn't recognize. This part of us accepts or rejects new information the same way our physical immune system accepts or rejects biological viruses. We call this subconscious idea immune system our *worldview* or *personal lens.*[4] This mental immune system is necessary for our survival. And it is also one of our biggest obstacles to positive change.

Our Mental Immune System

Religion is a fascinating case study in the potential for negative outcomes when we surround ourselves with like-minded people. Regardless of your belief system, I'm sure you can agree that those claiming to do "God's work" have used religion as a means to a self-enriching end for millennia. No method is as successful for motivating people to blow themselves up, no cause so versatile in justifying war, no tactic so efficient at picking the pockets of the poor. Some estimate as many as two hundred million people have died in religiously justified conflicts and wars. This is not to say that religion always leads to negative outcomes. On the contrary, countless examples exist of religious followers selflessly helping others and otherwise making our world a better place. Many spiritual people are among the nicest, most giving people you will find anywhere. Yet, to the extent that we surround ourselves only with other like-minded people, we increase the possibility that we may lose track of what is objectively real versus what is merely perceived as real by those in our circle.

People of all persuasions, religious or secular, tend to sort themselves into groups that align with their worldview. When it comes to faith, some call this church shopping. Others call it avoiding bad influences. But most do it merely because it's more comfortable and practical to hang around with people who have a similar worldview. Their mental immune systems reject beliefs that don't fit while they seek refuge in the company of those with similar views.

The variety of what constitutes sin is without end, changing from church to church, synagogue to synagogue, temple to temple, and denomination to denomination. The one similarity that you will find is that people tend to choose a religion, or sect within that religion, based on sharing similar beliefs with other people who prefer the same religion.

No matter what your worldview is on any given topic, you will have little problem finding a church, cult, or secular community with the same

---

4. And if you don't, you might now.

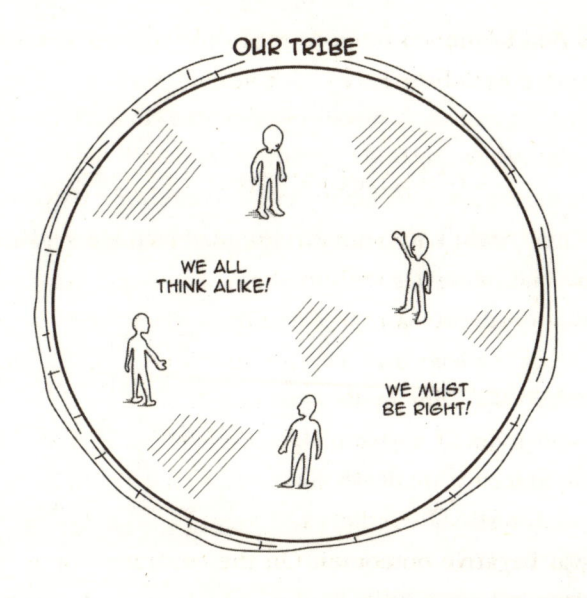

perspective. Those who struggle to find a geographically close-knit group that supports their beliefs can turn to books, discussion boards, podcasts, or YouTube channels. Quite conveniently, if we ever change our mind, we can easily change our affiliations.

In practice, we don't give much credence or consideration to the views that contradict our own. If one surrounds himself with others who believe in pretty much the same things,[5] it's easy to ignore the fact that many other people would perhaps die for their quite opposite beliefs—and if not die, at least operate their lives on the belief that their truths are mostly objective beyond a reasonable doubt. We find it uncomfortable to consider that the ideas we feel are well supported within our community are in direct contrast to what other people feel are equally well supported by their

---

5. Many religious sects allow, or even encourage, minor differences of conviction between followers. They might say, "We are free to disagree on the small stuff as long as we have consensus on the most significant pillars of our faith." But this perspective fails to consider the possibility that one believes in the significance of particular pillars of faith merely because one is surrounded by others who believe the same. This viewpoint also ignores the prospect that all aspects of religion are subjective, no matter how central an idea is to any one faction.

communities, so our mental immune system simply rejects these conflicting views as non-possibilities.

Once again, we can see how our brain works similarly to our biological immune system. When our body is working correctly, a collection of white blood cells work together to keep foreign contaminants from killing us. These T cells, neutrophils, and monocytes must distinguish the good organisms from the bad, ignoring the former and dismantling the latter to be repurposed or expelled from the body. But sometimes, our immune system gets confused. It can attack good cells, which can cause death via many types of illness. Other times, our body doesn't recognize the dangerous contaminants and allows them to thrive. Both types of malfunction are responsible for many common disorders, from failed organ transplants to Crohn's to arthritis to multiple sclerosis to diabetes to AIDS.

> "The difficulty lies not so much in developing new ideas as in escaping from old ones."
>
> John Maynard Keynes

Our mental immune system tends to only accept ideas if they are similar to what we already believe. The more different or threatening a notion, the more our cognitive immune system will combat it. In other words, we see what we want to see. If we want to reject an idea, we will discard it. If we want to believe something, we will find a way to justify it. We tend to seek evidence to support our existing desire or perspective because it's more comfortable. None of us wants to believe we are delusional, so we spend a lot of energy to justify our positions. And, of course, we find other people who believe the same so we all feel better about ourselves.

This is why arguing with the opposite side about politics or religion rarely gets us anywhere. Both sides' mental immune systems are so resilient against such radically different perspectives that everything that doesn't fit just bounces off. The longer we are alive, the more our worldview locks in. We have all seen how children are more likely than older adults to accept new ideas. Just as children's immune systems are weak and kids are more likely than adults to catch any viruses they encounter, so, too, are children's worldviews far more malleable. In a similar fashion, high school and college students tend to be more open to large changes in their worldview because they haven't yet fully formed one.

Our Existing Worldview

Our existing worldview is the biggest obstacle preventing us from accomplishing positive change. However, this lens is necessary for our survival. It enables us to operate in a complicated world without continually having to reevaluate every input from scratch. This is related to the part of our brain that forms habits. The simple act of walking requires our brain to recall what it learned when we took our first few thousand steps, so we don't fall every time we try. Language requires us to memorize words and meanings until they become so ingrained in us that we can speak without consciously processing all these sounds and meanings each time we repeat them. Without this magnificent ability of ours to consult experience, understanding even a single sentence would be impossible. And when we first learn to drive, we can easily be overwhelmed thinking about everything we need to monitor. Vehicles coming at us from any direction. The speed limit and our own velocity. Signaling a turn with the blinker. Multitasking is difficult while we're learning, making even casual conversation a dangerous distraction. This is why many states don't allow new drivers to have friends in the car until six months after obtaining a license.

> "They are loaded with prejudices, not based upon anything in reality, but based on ... if something is new, I reject it immediately because it's frightening to me. What they do instead is just stay with the familiar."
>
> Wayne W. Dyer

But over time, the habit-forming part of our brain moves these conscious thoughts to our subconscious. Before long, everything that was so difficult to track becomes second nature, and we can find ourselves driving for ten minutes as our mind wanders without once thinking about the task of steering, applying the brakes, using a turn signal, and so on. If we didn't have this habit-forming ability, every time we drove a car would be like the first time. You might have experienced something similar if you have ever driven in a country that uses the opposite side of the road than you are used to. Just that small change can cause our brain to feel like we must relearn how to drive. Conversations and a wandering mind become dangerous again. The moment we take our conscious mind off the task of driving on the opposite side of the road, we are likely to find ourselves back in our subconscious habits, which in this case could lead to a head-on collision (and almost did for me on more than one occasion).

Our lens is fashioned from a combination of every interaction we have. As our worldview forms, the lens through which we see life begins to color any new input. The effect of contact with another person's traits is mitigated by previous experiences and preconceived notions built upon past relationships. For example, two people with different lenses see the use of guns differently. This, in turn, affects their view on the issue of gun rights. Also, our age when we are exposed to ideas changes how likely we are to accept them. Hearing opinions on gun rights at the age of ten will have a different impact on a person than introducing the same ideas at the age of fifty. The middle-aged person's worldview had forty additional years to become established. Thus, they will be more skeptical of information that contradicts what they have come to believe over all those years.

OUR LENS AFFECTS HOW WE SEE GUNS

The Lens of Precedent

In the same way that we are prone to adopt inaccurate stereotypes, we often incorrectly categorize new ideas. We can dismiss a helpful idea because we assume it's just like another idea we didn't find beneficial. We can incorrectly assume a path is blocked because we wrongly apply a precedent to the current situation. We can ignore helpful people because our experience is incorrectly telling us to ignore certain kinds of people, though the reason we're ignoring them may have little to do with what we could gain from them. We are often too quick to feel we have already applied whatever we are hearing. Someone shares something that can help us, and our first response is usually to believe that we have already learned this lesson.

It's difficult to believe there is more to understand on a given topic that we feel we have already mastered. This is partly because of ego. Other factors could be laziness or fear. Perhaps we don't have the energy to thoroughly investigate something new. Or we're afraid of what might happen if we allow ourselves to believe there is more. By feeling that we have already learned a lesson, and perhaps that this lesson does not work as promised, we give ourselves a convenient excuse for not achieving what we desire. But this is mostly because of the practical limits of our imagination. Just as we cannot think of an idea that hasn't been made from others that already exists in our minds, we can't easily see beyond what we already know.

The way our brain uses precedent comes in handy in many aspects of everyday life, but we must learn to overcome this to make progress toward positive change. *Fortunately, there are ways we can retrain ourselves to accept new ideas.* Let's explore this topic next.

Retrain the Brain with Baby Steps

In 1968, the famous psychology researcher Albert Bandura published a study that examined how fear in one person is affected by exposure to people who show no fear in the same situation. He studied forty-eight children, ages three to five, with a significant fear of dogs. Some children watched videos of actors playing happily with dogs, while another group watched videos without dogs.

As you can guess, the children who saw people interacting fearlessly with dogs were more inclined to play with dogs themselves after this exposure.

Children are more open than adults to new ideas, partly because they have a less solidified worldview—their immune system for rejecting new ideas is still weak. But if the concept is too radically different from their existing experience, children will ignore the new direction just as adults will. In another study, children were exposed to an actor playing with a dog in person. If the dog was gentle, the children would watch the actor playing and become more interested in playing with the dog themselves. But if the dog behaved aggressively, they would hide their faces or turn away. Without exposure, they did not become any more likely to play with dogs.

Bandura's study illustrates the power of incremental exposure. Even as adults with strong worldviews, we can change a lot if we do so in small steps. Making a positive change in our lives often requires accepting new ideas that don't fit our existing worldview. Our first instinct will be to reject these ideas, even those that may be just the thing we need to accomplish our goal. But if we already knew what we needed to know or possessed the necessary mental ability, likely we already would have accomplished what we want.

OUR MENTAL IMMUNE SYSTEM WORKS LIKE A POLARIZED LENS

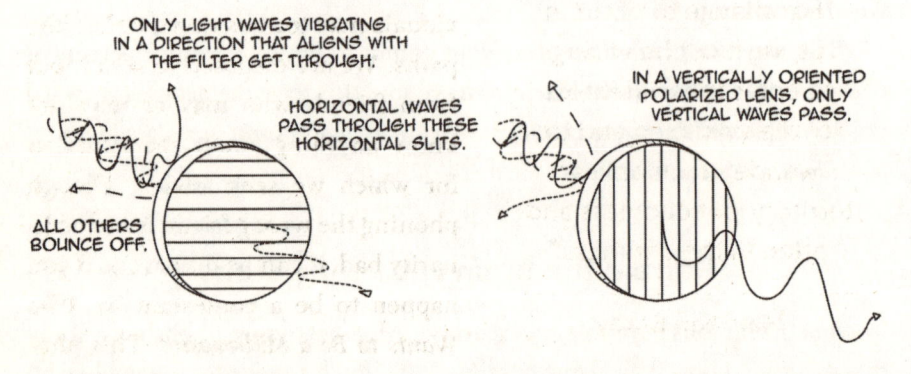

ONLY LIGHT WAVES VIBRATING IN A DIRECTION THAT ALIGNS WITH THE FILTER GET THROUGH.

HORIZONTAL WAVES PASS THROUGH THESE HORIZONTAL SLITS.

ALL OTHERS BOUNCE OFF.

IN A VERTICALLY ORIENTED POLARIZED LENS, ONLY VERTICAL WAVES PASS.

To better understand how this can work in our lives, let's compare our mental immune system to polarized sunglasses. These types of lenses have something like slits in them that are all oriented in the same direction. As a polarized lens is turned, only light waves aligned with its slits can pass through. Those vibrating in other directions bounce off. These kinds of lenses are helpful in many circumstances. For instance, light reflects off flat surfaces in a horizontal pattern. If a polarized lens is tilted so its slits are vertical, it filters out horizontal glare from roads, pools, and lakes—a handy feature when driving on a sunny day.

IF WE ROTATE OUR LENS OVER TIME IDEAS THAT BOUNCED OFF PREVIOUSLY WILL EVENTUALLY PASS THROUGH

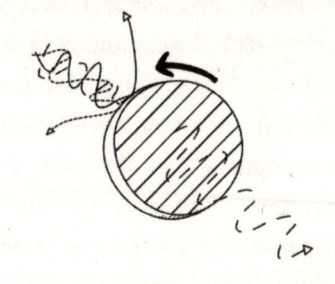

If we believe dogs are dangerous, we acknowledge inputs that support this view and ignore those that don't. But gradual exposure to new ideas helps us slowly accept these inputs. This is like turning the polarized lens a little each day over many months or years. What starts as an idea we reject outright is eventually accepted.

Trusting the Influencer

Another scenario that increases our likelihood of embracing new philosophies is when we trust the influencer. We are more prone to accept the direction of someone we admire or know well. However, trusted individuals may lead us down unhealthy paths. We are disposed to seek input from friends who may or may not know anything about the situation for which we seek advice. Though phoning the wrong friend is not ordinarily bad, it can be disastrous if you happen to be a contestant on *Who Wants to Be a Millionaire?*. This phenomenon can also explain why we are less likely to take the advice of book authors and others in unilateral relationships—we don't know and trust the influencer as we might a personal mentor, boss, or parent.

> "For change to occur in us, we must be willing to enter the wilderness of the unknown and to wander in unfamiliar territory, directionless and often in the darkness."
>
> **Maureen Brady**

We need to focus on the aspects of life we can change: our choices, our options, and, of course, our relationships. To change these, or even desire to change them, we need to learn to accept new ideas by overcoming our mental immune system to admit novel information. In many cases, this involves incorporating information we don't even know we need. In others, we must accept ideas that we currently believe are unhelpful, incorrect, or inapplicable. Easier said than done.

Before we move on, let's reexamine the game we are playing, this time adding a lens that shapes how we see our options. If we want to create positive change, we must become

> "Our first impressions are generated by our experiences and our environment, which means that we can change our first impressions... by changing the experiences that comprise those impressions."
>
> Malcolm Gladwell

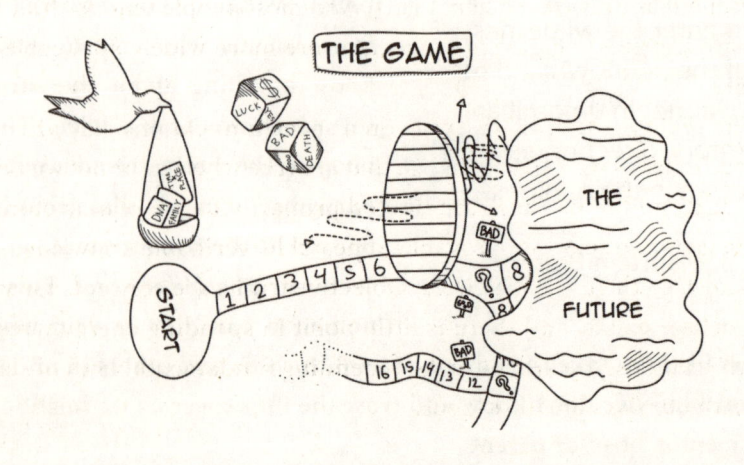

more willing to accept new beliefs that may not fit our existing worldview. We must somehow find a way to weaken our cognitive immune system to become open to information that has not been baked into us by friends and family from a young age. As discussed for Bandura's study or the polarized lens analogy, gradually exposing ourselves to different ideas can help us make significant changes to our lens over a long period. (Engaging with a highly trusted mentor can shorten this process.) Using these scenarios makes measurable, positive change more likely. When we adopt the belief that we could be wrong about anything we believe, we become more and more open, accelerating our ability to accept healthy ideas that are quite different from what we already believe.

Pause to reflect

- Are there any examples of when you came to accept a view you previously rejected? What factors led to this change?
- Which of your current views have more potential for fundamental change than you may have thought prior to exploring the topics of this chapter? If you're struggling with this question, consider the areas of your life in which you have few influences outside a supportive circle of like-minded individuals.

Objective Versus Subjective

Most ideas are neither universally good nor bad. Some are helpful for one person but unhelpful for another—like mild use of recreational drugs, antidepressants, or owning two dozen cats. Other ideas are more generally healthy or unhealthy—spending less than you earn (usually considered a good idea, unless you're the United States government) or corsets (organ damage is never in fashion). The problem comes when we get advice that is presented as universal when it isn't. And most people tend to think their ideas are the most helpful or correct, or are more widely applicable than they are.

The reality is that truth exists on a spectrum. On one side are objective truths, ideas we cannot change that are true whether or not we believe or understand them. These are limited primarily to the realms of mathematics, fact, and science—provable, repeatable, verifiable knowledge, such as calculating the area of a circle. Objective truths are concepts for which scant debate exists, and there is little point in spending energy wrestling with them unless we aim to make redefining fundamental laws of science and math our life's primary focus.

On the other side of the spectrum are subjective ideas, which exist outside the world of provable, repeatable facts. These kinds of positions are malleable. We can bend them to our whim, whether we recognize the power or not. To understand how other people might overestimate the universality of their ideas, consider your own opinions. We all decide what we believe is the truth about subjects that have been debated for centuries. We hear a monk recite the *Bhagavad Gita* and may choose to accept what he says. Or we may not. We read a headline in the *New York Times* and we may elect to label it fake news. Or we could consider it reliable.

> "People almost invariably arrive at their beliefs not on the basis of proof but on the basis of what they find attractive."
>
> Blaise Pascal

We define our reality as if we are the god of our own universe, able to judge right from wrong for ourselves and others. When we are caught up in this process unawares, we may believe we are discovering the truth, but we are creating our own reality. We all live in a dream, primarily constructed by our personal definition of truth—whether we realize it or not. The objective/subjective truth spectrum is illustrated in the figure on the next page.

The subjectivity of most ideas is a challenging concept to accept. We have been told all our life that truth is objective. From the time your ears were formed in your mother's womb to this very day, you have been bombarded with an endless stream of proclamations, often presented as far more objective than the evidence supports. It can be challenging to question people who are so convinced they are correct, especially when we trust them. On the other hand, you have to recognize your role in the process: whenever another person presents you with their truth, it is you, and only you, who possesses the power to accept or reject it.

> "We live in a fantasy world, a world of illusion. The great task in life is to find reality."
>
> Iris Murdoch

Each of us constructs a personal universe from countless choices. Thus, we all live in different universes. Given the myriad truths we choose for

SUBJECTIVE TO OBJECTIVE TRUTH METER

BASED ON THE QUANTITY AND QUALITY OF EVIDENCE

SUBJECTIVE — 0
- RELIGION
- POSSIBILITY OF ALIEN LIFE
- THE PURPOSE OF LIFE
- HOW TO BE HAPPY
- WHICH POLITICAL SYSTEM IS BEST
- UNPROVEN SCIENTIFIC THEORIES
- HOW TO BEST LOSE WEIGHT
- WELL RESEARCHED NEWS
- SCIENTIFIC LAWS
- MATH

OBJECTIVE — 100

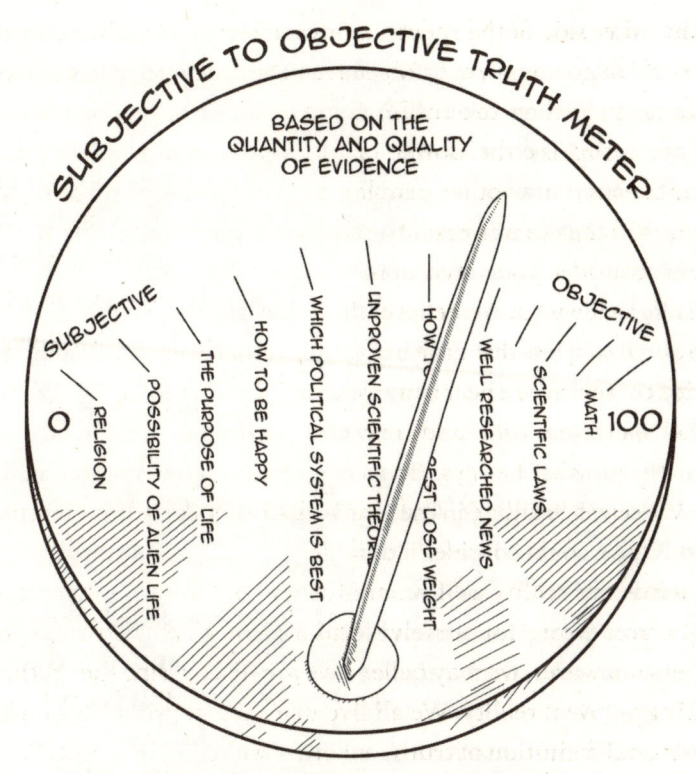

*NOT INTENDED TO BE A PERFECT REPRESENTATION OF WHERE THESE CONSTRUCTS WOULD BE FOUND ON SUCH A METER

ourselves, it's impossible that two people in history have ever lived according to the same set of certainties. Yet, if we're not careful, we can act as if we, of all the people who have ever lived, have discovered the real truth. We are prone to believe left is right and right is wrong without appreciating how, in the house next door, the opposite may be true.

Our instincts and desires can cause us to push our subjective laws for living on others. We often don't realize we're doing this. Perhaps we think our advice is best and subconsciously want to gain e-capital by spreading our ideas as widely as possible. Or, if we can relationshift someone else to adopt a bit of our truth, it validates our submission to the same ideas. Many other reasons exist for humanity's eagerness to peddle subjective laws as universal, many of them related to profit, power, and fame. Book sales, tithe baskets, and the funding of political campaigns are a few. Some of the most successful people in this world got to their position by developing their ability to convince others to subject themselves to so-called laws that are not nearly as objective as one might have been taught to believe.

Regardless of where our beliefs come from, we often don't realize how much of our reality is curated. As a result, we are prone to subject ourselves to ways of life that may not be good for us. We can easily find ourselves pining for a world that works more to our liking, not recognizing that we are actively choosing to live in a universe we don't like.

It is here that we discover one of life's chief sources of unhappiness: subjecting ourselves to arbitrary ways of thinking that cause discontent. It seems a very odd thing to do, and yet we practice it with regularity. We tell ourselves to abstain from a slice of blackberry pie because we don't like the way we look in the mirror. In reality, many people can enjoy sweets in moderation as part of a long, healthy life. Quite a number of folks believe money is evil but secretly wish for the freedom that wealth could provide. Some are certain they don't deserve more from life with no evidence other than their negative self-view. We can believe we're not amply intelligent to earn an A in chemistry, sufficiently charismatic to tell a story at a dinner party, or adequately attractive to catch the eye of that cute barista at our favorite coffee shop. But why couldn't the opposite of these be just as valid?

> "People will choose unhappiness over uncertainty."
>
> Tim Ferriss

It's easy to become stuck in a trap of our choosing. If we're not careful, we can find ourselves merely carrying on, unsatisfied at best, miserable perhaps, longing for luck to swing our way. Others place their hope in a life after this, one we are promised by those who are eager for the same outcome. But regardless of what we think happens after we die—and we can never be sure until we, too, are dead—we have only this current moment to enjoy. Giving up on this life, especially when it's not necessary to do so, for the hope of something we can't be sure of is not the best way to maximize contentment and happiness in our present state. We can all too easily opt in to these limiting worldviews, partly because they are so much easier than trying.

We cannot accomplish a goal that we believe is out of reach. We cannot achieve anything within a conceived reality that predisposes us to failure. The good news is that we have accepted our present reality choice by choice, so we also can select a new reality the same way. If we have a self-defeating worldview about getting into shape, our first step toward change is to admit that other people live in a different subjective existence. A million different realities exist, each one containing unique worldviews and ways of life. In some, people can eat what they want and stay thin by exercising more or eating less. In other personal universes, people eat as much food as they wish but tend to eat certain foods that make it easier to stay in shape.

The more evidence that exists to support an idea, the more the idea pulls to the fact side of the spectrum. But where there is a significant lack of verifiable, repeatable evidence, subjective truth abounds. This leaves more room for creating our own reality. Much of engineering is on the fact side of the spectrum; mathematicians reference scientific knowledge and complex formulas that have been tested for decades to determine, say, the size of beams necessary to keep a bridge from falling into a river. Yet people may disagree on how big to make the beams to compensate for earthquake risk.

> "The whole purpose of scientific method is to make valid distinctions between the false and the true in nature, to eliminate the subjective, unreal, imaginary elements from one's work so as to obtain an objective, true picture of reality."
>
> Robert M. Pirsig

Inversely, you will never find an engineer who got a six-figure deal for a book that explains the secret power of replacing steel I-beams with Jell-O—possibly because the bridge fell on said engineer before the book could be finished. Scientists have proven through countless experiments that a rainbow appears in the sky because of how light refracts within each drop of rain. This abundance of evidence places the idea on the objective-truth side of the spectrum. But if you ask ten people in a room to define love,[6] you will likely get ten different answers—everything from "love is what makes life worth living" to "love is bullshit." This result implies that the definition of love exists on the subjective end of the spectrum.

---

6. Check with HR before you use this as an icebreaking topic for your next executive networking event.

Countless volumes of research are available to aid one in their fitness goals.[7] However, various interpretations of these studies and conflicting results can confuse the matter. So we have some room to create our reality on this topic, but only within the boundaries of verifiable evidence. Researchers may disagree on whether or not gluten is terrible for us, but most people would agree that consuming a diet entirely of fried pork belly in corn syrup is not ideal for one's waistline or longevity.

Of course, just because there are many different opinions on a topic doesn't mean it's necessarily subjective. People can be dumb—myself included. We are easy to sway if we are ignorant or collect our information from unreliable sources. When available, verifiable evidence or expert opinion are much better indicators. If there is a disagreement between subject matter authorities and the general population, weight the experts' views more heavily.

For example, consider the debate on climate change. A quick Twitter search will yield countless opinions on the topic, ranging from the stance that humans are causing harmful warming of our planet to the belief that humans aren't doing and can't do anything to cause climate change. Of course, social media is hardly a bastion of factual accuracy. Thus, the opinions we see there should be weighted less than those from fact-checked, expert sources. Yet even among scientists, at least some level of disagreement exists on this issue. For example, the Oregon Institute of Science and Medicine claimed thirty-one thousand scientists posit that no convincing evidence exists to support the possibility of man-made atmospheric warming. On the other hand, a George Mason University poll of climate scientists found that 84 percent believe human interventions cause global warming. Based on these apparent disagreements among experts, we can't place the source of global warming on the objective truth end of the spectrum. But we also shouldn't throw our hands in the air and claim truth is undeterminable in this situation.

We can use the weighting system described in the previous paragraph to determine this topic's subjectivity by further digging into the disagreement between scientists. More precisely, the thirty-one thousand experts

---

7. Over twelve million results on Google.

cited by the Oregon Institute of Science and Medicine do not possess a commensurate level of knowledge about global warming, by their own admission. Only 12 percent of those thirty-one thousand indicated they had any affiliation with atmospheric science, and of those with an affiliation, nothing is specified about their level of direct knowledge related to global warming. As a result of this analysis, their positions on the topic must be given less weight than the study produced by George Mason University,

HOW TO MEASURE THE OBJECTIVITY OR SUBJECTIVITY OF A TOPIC OR POSITION

WEIGHT OF EVIDENCE

EXPERT OPINIONS — SCIENTIFICALLY VERIFIED EVIDENCE — NON-EXPERT OPINIONS

A TOPIC IS LIKELY SUBJECTIVE WHEN MANY, WIDELY RANGING OPINIONS EXIST

YES — ARE WE THE CAUSE OF CLIMATE CHANGE? — NO

BUT IF EXPERT OPINIONS OR EVIDENCE ARE AVAILABLE THEY SHOULD WEIGH MORE IN OUR ANALYSIS

YES — ARE WE THE CAUSE OF CLIMATE CHANGE? — NO

IN THIS EXAMPLE, EXPERT OPINIONS AND EVIDENCE GENERALLY AGREE, SUPERSEDING THE WIDELY RANGING VIEWS OF NON-EXPERTS. AS A RESULT, WE CAN CONCLUDE THIS IS A SEMI-OBJECTIVE TRUTH.

which surveyed only scientists who work in studying our climate. Given just these data points, the position that humans cause climate change can be comfortably determined to be more objective than highly subjective topics like religion. But, given the small amount of disagreement in even the George Mason University poll, this position should not be considered as objective as topics like math and well-supported scientific laws of nature.

Besides the number of opinions or the volume of evidence on a topic, we can also determine whether an idea is objective or subjective based on the number of times we have personally changed our view on the subject. If often, any positions we adopt concerning truth on this topic are likely to be more malleable. By extension, this subject should be considered on the subjective side of the truth meter. In contrast, people don't often change their minds about facts like how far the sun is from the earth, or the speed at which it is safe for an Airbus A380 to travel from San Diego to São Paulo.

Sometimes we cope with our changing views on subjective topics by considering the process "refining our understanding of an objective truth." We tell ourselves we're growing into a new understanding of the one truth, discovering how life works as we go, or finally realizing the ways things are. This requires us to consider that we were ignorant of the so-called truth before and now have finally discerned right from wrong, perhaps after being visited by a whispering unicorn in our dreams. And yet, in many circumstances, we have chosen this new truth just as arbitrarily as the truth we replaced. And we may find that we wish to change our position again and again, perhaps even switching back to an opinion we previously held.

Discovering our worldview's subjectivity is made significantly more difficult by our tendency to surround ourselves with people who affirm our beliefs. We thus may believe we are correct because we are not challenged

> "It becomes very easy to simply accept that something is true because enough of the people around you say it's true and accept that what you believe is right just because people around you say it's right."
>
> Joel Runyon

by conflicting views. But our desire to surround ourselves with like-minded people can cause us to dismiss different ideas without considering them fairly.

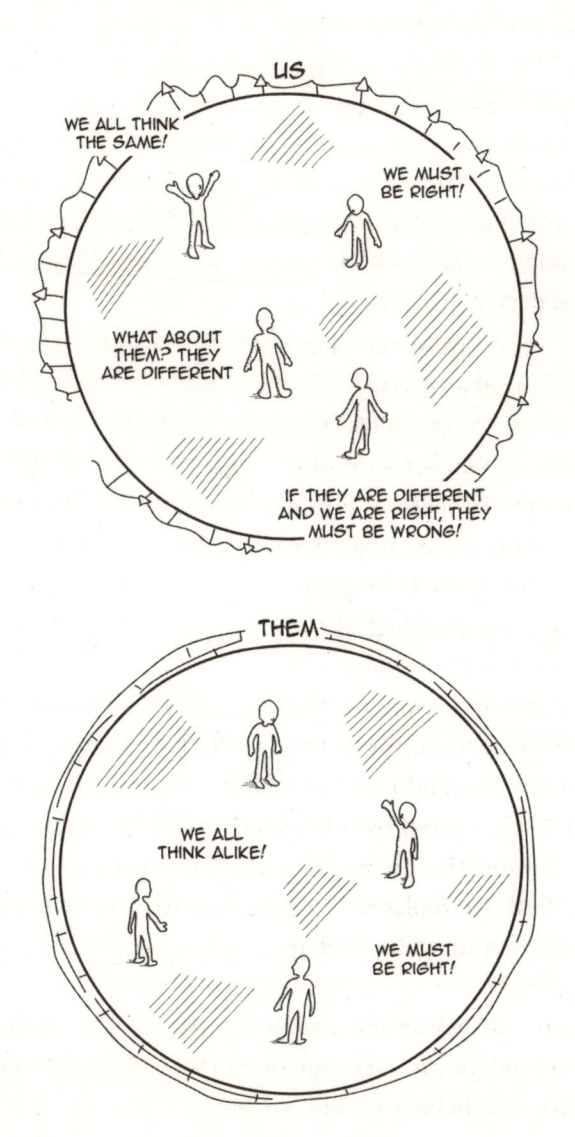

It's uncomfortable to live in a state of constant challenge, one in which we have no foundation. The world can be a scary or confusing place if it is a fluid river, in which everything is not black and white but countless colors and shades. So we seek comfort, and comfort means living in the company of people who believe as we do. When such people surround us, it's easy to forget that others have different beliefs. And though we sometimes recognize with chagrin that there are, in theory, other people out there somewhere who have a novel worldview, it's far too easy to assume they're wrong.

Accepting your power to create reality is an essential step in becoming who you want to be. Only after taking responsibility for the reality in which you live can you begin to construct a new universe for yourself. You can reject or accept the beliefs inside you, whether they were formed by chance or by the relationships that have been forced upon you. The more you see your universe as fluid, the more you will gain the ability to form it in any way you desire.

> "All that we see or seem
> Is but a dream
> within a dream."
>
> Edgar Allan Poe

To have these thoughts is audacious—to claim the ability to control your life story, to pen pages with wonders rather than fears, to fill chapters with beauty rather than ugliness, to form an ending you most desire, spun from the fragments of your favorite dreams. But since life is a dream anyway, a reality that exists entirely in your head, a nightmare or fantasy you have formed brick by brick, why not make it the best you possibly can?

Not Knowing What You Don't Know

One reliable sign that business isn't going well is when your suppliers are threatening to kill you. In the summer of 2008, the real estate bubble had just burst. I was in my mid-twenties at the time and was in the process of transforming several properties into subdivided suburban paradise. My construction company employed about fifty people and many more subcontractors. I had ridden a wave of success built on overconfidence, easy credit, and no understanding of risk.

When the banks first realized that the economy had been propped up on overpriced real estate, the first thing they did was freeze credit lines and loan disbursements for contractors like me. They wanted to see how things shook out before risking any more of their capital. The problem was I didn't have any reserves—I'd used the last of my cash to pay off a half-million-dollar credit line to lower my debt. As a result, I was running my company paycheck to paycheck. Now, looking back, many of my decisions seem so foolish. But at the time, I didn't see other options. I didn't have many mentors to teach me how to manage the finances of a rapidly growing company. And because of a combination of ego and ignorance, I didn't listen to those I had.

When payments from the banks froze, I called to access my credit line and pay my subcontractors. I was informed that the line had been revoked. As a result, I was unable to pay my subcontractors. Of course they also were worried about the economy, so they immediately filed liens against the properties we were working on together. This locked up my contractor licenses and made it impossible for me to complete the projects or draw any funds to pay anyone.

At the tender age of twenty-six, my success peaked. I had a fleet of trucks, enough property to build one hundred homes, a multimillion-dollar mansion, and a growing construction empire. I even owned a lake with its own island. In a matter of days, I lost everything. I went broke with no possibility of recovery. To make matters worse, people who own businesses don't qualify for unemployment. I didn't even have a modest safety net to catch me as I fell.

A few months later, the banks eased their reaction, and the government began to step in to help those who needed it. If I had saved enough cash or hadn't paid off my credit line early, I could have floated payments to everyone for a few months until the banks eased their overreaction. Instead, my business went bankrupt, my employees were laid off, and my contractors couldn't get paid for the work they had performed.[8]

I wasn't the only person seriously hurting for cash. Other general contractors were behind on payments to the same subcontractors I used on

---

8. Fortunately, most were able to get payment directly from the banks after the dust settled.

my projects. Some of these construction firms were also bankrupt and unable to pay their employees and other bills. A few of their owners were desperate for cash themselves. They came to my house, banging on the door and yelling at me from the lawn as I hid behind closed window shades. One guy promised to make me disappear if I didn't pay. Another spotted me turning on to the interstate and chased me at ninety miles per hour for a few miles while my heart beat out of my chest. When I decided to become a billionaire as a teenager, this wasn't what I thought business would be like at all! I was doing all I could to work with the banks to get them settled, even if it meant I got nothing. But my contractors had their own mouths to feed and bills to pay.

Reflecting on this season of my life, I realize now that my biggest hindrance was that I didn't know what I didn't know. This kind of ignorance exists in all of us. I was working hard, and I was learning on the job as I was able and made the time. I knew there was a lot more to learn, but I didn't know where to look, what lessons to seek first, or how to sort the helpful ideas from the unhelpful ones. In my case, what I needed to learn was how to prepare for a market downturn. I just didn't know it.

> "If you can't solve a problem, it's because you're playing by the rules."
>
> Paul Arden

By default, we play the game of life by a set of rules that society teaches us through the virality of shared ideas. These rules are extensions and interpretations of our evolutionary instincts. We become more like some people and less like others. We do our best to accumulate e-capital at all costs—sometimes even when it makes us miserable. We see our options through a lens that makes objective decision making all but impossible. And we surround ourselves with people who think like us.

Let's add these last few aspects of life to our game board, including how the magnetism of like-minded views can pull us in one direction or another. And with this, our game illustration is now complete!

Once we accept that our ideas have come from other people and that many of them may not be helpful, we can begin to deconstruct our lens and rebuild it in any way we see fit. This unlocks our ability to choose our own rules for the game of life. With this knowledge in hand, we can explore our goals, dreams, and life direction more freely, unconstrained by society's expectations and our deeply ingrained impulses. Redefining our purpose in a way that best helps us relationshift toward the person we want to be is, as you might expect, the topic we will explore next.

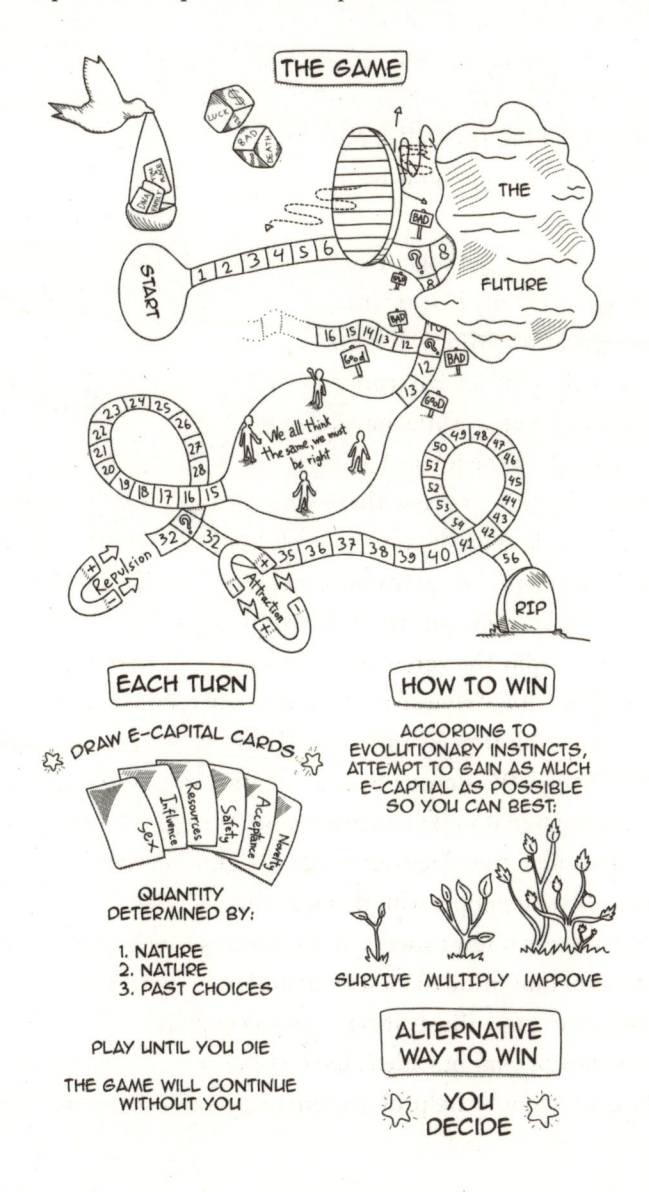

THE GAME

EACH TURN

DRAW E-CAPITAL CARDS

QUANTITY DETERMINED BY:

1. NATURE
2. NATURE
3. PAST CHOICES

PLAY UNTIL YOU DIE

THE GAME WILL CONTINUE WITHOUT YOU

HOW TO WIN

ACCORDING TO EVOLUTIONARY INSTINCTS, ATTEMPT TO GAIN AS MUCH E-CAPTIAL AS POSSIBLE SO YOU CAN BEST:

SURVIVE MULTIPLY IMPROVE

ALTERNATIVE WAY TO WIN

YOU DECIDE

Pause to reflect

- Have you discovered ideas you once thought were objective only to realize they were more subjective than you assumed? Which beliefs do you currently hold that may fit this description in the future?
- What knowledge are you lacking that most holds you back from living the life you want? How can you learn what you need to know to move forward more quickly or go further in your desired journey?
- Though this is difficult by definition, can you identify any areas of your psyche that limit you because you don't realize what you don't know?

CHAPTER 7

The Purpose of Your Life

"Things don't have purposes, as if the universe were a machine, where every part has a useful function. What's the function of a galaxy? I don't know if our life has a purpose and I don't see that it matters. What does matter is that we're a part. Like a thread in a cloth or a grass-blade in a field. It is and we are. What we do is like wind blowing on the grass."

Ursula K. Le Guin

Gertrude Bell (1868–1926) is one of the most remarkable figures of the past two hundred years. An accomplished linguist, archeologist, explorer, mountaineer, poet, photographer, historian, politician, and spy, Gertrude was Lara Croft with a flair for eloquent writing. She earned the respect of world leaders everywhere she traveled. Despite the persecution that women of her day faced, she was treated as an equal by many of the most influential leaders throughout Britain and the Middle East. A close friend of T. E. Lawrence, Gertrude has often been referred to as the female Lawrence of Arabia. Given her influence and impact, some historians have said it would be more fitting to call T. E. Lawrence a male version of Gertrude Bell than the other way around.

Her accomplishments make even the most successful among us look like underachievers. Born in Victorian times, Gertrude was the first woman to earn top honors at the University of Oxford for modern history studies. After visiting her uncle, the ambassador to Tehran, she developed a deep and lasting love for the Middle East. She traveled more than twenty thousand miles on camel, sometimes in great danger. Often robbed, jailed, and injured, she chronicled her journeys with photographs, maps she made, and notebook after notebook that would later prove critical to some of the most significant geopolitical transformations of her time. She summited many of the most challenging peaks in the Alps and became so well known for her adventuring that a mountain was named after her—a sure sign you've made it. So prolific was her writing that seventy-five feet of shelves in the Bell archive are filled with her letters, field notebooks, diaries, and published works. From excavating some of the earliest Christian churches, to being named a commander of the British Empire as the only woman serving in the military in the Middle East, to working with Winston Churchill to establish the nation of Iraq, Gertrude Bell left a mark on our world that lasts to this day.

> "All the earth is seamed with roads, and all the sea is furrowed with the tracks of ships, and over all the roads and all the waters a continuous stream of people passes up and down—traveling, as they say, for their pleasure. What is it, I wonder, that they go out to see?"
>
> Gertrude Bell

Gertrude undoubtedly was influenced by the liberal and anti-aristocracy views of her family. Her father, Hugh, with whom she was very close, encouraged her adventures at every turn. Even when Hugh didn't appear supportive—as was the case when Gertrude fell in love with an indebted gambler—her father encouraged her independence and strength. As a child, Gertrude was taught to consider herself equal to the most important people of the day, including Charles Darwin, Robert Louis Stevenson, Charles Dickens, and others of significance who called upon the family.

Complicating matters further, we are also formed by the interactions we don't have. In the case of Gertrude, the death of her mother was a noteworthy shaping force. The Bells were the sixth-wealthiest family in Britain, employing as many as forty-five thousand steelworkers who made railroads and bridges across the empire. If she had been born to most families of her day with similar stature, Gertrude likely would have been groomed as a debutante and fine courtier. She would have been taught to focus on parties instead of tradecraft, on running a large house instead of climbing mountains and stabilizing the Middle East. Instead, due to her close relationship with her father, she became strong-willed, opinionated, energetic, ambitious, adventurous, curious, and thirsty for life. Her transformation was so acute that later, when her father remarried, Gertrude's stepmother found her to be too unruly a child to have around—one reason Gertrude was sent off on trips around the world.

She valued honest appraisals of problems and candid debate about solutions. She chose a life of danger, adventure, exploration, diplomacy, and creativity over luxury, parties, and what she might have called shallow conversations with boring people. Whether she discovered her purpose by accident or by choice, she lived life on her terms. She was not swayed by intense peer pressure to act more like the important British ladies of her time. And she lived her life with a deep sense of purpose—apart from pure luck, accomplishments are impossible without direction.

When considering someone like Gertrude Bell, it can be easy to feel negative about our achievements. Few are capable of even a fraction of what Bell accomplished, partly because of the enormous wealth into which she was born. And yet, we can all love and be loved, find peace, live healthily, achieve goals, enjoy adventure, experience lasting happiness, and much more. The first half of this book gave you the tools to know who you are and how to change. Then, in chapters five and six we examined how ideas—both helpful and unhelpful—are passed between people, and how that's been happening for many thousands of years, carrying on the drivers that helped us become the species we are today. By now you should have a better understanding of how to launch from this point in your life in any direction you choose, free from any unnecessary motivations that your instincts, your peers, and society at large may be attempting to force upon you. The question is, how do you want to relationshift? Who do you want to become?

Once we understand the source of our core subconscious desires, we can begin to revise our approach to life to better fit with what we might want for ourselves. We can de-emphasize the instincts that make us miserable and focus instead on developing a worldview that brings us the most of whatever it is we want. We can release the need to accumulate possessions at all costs or fit in no matter how much it hurts, ignore unreasonable fears that have been holding us back, and hold on to the possibility of meaningful romantic love even when our current love life is far less than we might desire for ourselves. And once we let go of our outdated, unwanted evolutionary instincts, we create space to update our personal operating system.

This chapter is devoted to exploring purpose and direction. If you have no idea what you want to do with your life or how you might improve yourself, you're in the right place. It is possible to find purpose even when you have zero clues about the direction in which you might start looking. Or, if you have a sense of purpose, you may want to reconsider it in light of the idea that your goals and dreams may be built upon societal pressures, evolutionary instincts, or previous choices that no longer have a bearing on your life. No matter who you are, where you are, or what you've done, you can move *forward*—whatever that means for you.

Learning to Lean

When I was a kid, I loved watching the game show *The Price Is Right*. My favorite segment was Plinko. This mini-game involved a board covered in pegs with slots at the bottom. Contestants dropped a puck into the top. It would rattle down through the pegs, eventually sliding into one of the spaces at the bottom. The goal was for the puck to fall into the slot that awarded the highest dollar amount. Yet regardless of where the contestant placed the puck to start the game, she had very little control over where it ended up.

Life is a lot like the game Plinko. Whether or not we know which slot we might like to end up in, we keep hitting these pegs that force us to the left or right. Eventually, we land in one slot or another. But because the luck of life has been shoving us around, our destination is often far from where we might have wanted to go. It's easy to feel as if we are a Plinko puck, pushed this way and that by the forces of chance. You may wish to move from where you are to somewhere new, to reinvent yourself, to make a better life, to find happiness or riches, or even just a meal to survive another day. Even with great intention, you may look around one day and find you are wherever gravity has taken you. But this need not be your fate. To take control of your life, you don't even need a clear direction to take your first step. All you need to know is how to lean.

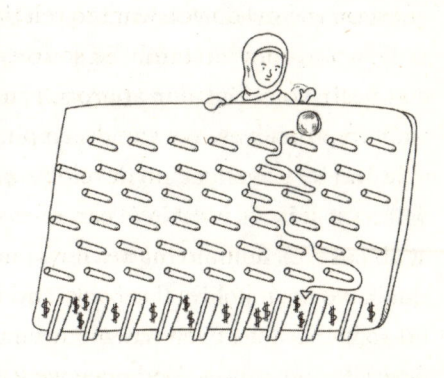

In Plinko, gravity pulls the puck downward in a way that gives it a 50/50 chance of falling to the left or right each time it hits a peg. As a result, it's impossible to predict or control where the puck lands.[1] Fortunately, the rules of life are more malleable than those of *The Price Is Right*. If we are a puck bouncing left and right randomly as we hit peg after peg, all we need to do to take control of our destination is change the direction of gravity. To do this, let's imagine we can tilt the Plinko board so down is now right. This is the equivalent of leaning in the direction we want to travel in life. While we may bounce around a bit because of chance or the unpredictable outcomes of our decisions, we can force the puck to the right over time. It's a bit messy, but it works.

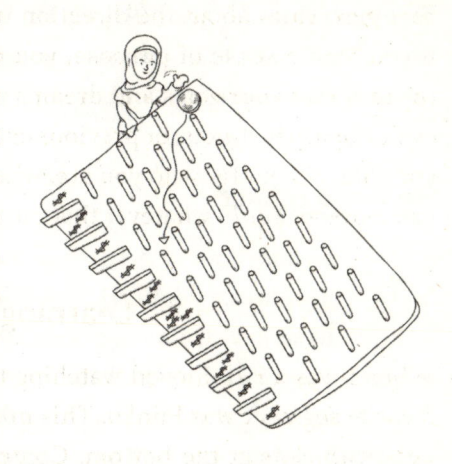

---

1. If you played Plinko long enough, you would find that the slot directly below where you dropped the puck was the most common destination. But with only five or ten tries, the puck would likely end up in a different slot every time.

Like tilting a Plinko board to change the direction of a bouncing puck, you can control your life direction by leaning into your desires. However vague your goals may be, you will find yourself slowly, incrementally making progress if you lean toward them. You will find clarity, direction, and everything else you need along the way, but only if you are moving. Some days you will feel lost, wandering in circles or falling backward. Other times you will find yourself moving toward your goals more quickly than you ever thought possible. Over months, years, and decades, you could find yourself experiencing life in a way you might never have even conceived when you set out.

> "When you turn your intention towards success, success will turn its intention towards you."
>
> Joshua Aaron Guillory

Leaning into your desires requires only intention. Ask. Read. Reflect. Share. Learn. Follow. Climb. Seek. Simply point your face in whichever direction seems closer to where you want to be, and push toward it until you find your feet moving under you. Give up the idea of finding shortcuts or straighter paths. Don't wait to know more, to be ready, or to overcome your fears.

Just do something. Anything.

Pause to reflect

- Given all we've discussed, from the origin of personal views to the power of evolutionary instincts, what goals have you been trying to achieve (subconsciously or not) that you are now reconsidering?
- Can you think of a time in your life when you leaned toward a goal and found yourself moving forward without realizing it?
- How can you lean in the direction you want to go in life more?

Eight Themes of Purpose

Without direction, our goals can become scattered and unfocused. Consider the person who has many dreams and ambitions but lacks a clear idea of where they want to go in life. They are likely to become distracted by one possibility while on their way to another, then become diverted yet again by a third. There is nothing morally wrong with this approach. A meandering life can be quite interesting; it just isn't likely to get you very far.

On the other hand, we could be the next Gertrude Bell if we live our life with purpose. Even with lesser ambitions, clarity of purpose gives us a much better chance of achieving what we want. Ideally, goals should be aligned like road markers along our way, letting us know we're on the right path. And with each goal passed, we're another step closer to our desired destination.

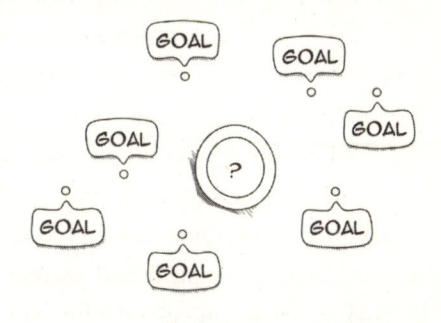

The problem is, hardly anyone knows what their purpose is. Studies show between 5 and 25 percent of people are confident of their purpose. Maybe you've studied books on the subject or discussed possible life directions with mentors but come away even more confused. Advice about purpose can be inconsistent and ambiguous. This can easily lead to a state of paralysis. But all these smart people have so many different beliefs about finding purpose because there is no single truth on this topic. Each person who offers their advice about direction lives in a different reality based on their unique lens, background, and advantages or disadvantages. What worked for them may not work for you.

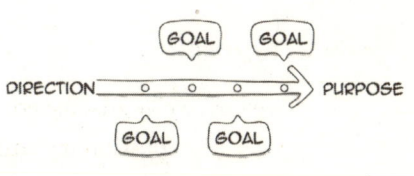

Recall our system for determining the objectivity of a topic from chapter six. Because experts have widely ranging positions on the matter, purpose should lie on the spectrum's subjective end. However, one's purpose is a multidimensional concept. Using the analogy of a two-dimensional teeter-totter is not sufficient to understand the complexities of the subject. Though opinions abound on how and to what we should aspire, the topic is not entirely subjective.

As part of my research for this book, I studied over twenty books on the subject of purpose and was surprised at how consistently specific themes appeared. Those that appeared most often can be considered the most objective. In contrast, many ideas about how to best direct our lives were not nearly so universal. According to our objectivity/subjectivity

SOME SUBJECTS HAVE MANY POSSIBLE POSITIONS.
IN THESE CASES, THE TEETER-TOTTER ILLUSTRATION FROM
PART THREE COULD BE SEEN AS A TABLE TOP,
WITH DIFFERENT IDEAS ALL AROUND

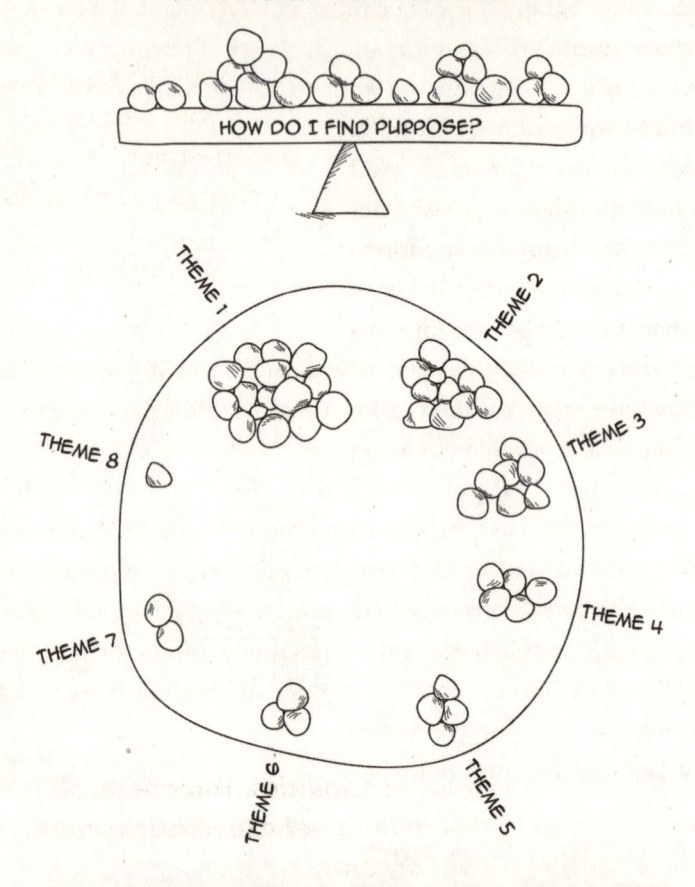

HOW DO I FIND PURPOSE?

THEME 1, THEME 2, THEME 3, THEME 4, THEME 5, THEME 6, THEME 7, THEME 8

WITH THE SUBJECT OF FINDING PURPOSE, EIGHT THEMES APPEAR
AGAIN AND AGAIN IN BOOKS ON THE TOPIC. EACH OF THESE EIGHT
DIMENSIONS HAS ITS OWN LEVEL OF OBJECTIVITY BASED ON THE
NUMBER OF EXPERTS WHO ARGUE THE THEME IS IMPORTANT.

spectrum examined previously, those that appeared in only a few books are the least universal and should be given less weight. As such, I include less discussion on the themes that are the most subjective. The following headings list the top eight recurring themes, starting with those that appeared in almost every book on the subject, followed by those that were less common, and so on.

To maximize our lives, we must first define our purpose, even if only vaguely. This gives us a direction in which to lean. Then, as we move forward, what we want and how we can get it becomes more visible.

I encourage you to embrace an open mind as you explore these eight recurring themes. Consider what possibilities you might desire in light of your freedom from outdated evolutionary instincts and the drive to collect e-capital at all costs. This is a chance to redesign your life path as you see fit. Or, if you don't have any idea what you should do with your life, these next few pages are the perfect place to start.

> "You cannot change your destination overnight. You can change your direction."
>
> Jim Rohn

1. You define and limit your possibilities. You are responsible for your reality. It's up to you to let go of expectations and create a world big enough for your dreams.

We tend to be our own worst enemy when seeking to achieve our dreams and live a great life. We feel the world pushes against us. We're more in love with our bed than the work required to build something lasting. How much easier it is to lie under a blanket smoking a joint than to go for that run. How much simpler to catch fish in *Animal Crossing* than to become an excellent fisherman. How much less risky to browse posts on FetLife by oneself than to build a lasting relationship.

We love comfort. We love the status quo. It's easier to allow the people around us to determine our dreams, what is right and wrong, what we should pursue and what we should let go, or what is possible. But the most exciting life directions are often waiting outside our current universe.

The next few pages contain six considerations that help us understand and apply this theme.

Dream bigger. Believe in possibilities over limitations.

One of my mentors, Rick Altig, often says: "No matter how big you're dreaming, you're probably not dreaming big enough." Your dreams are limited by your imagination, by what you believe is possible. And what you feel is attainable is determined by your experience. If you want to experience the most significant life possible, you must seek inspiration for your dreams beyond what you think is reasonable. You must climb to a higher vantage point.

In a universe so vast, we should assume there is always more. The space between planets, solar systems, and galaxies stretches on forever. Why would other aspects of life be tightly limited? Scientists continue to find smaller and smaller pieces of atoms,

> "The closer you come to knowing that you alone create the world of your experience, the more vital it becomes for you to discover just who is doing the creating."
>
> — Eric Micha'el Leventhal

WHAT IS POSSIBLE?

OUR VISION IS MOSTLY LIMITED TO
WHAT WE CAN SEE FROM WHERE
WE CURRENTLY ARE

WHAT IS POSSIBLE NOW?

THE HIGHER YOU CLIMB THE MORE POSSIBILITIES YOU CAN SEE

electrons, and quarks. Why would we not be able to drill ever deeper into our possibilities? We all too often project what we are capable of based on what we have already done. When we push into the unknown and find a boundary that is difficult to cross, we are likely to believe we've reached the end of the road.

Get into the habit of assuming there is always more—so much more that you can't even imagine what it might look like. Don't assume you understand what it means to be as happy as a human can be. There are likely entirely new realms of happiness waiting to be explored. Perhaps you need only push a little harder against the wall at the end of your understanding. Don't assume you're as creative, good-hearted, talented, smart, successful, or attractive as you can be. Chances are there are higher levels you could enjoy in all of these areas.

> "Few people have the imagination for reality."
>
> Johann Wolfgang von Goethe

Ignore society's rules and expectations. Other people don't have to live your life, so don't allow them to dictate it.

Of all the living creatures in the world, only you live your life. All those people who so confidently tell you what to do and what to believe aren't going to offer a refund on their advice if they turn out to be wrong. Gather advice from trusted mentors, but don't let them make your decision for you. In the end, you are the one who must live with your choices.

You must build your life upon your self-worth.

Significant accomplishments are difficult in even the best of circumstances. But achievement is impossible when you don't believe in yourself. If you feel your worth depends on a relationship, success, or gaining others' approval, you are destined for disappointment. Everything and everyone outside of your unshakable self-worth is going to let you down. Even *you* will let yourself down.

When our strength comes from self-worth, we can more easily rise after a fall. We can learn to stop seeing failure as a sign of our worthlessness, but instead, as a natural step

"We create with our consciousness. What we think about, pay attention to, focus on, and choose to believe . . . whatever goes on in our mind, is what becomes our reality."

Anthon St. Maarten

toward accomplishment. It's all right for failure to hurt. Denying pain is not the point. Allow yourself to feel sad while letting go of the need to punish yourself for every mistake.

When we err, we hope for forgiveness from those we have wronged. Yet we often do not extend the same mercy to ourselves. This self-harshness makes no sense. Why would we expect others to treat us better than we treat ourselves? Each failure, each mistake, each slip of the tongue—we can use these as whips, repeatedly beating ourselves with them. In many cases, even when everyone else has forgotten, we still remember.

> "Don't let someone else's opinion of you become your reality."
>
> **Les Brown**

Self-worth allows us to extend mercy to ourselves. Sometimes we need a reminder that we are as mistake prone as every other creature who has ever lived. We need to lighten up. Self-worth understands our imperfections. If we love ourselves, we can embrace our mistakes. We can learn from them and grow instead of ignoring mishaps or covering them up. We can even learn to laugh about our mistakes. Other people do; why not join in? In general, life is a lot more fun when we don't take ourselves so seriously.

We choose our reactions.

The actions of others are not our responsibility—only our response. The way people treat you and the things they say to you reveal more about them than about you. If someone is an angry person, they are likely to be mad no matter what you do. If they say you're worthless, they are desperate to find their worth. We cannot be nice enough to make abusive people stop swinging their fists at us. And if people love you, it's because they have love inside them to give.

Similarly, our reaction to a situation, or to a person's actions or words directed toward us, is a reflection of what is inside us. If we rise with courage when danger is near, we are revealing the strength inside us, a power that overcomes our fears and compels us to take action in spite of them. If we lie in bed all day or get drunk when we lose our job, we reveal the source of our worth—that we don't have value outside this occupation. If we are angry when someone slights us, we are announcing the anger that lives inside us. The greater our reaction of any kind, the more of that energy is inside us. If we overreact with rage when someone cuts us off on the highway, we reveal the turmoil that has been lurking inside us. If anger abides inside us, we can hide it for a while, but it's only a matter of time before it explodes.

We can learn to change our responses with mental toughness. Starve negative reactions by refusing to allow them to control you. It's okay to feel terrible. To want to give up. To feel angry or sad. You can't stop a feeling, and you shouldn't try. Instead, accept this part of you. Just don't give in and don't despair. Feed your positivity instead. Cultivate the reactions you want by practicing them despite how you feel. We do not have control of all the things that happen to us in this life or how people treat us. But we always have control over our response.

> "Winners never quit, and quitters never win."
>
> Vince Lombardi

Don't win at the wrong game.

Many people die with regrets. This often is the result of attempting to win at the wrong game. Instead, align your vision with your actions. You should be checking along the way to ensure you're getting what you want and going where you believe you will find whatever it is you are looking for. Examples of misalignment could include getting rich but feeling empty and lonely, rising to the top of your profession but neglecting the art that feeds your soul, traveling the world but not knowing your children, and helping millions get where they want to go but ignoring your dreams.

This isn't a moral issue. It's not a matter of whether your goal is right or wrong. What matters is whether the place you end up is where your holistic self wants to be. How you make sure of this is by simply being honest with yourself about what you want and whether you are taking the actions necessary to arrive there.

You could perform a test to see how well you have been doing so far by analyzing your progress over the past few years. No matter where you are, your choices played a significant role in the process. If you don't like where you are, you need to take ownership of your decisions that brought you to this moment.

Don't beat yourself up if you find you're not where you want to be. Whether your choices have led you to a dead-end job or an unfulfilling relationship, you are far from alone. Mediocrity is the natural state of humanity; to be anything else is, by definition, extraordinary. Most people talk about self-improvement. They might read books or go to workshops, but they don't get anywhere. Their choices are to blame. When they could be doing the hard work to change themselves, they choose instead to change TV channels.

If you're not happy with your progress, you can't keep doing what you've been doing. Perhaps you have gone far in life by one measure, but not in the way you most desire. Now is the time to correct your path. The choices and tactics you've been using have gotten you where you are today. Those same strategies aren't likely to get you anywhere else. Within yourself, you must find a desire strong enough to overcome the resistance you will face in the attempt. Or instead, learn to be content with where you are.

There is no one best move.

You can never really know whether a decision is good or bad, healthy or unhealthy, helpful or unhelpful until you see the result. Yet we often become constrained by pressure to make a perfect decision, one that will change the course of our life in the best possible way. Apart from luck, life doesn't work this way. Far better to rely on many small decisions where each one may move us toward our desired destination. In the process, we may sometimes find ourselves moving sideways or backward. That's normal. Make the best decision you can at the moment and keep moving forward. If you choose poorly, you will likely realize it soon enough. Then, after learning a valuable lesson, you can make a better choice the next time.

Very few decisions are so essential or irreversible that we need to worry about making a wrong move. If you decide to retire but realize you love to work, you can get another job. If you choose a college major you don't end up using, so what? Countless people have done the same and turned out fine. Let go of the need to choose perfectly. No one can, so why put yourself

WE THINK GOOD RESULTS HAPPEN LIKE THIS

BUT USUALLY GOOD RESULTS REQUIRE MANY ITERATIVE SMALL CHOICES

CHOICE

through the pressure of an impossible situation? Gather information. Consider it. Get advice from a trusted mentor. Then make a move and have fun knowing you are going to make lots of mistakes in life. Stephen King used to stick his rejection letters on a nail in his bedroom wall. He got so many before publishing his first book, he had to replace the nail. Of course, he also doesn't remember writing *Cujo* because he was so high on cocaine, so, you know, take one leaf from his story and not another. Learn to have fun in life, knowing you're going to make and recover from many mistakes. That's part of the journey.

2. Systems, strategies, and tactics will help you move forward despite the many obstacles you will encounter on the journey toward purpose.

Make use of systems, strategies, and tactics developed by sources you trust to help you keep moving forward no matter what you encounter.

Create clear goals and write them down.

Writing down our goals is a helpful way to make them more real. It also keeps us more accountable to ourselves. With a written record, we can look back and see whether we did what we could to accomplish them. Absent recorded goals, we can easily modify our memories or forget altogether while making little to no progress and not realizing it or being realistic about it. It's easy to achieve all of your ambitions when you have none.

Don't worry about having perfect goals, or even very many of them. Just write down anything you can think of, no matter how small, vague, or ambitious. Do this with full knowledge that you will be changing them as you go. That's part of the process. Remember that you can't act on experience you don't have. So, as you move forward and gain knowledge, you can use this information to modify your dreams. You may find new aspects of life that you didn't know were possible. You may want to modify a goal that isn't making you happy anymore. All of this is perfectly normal and doesn't negate the importance of writing down your goals, whatever they are right now. Don't worry about eloquence or perfection; we're not trying to be the next Shakespeare here (unless you *are* trying to be the next Shakespeare, in which case, feel free to record your goals in iambic pentameter).

> "The path to our destination is not always a straight one. We go down the wrong road, we get lost, we turn back. Maybe it doesn't matter which road we embark on. Maybe what matters is that we embark."
>
> Barbara Hall

Overcome your fears by subjecting yourself to them.

Allergies exist when the body has an overreaction to otherwise nonthreatening contaminants, such as pollen, nuts, or dust. Scientists have discovered that, by introducing small quantities of these allergens to the body, we could become accustomed to their presence and stop having the adverse reaction.

Fear is similar. We often overreact to situations that don't require that fear. So if we subject ourselves to whatever is causing the fear, we can become accustomed to it. In time, we will find we no longer have it. Start with small doses, then give yourself more exposure over time. Research shows that this is an effective method for reducing anxiety.

> "Our goals can only be reached through a vehicle of a plan, in which we must fervently believe, and upon which we must vigorously act. There is no other route to success."
>
> Pablo Picasso

If you'd like to review, we discussed overcoming fears in greater detail beginning on page 155.

Overcome natural resistance through a lot of hard work and investment.

Every improvement in this universe requires the investment of energy from another source. Weeds and pests overtake even the most beautiful gardens when their caretakers don't put in the work to keep the plants healthy. Rocks are hard and difficult to shape, but with enough time, even a gentle river can erode mountains. Defining your purpose is no different. Whether inventing or discovering, you must invest energy if you want to see results. This takes time, focus, and persistence. Having a good plan sometimes can increase the speed of results. For example, using a map makes the journey faster than finding a destination by trial and error. But if you want to have a clear purpose, you're going to have to put in the effort to find it.

3. Defining purpose is a lifelong process. You will never finish because there is no end to the journey. Regardless of your situation, the sooner you start, the further you'll go.

Be mindful of the present. Take action now with whatever information you have. Act as if you are already what you want to become. If you want adventure, love, happiness, enlightenment—find it. Then enjoy the journey. It's all you have.

Defining purpose happens through many small steps, not one or two significant realizations.

Too many people waste their time looking for a magic solution. Life doesn't usually work this way. Learn to make better decisions by moving quickly and improving as a result of your mistakes. With an iterative approach, you will find assurance of your direction in incremental steps as you keep moving.

Your path will change as you learn more about yourself, the world, and what you want from life.

Impermanence is life's only constant. Things change. You will make mistakes, learn lessons, and uncover new desires. None of this is a problem. Regardless of the reason why, if your strategy isn't working, change it.

Though you may be aiming for a destination, there is no end to the journey of purpose.

Direction is vital. Without it, you can't go anywhere. But you should hold your goals loosely. Your destination is likely to change many times as you move forward and discover more about yourself and what you are looking for in life. And even if you arrive where you aimed to, you will likely find yourself dreaming up a new, even more audacious goal. Embrace the ambiguity and instead enjoy moving toward a desire knowing it is likely to change as you go.

4. Purpose can be discovered or invented. It's up to you.

Listen to life.

Our vocation is not what we try, but what we become. We look back and see our calling as a trail behind us, like the churn of bright blue water boats leave in their wake. If you simply do what you love, you will find that purpose is not far off. Do what you're good at. Do what's fun. And always remember that purpose is not about how or what you do, but why you do it.

> "For me, becoming isn't about arriving somewhere or achieving a certain aim. I see it instead as forward motion, a means of evolving, a way to reach continuously toward a better self. The journey doesn't end."
>
> **Michelle Obama**

Trust your intuition. Don't worry about choosing between two good options. Just pick one.

A lot of people get stuck trying to choose from multiple options. They get frustrated because picking the best choice is hard. If this describes you, let go of the need for perfection. There is often no way to know how a choice will end. Luck plays a massive role in everything we do. And if all the options look equal, then our job of choosing is simple: flip a coin and go. We can always adjust course if we realize we might have liked another option better, but we will learn nothing while waiting.

Rekindle passions you had as a child or teenager.

Sometimes it's helpful to think back to what we were fired up about as a kid. As we get older, we can be prone to give up on our childhood dreams. This transition is a natural result of life's burdens weighing upon us. We have responsibilities, and life can be difficult. So we abandon those goals when they begin to feel foolish or unrealistic. However, childhood dreams can be an excellent source for discovering aspects of life that we're passionate about but have forgotten.

Purpose isn't about what you do or how you do it, but why.

Imagine your purpose is making people happy. You can do this as a bartender, a social worker, or a porn star. But it's often better to separate our purpose from our job. Getting cash to live out your dreams may be delightful, but fulfilled living costs nothing. If you focus on earning a living in a traditional job[2] and allow yourself to pursue a purpose outside of this, you are far more likely to get both money and happiness. Most jobs that have a great deal of meaning associated with them are in high demand. Many people are willing to do them for little to nothing. This drives wages down. And once you get that job that brings you a sense of purpose, you now have to do it every day, like it or not. You may get burned out or resent what once brought you joy. Instead, consider separating work from purpose. This will enable you to more easily control how much you give and adjust your energy based on other demands upon your time.

---

2. Just make sure it's a job that doesn't make you miserable. Every job has aspects we don't like. That's why we get paid. But we shouldn't hate going to work. That's not a great way to find our best life.

5. Embrace failure, tragedy, pain, and loss as a normal part of life, recognizing that it is often out of these that purpose reveals itself.

Adverse events shape us for better or worse, but they can become our most significant opportunities.

Failure is a critical component of becoming smarter and more decisive. Remember that you can lose a lot of things in life: jobs, friends, money. But you can never lose your knowledge and experience. Failure is a crucial ingredient of adventure. As the world's smartest butler, Alfred Pennyworth, once said: "Bruce, why do we fall?" Yes, this is a Batman reference. Bruce Wayne embraced failure, pain, and loss, and in so doing, found his purpose. This section is about how to be like Batman.

> "The most beautiful people we have known are those who have known defeat, known suffering, known struggle, known loss, and have found their way out of those depths."
>
> Elisabeth Kübler-Ross

Take risks.

Risk directly correlates to reward—the greater the risk, the greater the possible benefit. If you want to experience more, you're going to have to get used to increasing the risk factor in your decision making. But you don't have to chance financial ruin to earn more money. Take calculated risks that are commensurate with your ability to overcome any adverse results.

In many circumstances, the risks we face are entirely in our heads. For example, we generally feel nervous when asking someone we like for their phone number. But if we fail, we lose nothing but our pride, and our perspective controls even this. If you have a mindset of abundance, you know that there are many people in the world. Just because this one person is or isn't into you doesn't change the fact that there are millions of others with whom you might match. Furthermore, someone can turn you down for many reasons besides a personal judgment about you and your value. Recall our earlier discussion about how we are not responsible for others' responses, only our own. So if you adjust your mindset, the risk evaporates. Suddenly asking for someone's phone number becomes not a chance for failure but a chance to gain with little downside. One thing is for sure: the person who risks nothing gains nothing.

Sometimes the closed doors are our best guides.

Doors are closed far more often than open. But this doesn't mean you can't use these blocked passages as a guide. In scientific research, a well-designed study that finds no result can be helpful by moving other researchers one step closer to the goal, because they don't have to try what had no effect again. And when academics conduct their next study, they can revise it according to what didn't work the last time.

Imagine a hallway with many doors. Every closed passage you encounter is a sign for you to continue looking. If you repeat this process long enough, you will eventually find a door that opens. Thus, closed doors are as much a guide forward as open ones.

> "The person who risks nothing, does nothing, has nothing, is nothing, and becomes nothing. He may avoid suffering and sorrow, but he simply cannot learn, feel, change, grow or love. Chained by his certitude, he is a slave; he has forfeited his freedom. Only the person who risks is truly free."
>
> Leo Buscaglia

6. Relationships are critical to discovering your purpose.

Cultivating a giving attitude is the best way to find a mentor.

Though everyone wants to help others, few people are eager to sign up to be another person's official mentor. This is asking a lot—to sacrifice their time for you and help you achieve your dreams, time they could be investing in their happiness. This approach makes finding a great mentor a more challenging process. Instead, you can speed your journey by remembering to ask yourself, "How can I help this person get more of what they want as they are helping me get more of what I want?"

Having purpose draws people closer to you.

If you're having a hard time attracting friends or a romantic partner, consider what you can do to become more magnetic. Having a strong sense of purpose is attractive. As you develop yours, you will find that more people want you around. This plays on the concepts of e-capital explored in part two. A purposeful person appears confident and influential, and is likely to have more resources. All of these are attractive traits to others.

> "I can trust my friends. These people force me to examine myself, encourage me to grow."
>
> — Cher

Your relationships can hone your perspective.

Seek feedback and expand your worldview. This is possible only by exposing yourself to the ideas of other people.

7. One can live with purpose and earn a good living at the same time.

It's okay to admit that bills are real.

Maybe every dentist is a committed oral hygiene activist who found their true passion, but I suspect not. The world pays you for what you do, not for your passions. So if you want to make money, solve expensive problems that other people can't or won't. Work exists to support our life, not the other way around. But if you try to do only jobs that align with your purpose, you're likely to be competing against countless other people who want to do the same thing. This competition lowers the pay for everyone. As discussed earlier in this section, it's usually more comfortable and less frustrating to separate your income from your pursuit of fun and meaning. In this way, you can earn a good living while avoiding burnout on the things you love. When you spend all your time living out your purpose for little pay, you may also find little energy at the end of the day for your projects related to the same purpose.

Go into business.

If you want to make money as quickly and efficiently as possible, capitalism is your golden ticket. One can argue that our American survival-of-the-fittest economic system is making people miserable and is terrible for our planet. Still, it certainly has proven capable of making people rich. You don't have to love capitalism or sell out to use the system to your advantage and get what you want from life. Money is not evil, though people sometimes use it to do terrible things. If you want to, go ahead and get yourself some. Or a lot. Then use it to help people or make yourself happy. Not only that, if you make yourself a lot of money, you will likely have a lot more fun living out your purpose and, in the process, get more good done in the world.

8. Spirituality can be connected to purpose but is not required.

People feel more purpose when they are part of something larger than themselves.

Many people want to be part of something big, make a difference, or feel connected to the universe's mysteries. These desires can lead us to invest our energy in healthy directions, like helping others or improving our state of mind. Spirituality or religion are familiar sources of purpose. But finding our purpose in spirituality or religion can also cause us to become "so heavenly minded that [we] are no earthly good" (Oliver Wendell Holmes Sr.). In the worst-case scenario, faith-based purpose can make us miserable, sometimes without us even realizing it.

Say, for example, you read on Facebook that aliens will destroy Earth to make way for an interstellar highway construction project. In response, you and your friends decide to build a spaceship that will carry you to safety. You quit your job, sell all your possessions, and put everything into this urgent survival project. Some people claim the aliens aren't coming, but you figure, "Might as well be safe than sorry." On the appointed day of Earth's destruction, you and your friends climb into your shiny new spaceship and launch into orbit. You watch your old home through the windows, waiting for a big explosion of some kind, but nothing happens. You check your Facebook feed for updates and find that *The Hitchhiker's Guide to the Galaxy* fan club made the whole thing up. You have fallen victim to fake news. It could happen to any of us.

This story illustrates the potential pitfalls of finding our purpose in religion. While building the spaceship was a potentially safer choice, in the end, the danger was imagined. You had no way of knowing this until the day the aliens were supposed to arrive (or didn't), so your decision to act on a prudent plan to keep yourself safe was reasonable. But building the spaceship came at considerable cost. You had to sell everything and quit your job to get it done in time. Don't get me wrong; riding into space on a rocket is undoubtedly a fantastic accomplishment. If the joy of this ride was also part of the purpose, then maybe it all worked out for the best as long as the ride alone was worth the sacrifice. But if you were miserable the entire time you were building the rocket, if you tried to make other people feel guilty for not helping, if you gave up so much that you weren't able to help your tribe in more practical ways, then perhaps it wasn't wise to focus entirely on this single objective.

This is the problem with religion. No matter what you or I believe, we can't be sure. If the purpose of a faith-based belief system makes us happy, there is little reason to change anything. But we risk much when we choose a life that relies on faith, especially when we do so out of guilt, fear, or obligation. Sacrifices for this purpose may turn out to be a waste. Or worse, we could cause harm to ourselves and others. And we must also consider the possibility that, even if we are happy with our current life direction, we could be missing out on an even better life if we were more open-minded. Remember that experience limits our idea of what is possible.

> "I am an agnostic; I do not pretend to know what many ignorant men are sure of."
>
> Clarence Darrow

If you are happy finding purpose in your religion or spirituality, feel no pressure to change. I would simply argue that you should consider diversifying your portfolio of purpose. If any single direction turns out differently than expected, you will have had other experiences and outcomes to enjoy.

On the other hand, we can find great purpose outside religion. At one time, this didn't make sense to me. What point is there to invest in something that isn't part of a grander scheme? But this perspective doesn't allow for grand schemes of the secular variety. We can make our world a better place for those around us and generations to come. We can connect to everyone who is living and everyone who has come before us by contemplating that we are all made from the same pieces and part of the same universe. Everything we do affects everything else and has been affected by all that came before us. And, of course, we can find purpose in merely enjoying life for every moment that it is. These may seem cold or pointless to you if you come from a strong religious background. But if you allow yourself to consider them thoroughly and with an open mind, you may find, as I have, that many forms of purpose outside religion can be meaningful and rewarding. The best thing about purpose is, in the end, it's entirely up to you.

Start at this moment, and refine your direction as you go.

Clarity and empowerment come from accepting that this one moment in which we live is the only real time to be alive. We know we cannot change yesterday, nor live it again. We cannot foresee tomorrow, how we will exist within it, or whether it will exist at all. When we embrace these truths, we become free to focus on this one page of our story that we can control and enjoy. When it comes to choosing our purpose or making big decisions, the temptation to wait is a trap that can forever lull us into losing out on life. Yet we all too often wait, which is just a way of saying no to our dreams.

No matter how good we feel our excuses are, we and only we are giving up on the one moment we have. Sometimes we wait because we do not know how to proceed. Other times we fear making the wrong choice. And often, we don't even know where to begin. But when we do not take action, we fail to see that achieving is possible only with movement.

> "We cannot change yesterday, and we cannot predict tomorrow, but we can live today. So be alive. Never let one day pass by without a smile."
>
> Nishan Panwar

Remember that your purpose is going to change as you learn more about life. You can't take action on any ideas you don't currently possess. Once you've begun to move toward purpose, you can use relationshift to refine your direction. That's all part of the fun. As clichéd as it might sound, purpose is about the journey more than any kind of destination. We humans evolved to need a big goal. When we have one, we feel more satisfied with life. Start with whatever makes the most sense at this moment, and then learn to find the joy in revising and reiterating your purpose as you move forward. No one has ever arrived anywhere without setting foot outside their door. So why not start today?

EIGHT THEMES ON FINDING AND LIVING WITH PURPOSE

- YOU DEFINE AND LIMIT YOUR OWN POSSIBILITIES
- TOOLS, STRATEGIES AND PROCESSES HELP YOU LIVE WITH PURPOSE
- SPIRITUALITY CAN BE CONNECTED TO PURPOSE, BUT IS NOT REQUIRED
- FINDING PURPOSE IS A LIFE LONG ADVENTURE
- YOU CAN LIVE WITH PURPOSE AND MAKE A GOOD LIVING AT THE SAME TIME
- PURPOSE CAN BE DISCOVERED OR INVENTED
- RELATIONSHIP ARE KEY TO HELPING YOU FIND PURPOSE
- FAILURE AND LOSS CAN GUIDE YOU TO PURPOSE

Pause to reflect

- Can you think of any examples when you believed a ceiling limited your possibilities, only to discover more was achievable?
- In what areas of your life are you most likely repeating this mistake now?
- What fears or insecurities are holding you back? How can you use the principle of incremental exposure to overcome them?
- How can you balance aiming for a goal, whether large or small, without losing out on the enjoyment of the present moment?
- Rather than making resolutions every January 1, consider five to ten goals you would like to accomplish and can achieve in the next few months. Do the same on a twelve-month timeline and again for a more extended period—say, five years. Keep track of these goals and celebrate when you achieve them. Change them as you like and replace those you complete.

Define Your Pillars

Defining direction is not often an easy task. We tend to get ahead of ourselves, trying to solve problems that don't exist yet. Instead, we can define a general direction and become comfortable figuring out the details as we go. This significantly reduces the complexity of the process. You can have a moderately defined idea of your life direction in about an hour with the right exercise. Remember, your focus is going to change many times in life. So it doesn't do much good stressing about getting it perfect at this very moment, because it's likely to vary slightly by next week and still more the month after that.

If you feel overwhelmed—most people would when faced with the idea of writing the entirety of their life story before it has unfolded—do not worry. We are going to take this one small step at a time.

The easiest way to get going is to break your vision into pieces. For example, your wholeness may be affected by your health, mind, spirit, and bank account. You can think of these as pillars. If they are out of balance, if one pillar is weak, the whole suffers.

> "I may not have gone where I intended to go, but I think I have ended up where I needed to be."
>
> Douglas Adams

People who do not have balance across their pillars can end up being rich and miserable. Or emotionally balanced but unable to pay their bills. To be completely whole, you want all your pillars to be healthy and strong.

As you consider the eight themes of purpose, think about what pillars might best suit your particular flavor of life. Title these pillars however makes the most sense to you. You may find it frustrating trying to categorize so many different aspects of your life into groups that make sense. In the end, it doesn't matter what you call your pillars or how many there are. You can change them whenever you want. For now, you are merely attempting to get started.

Here are a few examples of pillars that might get you moving:

- body
- career
- money
- balance
- purpose
- mind
- romantic love
- influence
- beauty
- environment
- spirit
- energy
- lifestyle
- politics
- diversity
- simplicity
- school
- family
- relationships
- expertise
- retirement
- legacy
- character

As you might see when you start exploring which of these pillars best suit you, there is considerable overlap. Each pillar contains multiple aspects of your desired future state. The point is not to get this perfect. You couldn't if you tried. Instead, simply pick a few and try them on for size. While there is no ideal number of pillars, I recommend choosing at least four and no more than seven. These numbers are arbitrary, but I've found that too few pillars can leave large parts of your life undefined, and too many can become too complicated or cumbersome to keep track of and bring to mind regularly. Restricting yourself to between four and seven categories means that some pillars will include several similar parts of you, like emotions, spirit, and balance. Or career, money, and influence. Don't worry about combining categories. You will define what those categories mean to you in your descriptive paragraph.

After you define your pillars, write a paragraph description of the ideal version of yourself within that category. This step is more important than what you call the pillars because it is here that you define your vision and how you will know when you have achieved your desired state. Your paragraph should include how you will feel when you've arrived, some benchmarks to track your progress, and how being in this state will enable you to live the life you most want to live.

> "As long as you are alive, anything is possible. The only valid excuse you have to give up is if you are dead. As long as you are alive you have the choice to keep trying until you finally succeed."
>
> **Unknown**

A BALANCED LIFE IS BUILT ON A NUMBER OF EQUALLY STRONG PILLARS OF PURPOSE

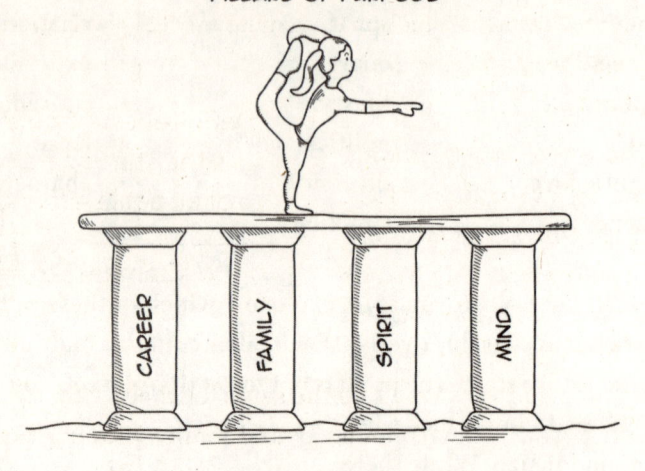

WHEN SOME PILLARS OF PURPOSE ARE UNDEVELOPED OR MISSING, ONE CAN FEEL OFF BALANCE AND DISSATISFIED WITH LIFE

Let's look at examples of defined pillars, along with their descriptive paragraphs. These are not personal examples, but I use the first person in these fictional pillar descriptions because I suggest you do when you create these for yourself.

Body: I weigh 120 pounds, run a marathon yearly, and walk twenty flights of stairs a day. I dance freely at concerts without being embarrassed and do yoga workouts weekly without being stressed or uncomfortable. I feel good in my skin. I'm awake and alert throughout the day and sleep well at night. I eat healthy foods that make me feel good, though I feel free to enjoy treats from time to time without any guilt.

Mind: I have friends with whom I talk about serious matters often, debating politics, philosophy, and the environment. My friends challenge me to be more open-minded, introducing me to new ideas and points of view, and I do the same for them. I am sharp mentally, contributing to my community and family with my experience and wisdom. I teach classes at the community college to engage my mind with the energy of young people.

> "Definiteness of purpose is the starting point of all achievement."
>
> W. Clement Stone

Character: I have embraced the challenges of life to build my character. I can handle new challenges with poise. Though I still struggle at times, I have perspective because I've overcome much in my life. I am known as a person who can be trusted, who is responsible. I'm loyal to those I love and forgive those who hate me.

Family: Multiple generations of my loved ones surround me. My children and grandchildren love me. I know this because they want to spend time with me. I am not close to everyone in my family, but everyone knows that I love them and would do anything for them. I spend a great deal of time with my family, enjoying their company, mentoring them, and learning from them.

> "The purpose of life is to live it, to taste experience to the utmost, to reach out eagerly and without fear for newer and richer experience."
>
> Eleanor Roosevelt

Romantic Love: I have a partner whom I consider to be the love of my life. We both know how much we mean to each other. I do not feel jealousy when they are out with friends, and they give me space to pursue my relationships outside the partnership. We are not married because labels aren't necessary, but we are committed to each other for the rest of our lives. We know each other so well we sometimes finish each other's sentences. And more importantly, we both can tell when the other person needs a hug, a laugh, or a smack on the ass.

And so on.

At this point, don't worry about how short or inadequate your pillar descriptions might be. Avoid the trap of overthinking, perfectionism, and paralysis. The trick to taking action on where you want to go is focusing on what you know rather than what you don't know. What have you enjoyed in your life to this point? What are you good at? What are people willing to pay you to do? What do you want to do when you don't have anything else to do? How would you describe your perfect day? What kind of work do you want to do right now? How do you want to feel today?

> "Don't waste your time on the little insignificant things, because they will only become important if you can get them down to the T, but even then they will still prove to be a waste of time."
>
> Gebru Villars

These are the perfect places to start. Once you have an idea of where you want to go in life, you are ready to begin considering which people are helping you get there—and what kinds of people you need to add to your inner circle to refine or accelerate your journey.

Pillars and Mentor

For each of your pillars, you need people to help you grow. Each pillar has its own point A, where you are now, and point B, where you want to go. Given that most pillars don't require difficult-to-reach people as mentors, the chances are high that you already have in your network those who can help you move forward more quickly in several aspects of life. If you're seeking relationships with high-gravity individuals like famous or highly successful people, these can take quite a bit of time and effort to build. Because of this, consider leveraging connections with those who are not as far along as you might like while you continue to invest long term in relationships with your ideal matches. Those who are just a little further along may not pull you quickly, but are likely to be more helpful than no relationship at all.

Start with who you already know. Take an inventory. Consider those you are in regular contact with and also those who are likely to pick up the phone if you call. Then add friends of friends, people you could be introduced to

EACH PILLAR HAS ITS OWN STARTING AND ENDING POINTS
WE OFTEN NEED DIFFERENT MENTORS TO HELP US ON EACH PATH

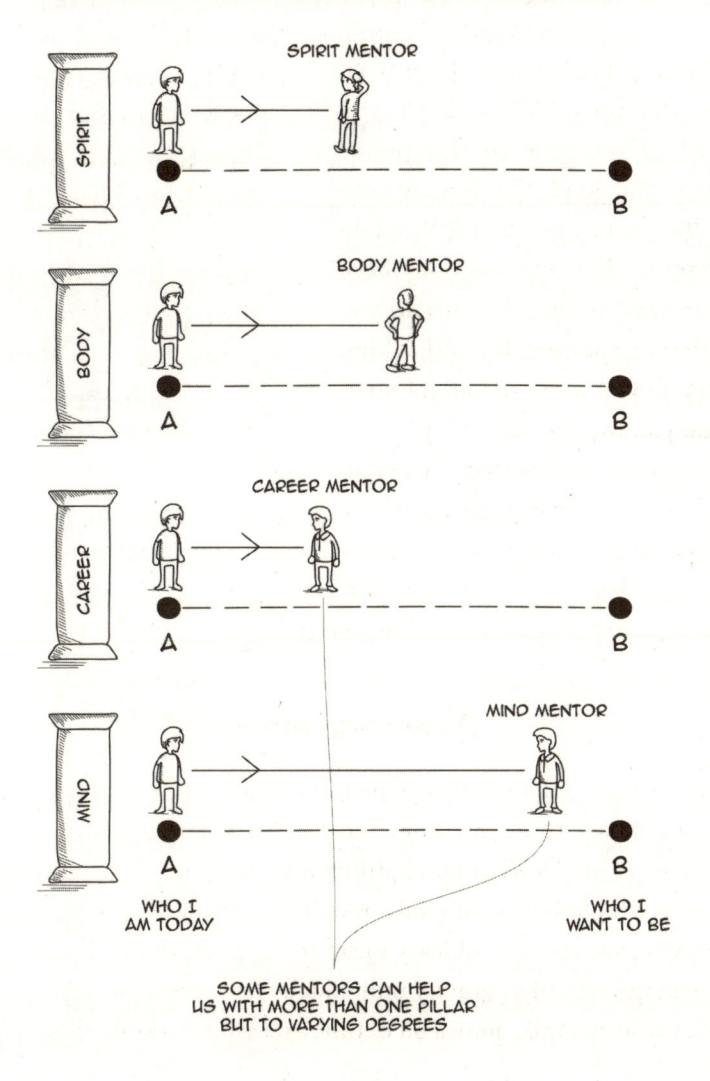

SPIRIT — SPIRIT MENTOR — A — B

BODY — BODY MENTOR — A — B

CAREER — CAREER MENTOR — A — B

MIND — MIND MENTOR — A — B

WHO I AM TODAY   WHO I WANT TO BE

SOME MENTORS CAN HELP
US WITH MORE THAN ONE PILLAR
BUT TO VARYING DEGREES

without much trouble. It may help to create a list or use a spreadsheet. You could write notes about how well they match with your goals, which pillars they can help you with, and the strength of your relationship.

Then consider any pillars that aren't well supported by current connections or people you have access to. This is where you have an opportunity to add new relationships that will help you on your journey. Make another list of people who would be ideal for your network. If you don't have specific names, describe what traits you think these people would have to be a perfect match.

Lists and spreadsheets may feel too robotic for you. If so, skip them. You can organically apply these principles. Simply keep in mind the traits you would like to have in your relationships. Then keep your eye out for people who might fill those gaps as you move through life. When you find someone who piques your interest, ask them out for coffee. If you have the chance to work for a manager who is an excellent match for one or more of your pillars, take the job. When picking partners for a school project, ask students who seem to be a great fit for your inner circle. If you have access to a high-caliber person through a friend of a friend, ask for an introduction. Then take a little more time to make a great impression. Ask people for advice. Offer to help. Don't waste the chance to make the most of opportunities when they pass your way. And remember, you can improve quite a few aspects of life simply by emulating those in your life who embody the traits you want more of, as I described in the introduction to this book. This remains the most common application of relationshift in my personal life on a daily basis.

> "What goes around comes back around."
>
> Beyoncé

Whatever approach you take, avoid a transactional or using mindset. Relationshift doesn't work if you are only out for yourself. The people you most want in your life will sniff out overtly selfish motivations and avoid you. It's possible to be aware of the traits you desire in your connections without seeking to exploit people for your gain. Foster natural reciprocity. Seek rich and rewarding friendships. Give first, and don't expect anything in return. You don't have to believe in karma to understand how generosity has a way of coming back around. Goodness and unselfishness are attractive. Plus, life is more enjoyable with an abundant and kind spirit.

Pause to reflect

- Take time to define your pillars. Which categories best encompass your various goals? Write a paragraph describing your desired future state in each. Don't worry about getting it perfect. You will undoubtedly be changing these as you move toward them.
- For each pillar, think about who is influencing you—for better or worse. How can you minimize the negative impact and maximize the positive in each scenario? Should you be spending more intentional time with some people than you are now to accelerate your growth in these aspects of your life?
- Consider any gaps in your inner circle that are holding you back from maximum growth in each of the pillars. Can you think of anyone to connect with more to fill these gaps? How will you approach those people? What can you do to help them achieve their own goals and, in so doing, foster a trusting and mutually beneficial relationship?

Changing My Worldview

I wish I could say I learned the lessons we've been discussing easily. Or even willingly. The truth is, life forced me to reconsider the choices, instincts, and desires responsible for making me into the person I had become. The decision came down to either letting go of everything I had ever believed or ending my life.

Throughout my teenage years and well into my twenties, I was generally a positive person. From time to time, I felt down for a day or two. But due to responsibilities or personality, I always managed to pick myself up and keep moving. In my early thirties, however, depression began to take deeper root in me.

I was finishing up my doctorate at the University of Maryland while running my latest business. Somehow, I even found time to play in the worship band and publish a popular blog on church leadership. Through it all,

I always made time for my family, which was my greatest source of joy. But I was wearing out fast. And more than this, I felt a growing sense of loneliness. This didn't make sense. I had a kind and easygoing wife, three beautiful children who loved me, and even a few church friends.

For the first ten to fifteen years of my marriage, I was in love and quite happy. My wife and I went on dates regularly. We enjoyed trips to Paris, Hawaii, and other romantic locations. Often hand in hand, we strolled our neighborhood or watched movies. I was confused as to why I would be feeling a growing sense of unhappiness with my relationship. Since I had been married to the same person for my whole adult life, I didn't have experience with other romantic relationships. So as I began to grow lonely, I couldn't compare my marriage to what might be considered a normal, rewarding relationship.

Several years passed like this before I began to realize the source of my unhappiness. Though my wife and I were kind to each other and did fun things together, I didn't feel any sense of romantic connection to her. We met when I was fifteen and got married two years later—my first serious relationship. In circumstances like those, one can feel a great deal of passion and love for another person built on little but the excitement of having someone feel the same in return. As I grew older, I realized we were very different people who likely wouldn't have gone on a second date, let alone gotten married, if we had met later in life. We didn't have anything in common apart from sharing a deep love for our children. But what really fueled my depression was the idea that I could never change my situation.

Growing up as a conservative Christian, I learned from my pastors and family that divorce is one of the worst sins in the book. Pretty crazy when you think of all the *really* terrible things one can do. However, the Bible is quite clear on the subject. "What God has joined, let not man separate" was regularly repeated by my peers and pastors. I believed these ideas were the absolute truth and even preached on the subject as a young minister. So engrained were these teachings, I myself regrettably came down hard on a friend when I learned she was separating from her husband.

As my loneliness and depression grew, I became increasingly frustrated with God over his anti-divorce stance. I was taught God hates sin because it's terrible for us. This is different from what many non-Christians believe:

that God enjoys being a spoilsport and taking away all the fun stuff. However, the Christian view on sin—that it is bad for us and will eventually ruin our lives—didn't fit with my own experience. Following God seemed to be making me even more miserable.

I went to my pastors, read my Bible cover to cover, and confided in my friends. Their message was consistent: "Marriage is hard. But God uses this difficulty to shape us into better people." They counseled me to sacrifice my desires to do what was right. I should be like Jesus and give up my happiness for the benefit of others. My friends and family promised me that God would give me strength and relief if I followed his commandments. Yet, with each passing day, I grew lonelier and more depressed.

To earn a doctoral degree, one must write a dissertation and then defend it before a panel of professors. This is a highly stressful time for postgraduate students; for me, a heavy load of nonacademic responsibilities amplified my anxiety. I pushed myself to the limits and beyond until my body finally told me enough was enough. I had a physical breakdown that landed me in the emergency room. Over the next three months, I could barely leave my bed. I was in constant pain and couldn't work. I saw seven specialists, took a medicine cabinet full of prescriptions, and lost thirty pounds.

During this time, my depression enveloped me entirely. I began to see suicide as my only way out. But suicide is also a sin, one that many Christians believe is unforgivable. I became unbearably frustrated with God. His rules seemed cruel, bordering on torturous. I couldn't get a divorce no matter how unhappy I was. And I couldn't kill myself to escape my suffering. It felt like I was living in some version of hell on earth, forced to remain alive and suffer until my master allowed me a merciful death.

I was very close to acting on my suicidal thoughts during those dark days. Thankfully, my drive to experience life to the fullest, be there for my kids, and a substantial fear of death saved me. I didn't want to die. I wanted to live and to live happily. I wanted to enjoy my family and be healthy.

One day I found an article in which the author described how he had divorced his wife and found God's grace after. I remembered hearing other stories like this. It made me wonder who was right: all of those people who had told me God hated divorce, or those who said there was grace for sinners who couldn't remain in a relationship.

This simple thought was the loose thread that eventually unraveled everything I'd ever believed. How could I know which opinion on divorce was correct if there were multiple positions on the topic? At first, I considered that the view with the largest number of followers was likely to be the most accurate. But this line of logic I quickly cast aside. The Kardashians have hundreds of millions of followers. This fact does not make them reliable. I remembered that even the Bible holds that popular opinion isn't always right. Alternatively, I could try to consider who was the most faithful Christian and go with their stance. But this, too, was problematic. How could God expect me to determine who the best Christians were in order to discover the truth on a matter? Why would God allow or create such confusion over his principles that his followers couldn't determine right from wrong with confidence? And if Christians disagreed about the consequences of divorce, why shouldn't I side with the opinions that might free me from depression?

This was the moment I realized I had been opting into a belief that was making me miserable. Meanwhile, other Christians were enjoying the freedom of interpreting God's rules a little more loosely. Most of all, if seemingly faithful Christians had conflicting opinions on the same subject, how could God judge any of them for choosing one side or the other? He was the one being, after all, who could clear it all up if he wanted.

I began to see how somebody could apply this same thought pattern to a wide variety of sins. For example, the Bible says homosexuality is wrong. Yet some Christians believe God doesn't mind if people have sex with whoever they like. No objective method exists to determine the truth on this matter. So, according to my new understanding of godly subjectivity, it seemed favorable to choose love and acceptance over judgment and hate.

In another example, the New Testament is clear that women should not speak in church. The Bible has many other shocking opinions about women's rights: a woman can be compelled to marry her rapist, women should dress modestly, women are responsible for the downfall of humankind, women should not be allowed to teach men, and men may divorce their wives by accusing them of lying about their virginity and then stoning them to death. I could go on, but will spare you. Most societies today find all of these positions abhorrent. As a result, nearly all churches using the Bible as their guide have done away with these practices. Yet some conservative churches and orthodox religions practice a few of these commandments to this day. Disagreement persists. Most Christians ignore the Bible's misogynistic flair. A smaller number have abandoned their hate toward those with alternative sexualities. We can only hope that, in time, Christians will leave all their archaic and hateful opinions behind as most have with their views toward women.

I decided to check out a bookstore to see how many different opinions there were on God's commandments. The religion section took up both sides of an entire aisle. Thousands of books filled the shelves. Not just Christian ideas, but Jewish, Hindu, Muslim, New Age, Buddhist, and many others. I realized that every single one of those books must disagree with the others on at least one point. If two books were in complete agreement, why have two books? So here were the opinions of hundreds of history's most influential religious leaders. And not a single pair of them agreed on everything. With no way to objectively determine who was correct about what, how could God hold me accountable for being wrong about anything? Some might say, "Look to the Christian Bible." But this is just one of the countless opinions. You might recommend with equal conviction that I should look to the Quran, the Tanakh, the Sutras, or the Vedas. Who decides who is correct? And who decides what interpretation of these texts is the one that gets you into heaven?

For the next two years, I pondered, prayed, sought mentors' advice, and went to marriage counseling with my wife. With each month that passed, I felt only sadder and lonelier. I tried to make friends to fill my companionship needs, but this, too, proved tragically problematic. One friendship developed into an affair—a mistake I'm deeply sorry for, but also a clear sign that I needed to address my depression in a healthier manner. Anna was a saint through all of this and deserves the utmost credit for doing all she could to keep our marriage together. But, in the end, what could she do? It wasn't her fault I was unhappy. My emotions and my path were my responsibility, and I needed to find a way to live honestly while also giving myself a shot at rediscovering happiness.

Asking Anna for a divorce and telling my three teenage daughters their parents were separating was the most painful moment of my life. My pain grew worse as I saw how my choice hurt so many friends and family members. Thankfully, I had the comfort of knowing Anna was well supported.

Since it was me who sinned, our friends and family sided with Anna completely.

Fortunately, time has healed my relationship with my kids, and I count them as my best and closest companions in all this world. My relationship with my ex-wife is amiable and supportive. I'm grateful that my income had recovered enough by this time that my ex-wife and I could maintain the same standard of living. My parents and siblings have forgiven me, though I think they still pray for me to leave my sinful ways behind. Everyone else I knew from before the age of thirty-four is gone from my life now. Divorce may not be a sin, but it certainly can come with a high cost.

Though leaving my wife was the hardest decision I've ever made, I also consider it to be the best. I have since overcome my depression completely, discovering happiness and contentment on a level I didn't even know was possible. I love myself and my life. My love for my children, family, friends, and even my ex-wife is purer than ever before. Now my love is given freely and out of abundance, not because of religious or societal expectations.

One surprising lesson I took away from this experience is that drastic changes to one's worldview are possible at any point in life, and that dramatic life improvements are achievable at any age, too—but only if we find a way to dig to the very core of our deepest assumptions. When we want to change, we usually consider only the most superficial aspects of our existence. For example, if I want to get into shape, I should run more or eat less. As you may have experienced with any of your struggles, this kind of thinking rarely works. We need to dig deeper. With the example of getting into shape, perhaps we need to evaluate our level of self-love or whether we really believe we can attain this goal.

Our propensity to focus on cursory-level thinking is why we can become increasingly locked into our ways as we age. The process of digging deep becomes more difficult as we add layers to our subconscious over time. If we want significant change, we must be willing to challenge our most closely held assumptions about how life works. We can mistakenly believe life's rules are more objective, logical, and universal than they are when we stay on the surface of our psyche. But when we dig deeper, we can more readily rewrite our hardwiring and make considerable strides very quickly.

Let's consider my views on divorce as layers of a cake.

Digging deep into our most fundamental beliefs can be painful or scary. We may discover we've been living according to subjective rules that have been making us miserable. And once we realize what is possible, we face the even more difficult task of acting on those new beliefs.

This process of unwinding our most foundational assumptions and taking action on our new, freely conceived vision can take many years. Three years passed between the time when I realized I might be living according to rules that no longer made sense to me, and when I was able to construct a new worldview that enabled my current, much happier life. Over those three years I got divorced, transformed countless insecurities into steady and satisfying contentment, overcame suicidal levels of depression to become fully happy and at peace, found adventure and beauty in my travels

THE UPPER LAYERS OF OUR BELIEFS ARE ONLY LOGICAL IF THE UNDERLYING ASSUMPTIONS ARE TRUE

- SHOULD I GET A DIVORCE?
- THE BIBLE SAYS DIVORCE IS A SIN
- GOD LOVES ME AND GUIDES ME TO DO WHAT IS RIGHT BECAUSE ITS GOOD FOR ME
- GOD IS REAL, POWERFUL, AND MADE THE UNIVERSE

WE TEND TO STICK TO THE UPPER LAYERS OF OUR WORLD VIEW WHEN MAKING DECISIONS

IF WE WANT TO EXPLORE ALL THAT IS POSSIBLE WE HAVE TO DIG DOWN TO OUR UNDERLYING ASSUMPTIONS across six continents, conquered fears, changed careers, reimagined every goal, and converted from Christian preacher to atheist.

These immense changes were only possible because my fear of suicide forced me to challenge my most fundamental beliefs. If you look deep inside your subconscious and do the same in your life, you will undoubtedly find a unique path from mine. Perhaps you will transition from atheist to Christian or from capitalist to communist. You might keep the same belief system, but change other aspects of your life. You can't possibly know what might happen until you take the plunge. However, I'm confident of this: if you undertake this task, you will find more of whatever it is your deepest self is searching for. I know it's possible because it happened to me.

CONCLUSION

> "This life is what you make it. No matter what, you're going to mess up sometimes, it's a universal truth. But the good part is you get to decide how you're going to mess it up... Just because you fail once, doesn't mean you're gonna fail at everything. Keep trying, hold on, and always, always, always believe in yourself, because if you don't, then who will, sweetie? So keep your head high, keep your chin up, and most importantly, keep smiling, because life's a beautiful thing and there's so much to smile about."
>
> Marilyn Monroe

Remember how long it seemed to take to drive to Grandma's house when you were a child? Or how it seemed like your birthday would never come? We have all experienced how life moves faster as the years tick by. Scientists have recently discovered the reason why.

Every moment we are alive, our brain is forming synapses. These synapses allow one neuron to pass an electrical signal to another. Memories are a collection of neurons that light up in a unique pattern. When you recall something, these brain cells fire in the same way they did when the original experience happened. Every moment we are alive, we are forming permanent connections between neurons. Though we lose conscious recollection of most memories over time, we retain every one of them until our brain is damaged or we die.

When we are young, our brains are in peak synapse-forming shape. Children have a lot to learn about the world to operate successfully, so they form synapses much more quickly than adults. As we age, our brain degrades. This makes us less capable of creating new connections between neurons.

Our brains work in a similar way to video. Most movies are filmed at twenty-four still images per second. Some, like *The Hobbit*, are forty-eight frames per second. This allows for better clarity in scenes with a lot of action. But filming with a high frame rate requires more money. The cameras are more expensive, and the software used to process all those images must be more powerful.

A child's brain is like a high-frame-rate camera. Children capture many moments every second because their brain is operating at peak performance. As we get older, the frame rate slows. Our brain becomes like older technology, incapable of processing all that information at the same speed as when we were younger. Though time continues to move at the same rate, we capture fewer moments, making us feel as if time is moving faster.

Time is not nearly as concrete, universal, and steady as we think it is. Einstein's theory of relativity proves that time slows down when we speed up or move closer to a dense gravity source. If you could hitch a ride on a light particle, you would experience time's movement differently from those you left behind. So time is irrelevant. We can't even perceive it accurately. All we can do is measure the number of moments we capture.

The first time I jumped out of a plane, I experienced how adrenaline caused my perception of time to move more quickly.[1] My brain diverted

---

1. One must travel close to the speed of light to experience measurable differences in the movement of time. In this example, my perception of time changed, but I wasn't moving fast enough to actually experience a difference in the movement of time from those watching from the ground.

MOMENT
CAPTURED

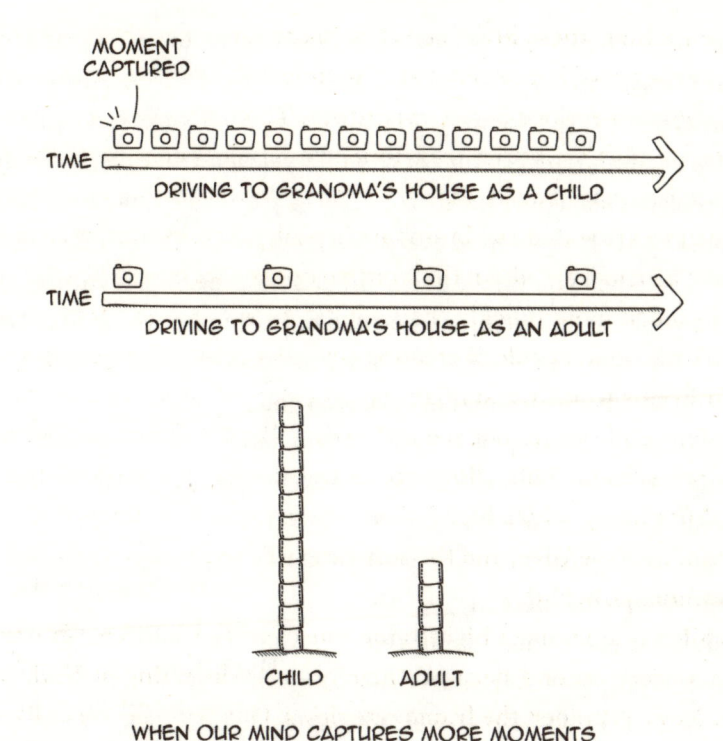

TIME [ooooooooooooooo] →
DRIVING TO GRANDMA'S HOUSE AS A CHILD

TIME [o   o   o   o] →
DRIVING TO GRANDMA'S HOUSE AS AN ADULT

CHILD   ADULT

WHEN OUR MIND CAPTURES MORE MOMENTS
WE FEEL AS THOUGH MORE TIME HAS PASSED

energy from forming memory synapses to averting death. As a result, I barely remember the drop—a good reason to, if you can afford it, pay the extra hundred bucks for a video. At other times, like when we are waiting for the workday to end, our brain is bored, so it spends all its energy forming memories of the second hand slowly ticking by.

We tend to measure life in months and years. We say to teenagers, "You've got your whole life ahead of you." At forty years old, we think we're about halfway through the ride. A terminal patient may be told, "You have six months to live." But none of these are accurate. Life is a series of moments that you experience one at a time. It doesn't matter how many more moments are coming your way or how many have passed. All you possess is now. So each is equally valuable, whether you're taking a middle school spelling test, holding your child for the first time, or lying in a hospital bed saying goodbye to your loved ones.

The present moment grows even more valuable when you realize you don't share anything with the person you were in the past or hope to become in the future. Not only do your thoughts change, but so does your body. Every atom in every one of the thirty-seven trillion cells that make you up replaces itself over time.[2] Your pieces are always changing. You leave a seventh of your body behind every year, replaced with entirely new atoms and cells. So when you worry about the past or pine for the future, you are giving up your current moment, one of a finite number you will possess, in exchange for worrying about some other moment that was or will be experienced by a body and mind that isn't even you.

The relativity of time is helpful to understand as we consider how to approach our one precious existence. Maximizing the positive impact of relationshift is, in many ways, centered on making the most of your moment. Enjoy the person you are today and the people you have in your life. You'll be happier and more content when you let go of the need to collect e-capital at all costs. You can love yourself more in the present when you let go of societal pressures based on evolutionary instincts our species no longer needs to survive. At the same time, you can invest in your future self by jumping at the chance to add an ideal match to your inner circle. Or by reducing the harm of someone close to you who isn't heading in the same direction. Someday, you'll be experiencing a different present moment, one that is affected by your choices today. Make decisions that make you happy today and also cause your future self to be thankful for your present self's wisdom.

> "Do not dwell in the past, do not dream of the future, concentrate the mind on the present moment."
>
> Buddha

Relationshift happens to all of us, whether we are aware of it or not. To take control of the process, and sum up this entire book, we need only remember three steps.

---

2. The only exception is brain cells, which do not replace themselves. We simply lose them over time. Smoke 'em if you got 'em!

1. Understand how you became you. This will help you determine which parts you want to keep and which you wish to change.
2. Revise your life direction based on what you want, free from societal pressure or ancient instincts that aren't a part of your new worldview.
3. Invest in relationships with people who align with your revised life goals.

Who you are has been affected by a great many factors outside your influence. But who you become from this moment forward is entirely within your control. It doesn't matter if you're twenty years old or eighty. You can enjoy each moment as if it's the only one you have because, well, it is. And no matter which path you choose, I hope you enjoy it fully.

• • •

My apartment is on the top floor of one of the many new towers built during the tech boom in Seattle. After my divorce, I needed a place to live in a hurry, and because so many people were moving to the city at the time, I had to lease it unseen. When I walked in for the first time, the beauty of the skyscrapers, lakes, and mountains all around struck me. It had always been a dream of mine to live downtown. This would have been the perfect opportunity to host a big party for all my friends and share the fantastic view.

> "Know the rules well, so you can break them effectively."
>
> The Dalai Lama

The only problem was, I didn't have any friends—I'd lost them all in my divorce. But why let that small detail stop me? So I set a date a month out and went to work finding some partygoers. Fortunately, plenty of people in my new neighborhood use hashtags on Instagram. I searched for tags like #seattlemusician and #seattlewriter and began sending invites. My pitch was simple. The party was to be called Art on the Rooftop. I intended to feature a few local musicians, poets, and painters. Donations would support the artists.

I invited about a hundred people. Some accused me of spamming—others, of having more nefarious intentions. But many were excited. They said my idea was just the thing this cold, unsocial town needed.

On the day of the event, I stocked my counters with cases of Rainier, White Claw, and a magnum of Kirkland vodka. An hour before the event was set to begin, my new friend Ingrid, whom I'd met a few weeks earlier on Tinder, arrived with her Australian shepherd, Daisy. The dog skidded across the floor, slipping on foam that was pouring out the sides of my dishwasher. I had no idea why this was happening, so I shut the suds in and hoped no one would try to open it during the party.

The official start time, nine o'clock, came and went. But no one showed up. Even the artists who had promised to perform weren't responding to my messages.

I stared at the cases of booze, wondering how long it would take Ingrid, Daisy, and me to drink it all. Then a knock came. One of the artists I'd connected with on Instagram, Spence Hood, was at the door, guitar in hand, with a few friends. He noticed the apartment was a little short on guests.

"You know how everyone wants to be fashionably late," I said with the most confident grin I could muster.

Minutes later, another group arrived. Several other featured artists appeared, as if by magic, hovering near the alcohol. Spence started playing his set as the room filled up. Everyone had a different story for how they had heard about the party. A few had received my messages, but many had been invited by friends—or by friends who had been invited by friends.

Quite a few guests laughed sheepishly when I asked what brought them. Many thought it was going to be some kind of sex party. Everyone seemed to agree that the whole thing was quite strange: going to some random guy's house based on an invitation from a friend of a friend on Instagram. And yet they came. By ten o'clock, over fifty people were crammed into my apartment, pouring out onto my balcony, sitting on counters and each other's laps. Someone brought a toddler who seemed endlessly entertained by feeding Goldfish crackers to Daisy. Between the giggles and Daisy's happily wagging tail, the two of them nearly stole the show.

The room was getting hot. I told everyone to grab a few drinks between acts, and we took the party to the roof. Around midnight, another artist I found on Instagram, Cha Wilde, played the last set by firelight with the city and stars glistening behind her. When she finished her last song, someone grabbed the mic and made an impromptu speech. He teared up talking about how difficult it had been for him to make friends in Seattle and how much he appreciated an event like this that brought people together around a shared love for music and art. Everyone cheered. I was embarrassed but pleased—if for nothing other than relief that I didn't have to drink all that alcohol on my own. But my humiliation grew as a second person took the mic and made a similar speech. Then a third person. I finally said a few words of thanks and hid the mic so no one else could mortify me further.

Since that first party, I've hosted many more—each one progressively more exciting, extravagant, or strange than the last. Some of those who came, including Spence and Cha, have become close friends. In a few short years, I went from being friendless, divorced, and alone in my first apartment to being part of a growing community of loving, happy, creative, and openhearted people. I've heard stories of many who met new best friends, business partners, band members, and lovers at Art on the Rooftop. People thank me for hosting, but the truth is I do it for myself.

Over the last ten years, as I discovered and applied the principles of relationshift in my life, I've been transformed from brokenness to abundance—not because I got everything I once wanted, but because I'm now content with who I am. I have mentors, peers, and protégés who enrich me and push me. They're helping me live the life of my dreams just by being themselves. I've experienced a wealth of love and acceptance my former self never dared to dream was possible. I was able to sell a business and start a new company with talented advisers. I realigned my goals and purpose to create a reality that is full of joy, peace, and contentment. Through it all, I discovered that so much more goodness is available in this life than I could have ever imagined just a few short years ago.

Of course, my life is far from perfect. I still get down or feel lonely sometimes. I have bad days at work now and then. I catch myself regretting a past mistake or worrying about worst-case scenarios that haven't yet come to pass. I haven't arrived at my ideal destination—but that's not my goal. The difference is, now, I love being alive.

I wrote this book so others who desire more, who are searching for a better life in any way, shape, or form, can experience transformation. As you think about applying relationshift in your life, remember the story of Eddy, Bobby, and David. Though the brothers lived geographically close to each other and enjoyed fame together for a while, Eddy could never shake the feeling of being an outsider in his own family. Eddy's death is a tragic example of how one can be surrounded by people and yet feel so lonely that they see little reason to continue living. And if you think you were born with a bad hand of cards, one that is holding you back and making life impossibly challenging, remember the story of Frederick Douglass. He rose from great adversity to become a hero, and he made our world a better place in the process.

When you think about your future, you may see only fog and uncertainty. You may feel a great deal of pressure to be what other people think you should be. Don't give in. Instead, recall how the brilliant pioneer Gertrude Bell lived life on her terms. She didn't waste time appeasing her contemporaries. Instead, she did what she wanted and created a life filled with extraordinary purpose. Or think about the story of Siddhartha Gautama. He didn't like the rules of life as taught by his parents and culture. So he left everything and sat under a tree until he discovered his own way of living. Hundreds of millions of Buddhists have followed his teachings to this day.

> "To live is the rarest thing in the world. Most people exist, that is all."
>
> Oscar Wilde

If you're looking for a friend who makes you better, remember how a single player for the Golden State Warriors, Draymond Green, affected his teammates more than any other. You want colleagues like Draymond, people who will make you better simply by being around. And if you want to achieve fame and success at the highest levels like the Beastie Boys, you're going to want to have a few Madonnas, Rick Rubins, or Russell Simmonses around to help you on your way to that big break.

In many video games, users can select a difficulty setting. New players can try the easy mode until they get some practice. As they become more experienced, they may increase the difficulty setting to create more of a challenge. Life, too, has a selectable difficulty setting. And while the situation of our birth greatly affects the quantity and magnitude of the challenges we will face, we can't change this aspect of our life. We can only choose how we approach the life we have.

When we try to go through life alone, like someone with a broken leg refusing the help of a doctor, we choose the challenging mode. When we attempt to live life according to unhelpful societal pressures and instincts that should have died with the dinosaurs, we choose a far more difficult path toward happiness and contentment. If we are waiting around for luck to strike, we play the game of life in hard mode. To switch to easy mode, we must look to our relationships. They have all we need to do anything or become anyone.

Taking control of relationshift is a messy, long-term process. And since we're talking about real people and real relationships, it's not going to be simple or straightforward like a video game. Accepting this long, meandering journey is an essential lesson of relationshift. You won't often see these principles working in day-to-day life. But, given time, you will look back and see how the progress you've made weaves through every relationship you have.

• • •

In closing, I'd like to reflect with you on the state of our world and how our knowledge of relationshift can play a part in the healing of our species and our planet. I used to believe it was a given that the future would be better than the past. And though this trend may have held for thousands of years, we can't assume it will continue. We face challenges confronted by no human before us. We don't know how our species will respond in the face of the rapidly accelerating change we now regularly experience. Yes, life has survived meteors, climate change, continental shift, pandemics, world wars, genocide, and who knows what else. But we have never before faced Twitter or artificial intelligence or 3D-printed firearms or ever more advanced government and corporate surveillance or drone-delivered Happy Meals from McDonald's. We simply don't know how our exponentially growing knowledge and technology will affect our future.

One could be forgiven for thinking social media, fast internet connections, free video calling, instant news, and constant access to an unlimited volume of information would bring us together. Yet all this connectivity and access has only given us more opportunity to misunderstand and hate each other. The political divide between left and right grows more extreme with each election cycle. To this day, shooters continue to murder schoolchildren, terrorists remain committed to blowing up public places, and the factories that create missiles and bombs are as productive as ever. We are further apart than we have ever been.

Those who came before us have been adapting and improving for millions of years. They passed that ability on to us. Our ancestors had to learn to work together in groups of fifty or one hundred to survive. So, too, must we join together to survive what is coming next. But this time, it will take all eight billion of us. We must learn to set aside the evolutionary instincts that have helped us get to where we are today—our desire to accumulate e-capital at all costs, dominate each other, and hoard resources at the expense of those with more pressing needs. We must eliminate our us-versus-them mentality and our eagerness to kick problems down the road for future generations to solve. We must learn to fear ignorance and apathy more than upsetting the status quo.

Proper use of relationshift is more than an opportunity to live a better life. It's a responsibility. We would all benefit from removing the polarization of our lens. We should all strive to become more open to understanding people of different backgrounds. If each of us were willing to step outside our comfort zone to meet those of different persuasions, we might stop hating and hurting each other. A tribe at war with itself will fall. This civil war our species has been fighting for millennia must come to an end.

My final challenge is for all of us. Let us make friends with people who are different; listen to people we don't understand; love the family members who share conspiracy theories on Facebook; have lunch with people who vote opposite of us and listen to why; and avoid judgment when someone does something we disagree with. Instead, we should ask them to tell their story. We can envision any future and make it a reality—a future without violence, hunger, poverty, sickness, hate, or fear. We can do all of this through the power of a single connection between two people, multiplied countless times across our planet.

Whatever our species becomes next is up to you and me.

> "Too often we underestimate the power of a touch, a smile, a kind word, a listening ear, an honest compliment, or the smallest act of caring, all of which have the potential to turn a life around."
>
> Leo Buscaglia

APPENDIX

A Discussion of Common Objections and Questions About Relationshift

As I've presented the principles of relationshift in seminars to students, business owners, and conference-goers, I've heard various questions, ethical concerns, and other objections. Here I take the opportunity to address the most common of these in case you've had the same thoughts as you read the book.

This philosophy is obvious. I already use these principles.

When I first began to present these ideas, almost everyone I spoke to was eager to tell me how much they already had been using relationshift: "This is so true; I've been doing this for years," or "I'm cautious about who my friends are and cut out anyone toxic." I had the same objection to these ideas as I began to explore them myself.

The truth is, relationshift *is* common sense. We all know intuitively that people in our lives will affect our mood and opinions, perhaps even color our worldview. But I found that I didn't apply this understanding as much as I thought I did. Sometimes I would look back and wonder why I let a particular high-caliber person slip from my acquaintance. Or I would avoid networking events because I felt they were a waste of time. Or I would meet someone who could be an excellent match for my inner circle, but I would neglect to follow up. I would avoid the hard work of trying to help people I wanted in my life because I was too busy or too lazy.

I found that it's often the commonsense ideas that we neglect the most. They're so familiar, we no longer perceive their importance. With relationshift, the question I ask myself now is not, "Do I understand this?" but rather, "Am I making the most of it?"

Relationshift sounds like using people.

These ideas have been compared to social climbing or using people for one's gain. Some people attempt to use others to gain social standing, access opportunities, or elevate themselves unethically. But these are not the principles of relationshift. Throughout the book, we discussed the importance of giving back, having a generous spirit, and being genuine. These mindsets aren't just useful for reducing the potential for selfishness within a relationship. They also make you more attractive to high-caliber people and may help you go further in life. So I would never advise anyone to attempt to take more than they give, if for no other reason than that I think it doesn't work. Neither is it a path to happiness or contentment, states of mind built primarily on thankfulness. Rather, relationshift is based on reciprocity. So, if you have the right approach, these principles aren't any more selfish than any other strategy for ethically enriching one's life with the company of another person.

How can I be expected to abandon people I love just to improve my situation in life?

One of the most challenging aspects of relationshift is confronting the idea that some people in your life could be holding you back. If you realize you're in such a situation, how you respond is entirely up to you. You may decide to keep someone in your life who is hurting you. I would never try to change your mind. But be honest with yourself about your exchange—you are trading your goals for a relationship. There is nothing wrong with this if that's the trade you want to make.

Every relationship is unique. Only you know how much someone is lifting you or holding you down. It's a wide range, and there is room for lots of people in your life—they don't all need to be ideal for you to enjoy growth. But if someone is hurting you or severely reducing your chances of happiness in this life, then for your own sake consider a few of these questions:

- Will this other person appreciate all you've given up for them?
- If you have been helping them, are you seeing any lasting signs of progress?
- Is their benefit of your presence equal to or greater than your sacrifice?
- Are you keeping this person in your life because you fear being alone or their judgment?
- Are you giving up your dreams because you believe in this other person, or because you don't believe in yourself?

If your relationship with someone is not hurting you terribly, and you don't want to just cut them out of your life, try this approach. Rather than thinking about who you must cut out of your life, focus instead on who you want to add or spend more time with. Give yourself as much as you can or want to the people who are helping you become who you want to be. As you are able, continue in the relationships that may not be a part of this. Perhaps in time, the negative relationships will fade away as you turn your energy to more positive connections.

Isn't it judgmental and mean to rate people based on my perception of their e-capital?

Yes, it is judgmental, but it doesn't have to be cruel. The fact is we rate people whether we realize it or want to admit it. For example, I'm guessing you would not marry, vacation with, or start a business with any random person. You look for people who you want to do these things with—nothing wrong with that. It's not immoral to tell someone you're not interested in a second date if the first didn't impress you. And suppose a business partnership isn't working out. In that case, you can dissolve the relationship without hurting the other person by ensuring they are fairly treated and compensated in a mutually agreed-upon manner.

Rating people subconsciously according to how we perceive their e-capital is an instinct we all have. But through enlightened thinking, we can choose not to act on those instincts. If we make a decision based on how we see someone, we don't have to be cruel about it. It helps if we modify our internal rating system to think about people as matches or mismatches rather than better or worse, which are subjective terms, after all. And as we discussed in part two, with practice we can let go of our instincts to accumulate e-capital. As we do this, we can also learn to see people differently, based on whatever we decide matters to us.

Relationshift is too much work. I don't have time for it.

Networking events, trying to figure out how to attract high-profile people's attention, and going to ten coffee meetings a week *is* a lot of work. But these things aren't necessary to apply relationshift. It all depends on which pillars you prioritize and what vision you have for your future. If you want to be a top 40 musician, you're going to have to work your ass off. But that's true with or without making the most use of relationshift. And in this example, using relationshift is a better path toward this goal. You will have a far more straightforward approach if you work your way to the top through relationships as the Beastie Boys did than if you attempt to do so without the help of other successful people.

Similarly, if you want to become a better chess player, you could probably find quite a few excellent players at a local chess club. Keep in mind one of the essential ideas within relationshift is being ready to capitalize on a great match when it comes your way. So, most aspects of applying relationshift are not so much about working day and night to build connections, but more about making the most of the people in your life and opportunities as they present themselves.

And if you still find this all too difficult to make use of on a regular basis, you can at least try to emulate traits you see in people who embody aspects of life that you want more of in yours. This is the simplest and quickest way to improve your life by making use of relationshift without any planning, strategizing, networking, or spreadsheets.

I'm content with my life. Why should I care about any of this?

If you're perfectly content with your life, congratulations. But for the sake of exercise, allow me to challenge you. In my experience, many of those who feel they have everything they want are often not examining all the areas of their life that could be improved. Or they don't know that more is possible because, as we've discussed, our view of what is possible derives from what we have experienced. Or they don't believe more is possible because of any number of reasons such as a lack of self-love or a history of hearing they don't deserve better from people in their life. If any of these could be true, consider the prospect of expanding your view of what is possible for you.

Even if you feel you are perfectly content with your life and have no need to apply relationshift to improve any aspect of your life, I argue you can still benefit from a slow, content, and steady approach to leveling up one area of your life or another. No matter how great my life, I figure there is little reason not to strive for more—as long as I'm not unsatisfied with what I currently have. When you are content with your life, you're in the best possible position to level up. Why miss the opportunity when it's just sitting there, waiting for you to take it?

In the final analysis, you are the author of your own story. So, if you like the plot the way it is, don't let me or anyone else tell you what you must change.

I'm not happy with my life, but I don't have enough drive to want to change anything.

This is a common place to be. If you feel this way, don't beat yourself up. We can easily find ourselves wanting something without enough desire to take action. However, it's essential to recognize that only you can activate your internal drive.

We discussed in chapter seven the idea of life being like a Plinko board. If gravity is pulling you down, tilt in such a way that down is moving you toward something you want. For example, if you feel no drive, try using what little you have to find and hang around highly motivated people. As you begin to feel a little more energy, use it to add people to your inner circle who get things done. Remember the difference between drive and ambition. Many people have big dreams, but you want people in your life who are doing something to make their ambitions a reality.

Or you can simply accept that you don't have the push to change yourself. You could instead learn to be happy with who you are and the life you have. The least helpful response is to complain about not having something while also not taking any action to get what you want. In any case, these are not questions of morality. Your choice for how you live your life is entirely up to you. Realizing that you are the only one capable of generating motivation is the first step forward, whether toward accepting who you are or finding a way to move forward.

> "The most difficult thing is the decision to act, the rest is merely tenacity. The fears are paper tigers. You can do anything you decide to do. You can act to change and control your life; and the procedure, the process is its own reward."
>
> **Amelia Earhart**

ACKNOWLEDGMENTS

In a book about the impact of relationships, I could fill chapters with all the people who have helped me develop these ideas and enriched my life in the process.

To my daughters, Lily, Emma, and Mackenzie, you inspire me more than anything or anyone else to live better every day. You are my mentors, my peers, and my protégés all in one. You have taught me what is essential in life. You share in my daily joy as the best of friends. And I have had no greater pleasure than to watch you grow into the amazing people you are today.

To my wife, Anya, thank you for your support and positive energy as I worked feverishly (and sometimes procrastinated chronically) to complete this manuscript. Your fingerprints are all over these pages, from helping me work through my research, to giving thoughtful feedback at every stage of development, to offering encouragement whenever I needed it most. Most of all, you embody positive relationshift more than anyone I know by drawing me every day to enjoy life to the fullest.

If not for my agent, D.J. Snell, and the fantastic team at Matt Holt Books, this book wouldn't exist. Specifically, I'd like to thank Matt Holt for his leadership and vision, Katie Dickman (senior editor), Joe Rhatigan (content editor), James Fraleigh (copyeditor), Jay Kilburn (production editor), Mallory Hyde (marketing), and Brigid Pearson (cover design). I'm also grateful for talented photographer Natalia Sakhnova and my illustrator, Billy Santoso, who brought to life the concepts of relationshift so perfectly. Thank you all for believing in my work and investing your capital, time, and talents to make it a reality.

Thanks to Gabriella Condarco for many conversations that contributed significantly to this book's concepts and for helpful feedback on nearly every page. And with a great example of this book's theme in action, I'm thankful that Gaby introduced me to Alex Gonzales, who provided intelligent insights that have improved this book in many ways. Thank you, Alex, for your contribution.

I would be nothing without my excellent associate Armaghan Adil. He assisted with countless aspects of the book, from organization to research to finding and setting up appointments with sources to getting all the details in place for submitting the final manuscript.

I want to extend my gratitude to those who have given their time and talent to reading and commenting on early versions of this book: Antonio Smith, Crystal Choi, Elizabeth Cunningham, Frank Coker, Jason Yan, Jesse Bauer, Keiron Nicholson, May Qiang, Nasrin Hassanlou, Oviya Thirumalai, Rachel Luoto, Sarah Hannan, Sasha Gordon, and Stephanie Sun.

And finally, I am sincerely grateful to all my mentors, teachers, family, and friends who have relationshifted me into the person I am today.

DEFINITIONS

Altruism

A regard for the well-being of others. Unlike the conventional definition, altruistic choices retain a degree of selfish motivation. The giver does so to receive something in return, such as affirmation, rewards in heaven, or assurance of the tribe's survival.

Attraction

The power or ability to gain interest or response from someone. The level of attraction between two people also affects how much they change each other.

Bilateral Relationship

A relationship that affects or involves two parties who know each other and invest a similar amount of energy or time into the relationship.

Bridge Relationship

A connection between two people who share few, if any, mutual links. Bridge networks provide access to the relations of other well-connected people.

Closed Network
A group of interconnected people that includes few outsiders. These networks are sometimes called a clique.

Conditioning
See *nurturing*.

Conscious Decisions
To be aware of the process of decision making, to more objectively consider one's options, and to minimize any subconscious impulses that may drive one to make a different choice.

Consciousness
A person's state of awareness of their existence, thoughts, and surroundings.

Direction
The desired life destination within a specific pillar of purpose.

DNA
The fundamental and distinctive characteristics or qualities of someone installed at conception. Similarities between two biologically related people like siblings can be attributed to DNA.

Domestication
See *nurturing*.

E-capital
What our evolutionary instincts drive us to accumulate for the purpose of surviving, multiplying, and improving ourselves and our species. By default, we are motivated to generate e-capital to varying degrees within six dimensions: safety, sex, acceptance, resources, influence, and novelty.

Evidence
The available body of facts or information indicating whether a belief or proposition is correct or valid. Evidence should be independently verifiable.

Evolutionary Instincts
The impulses we developed over millions of years. These have assured our survival and rise to dominance but are not necessarily helpful in our modern world.

Free Will
The ability to make choices without interference. Our free will within any given situation is affected by our worldview, which has been colored by past decisions and the people in our life.

Game of Life
Our approach to living. Natural impulses and societal pressures push us to obey subjective rules, but we can change these rules to better suit our desires through enlightenment.

Genes
Components of DNA responsible for passing some of a parent's traits to their offspring.

Goals
An objective, desired destination, or future state one can invest energy toward achieving.

Gradual (Incremental) Exposure
To slowly experience a new idea that our mental immune system otherwise would reject. This is one method by which we can change our worldview.

Healthy Versus Unhealthy Ideas
Morality is a societal construct. So, in many cases, beliefs should not be considered moral or immoral. Classify ideas as either healthy versus unhealthy or helpful versus unhelpful. This approach allows one to focus on whether or not a belief moves them toward or away from a desired state.

Helpfulness
The act of giving or being ready to assist or aid.

Heritability
The degree to which a trait is inherited from one's parents through genes (DNA).

Ignorance
The condition of being uneducated, unaware, or uninformed. This condition is exacerbated when one doesn't know what one doesn't know.

Influencer
A person who has the power to impact other people through public or private platforms, including social media, podcasts, blogs, or public speaking.

Inner Circle
A small group of mentors, peers, and protégés who most impact one's worldview and life course.

Instinct
Our natural tendencies and drivers. See *evolutionary instincts* for more.

Lens
See *worldview*.

Luck
Results that rely entirely on chance. Good and bad luck happen to everyone. We can make decisions that improve our luck as we move through life, but to avoid disappointment, we should avoid relying on things outside our control.

Magnetism
The level to which someone attracts the trust, attention, or desire of others.

Mental Immune System (aka Idea or Cognitive Immune System)
The feature of our brain that prevents us from accepting new ideas. Though in many ways this is essential to living, it also must be overcome to modify our worldview and expand our possibilities.

Mentor
An experienced or trusted teacher or guide. Someone who is on the same path as us within a specific pillar, but further along in the journey.

Mentoring
The practice of advising or guiding a protégé, child, student, or employee.

Networking
The process of building and maintaining relationships to achieve positive outcomes such as improving access to opportunities or expanding one's worldview.

Nurturing (aka Domestication or Conditioning)
The process by which we attempt to teach and control each other to improve an individual's or a tribe's ability to survive and multiply.

Objective Truth
An idea based on facts. The more evidence that exists from reliable and verifiable sources, the more objective we can consider a truth.

Open Network
A series of connections between people who are not highly interconnected. Those in open networks come and go more freely than occurs in closed networks.

Options
The possibilities we consider when we are making a choice.

Paralysis by Analysis
When someone is unable to move forward with a decision due to overanalyzing data or overthinking a problem.

Path
A specified course one aims to take through life.

Peer
A person who is heading in the same direction and is about as far along in the journey. The same person could be a peer in one pillar and a mentor in another.

Peer Pressure
The influence of a person or social group on an individual.

Pillars of Purpose
A dimension of ourselves that we intend to define an ideal future state and toward which we invest.

Plinko
One of the most popular games on *The Price Is Right*.

Plus/Minus Statistic
A sports statistic used to measure a player's impact on the game, represented by the difference between their team's total scoring versus their opponent's when the player is in the game.

Polarization
A specific type of glass that filters light based on the direction in which the light is vibrating. For instance, horizontally oriented polarization only allows horizontally vibrating light to pass through.

Precedent
An action or event in the past used as a guide for a current or future decision.

Protégé
A person we spend time with who we believe is heading in the same direction as us within a particular pillar but isn't as far along as we are.

Purpose
What guides our life, gives us direction, and helps us determine which relationships will help us get there.

Rapport
A sense of familiarity and commonality between people. Whether real or imagined, rapport develops a sense of shared tribal citizenship, which can cause people to want to trust and help each other.

Reality
What we perceive to be the platform on which we live. Many aspects of our reality are subjectively chosen, though we are often unaware of this.

Relationship Strength
The level of trust between people.

Resources
What we hope to accumulate, often at any cost, whether we need more or not. We do this to satisfy our natural impulse to generate e-capital, though we can let go of this instinct through enlightenment.

Rules of Life
A set of guidelines that society wants us to live by. These are not always helpful to us or our tribe. We can change or ignore many of the rules, adopting instead a way of living that better aligns with our vision.

Science
A system that relies on verifiable evidence as building blocks to form theories or suggest truth. Scientific thinking demands that we do not make assumptions or overinflate the objectiveness of that which has little to no proof.

Self-Awareness
Conscious understanding of one's character, feelings, motives, and desires.

Selfishness
Seeking or concentrating on one's advantage, pleasure, or well-being with little regard for others. This is a natural state for all life forms and, as such, shouldn't be vilified. But we should avoid selfishness when it begins to limit our happiness or progress toward a goal.

Shortcuts
A method or means of accomplishment that gets results faster. Some paths are sold as shortcuts when, in fact, they lead nowhere. A real shortcut must get someone to their desired destination more quickly or efficiently than other available options.

Social Capital
The value one can derive from their relationships.

Societal Code
A set of standards that are followed by a group of people or community.

Spectrum
A measurable trait that varies incrementally from one extreme to another.

Strong Relationship
A connection built on high levels of trust.

Subconscious Decisions
We make these when we aren't aware of the process used or the instincts behind evaluating our options.

Subjective Truth
An idea based on one's belief, feelings, or perspective when little verifiable evidence or agreement exists among experts on the subject.

Transformational Gravity
The power someone has to relationshift you, for better or worse. Some people can help you get much closer to your goals than others, while others have a greater ability to pull you further away from your goals. This can also be referred to simply as one's gravity.

Tribe
Traditionally this was a group of fifty to one hundred people, often consisting of related families, who lived with each other for companionship and to improve their mutual chances of survival. In our modern world, large tribes still exist in many parts of the world. Yet, regardless of whether or not we are part of a cultural tribe, most of us still perceive tribal membership in the same way our ancestors did. Today, however, the perception is based not on living together but the sharing of abstract or tangible commonalities.

Trust
Belief in the reliability of someone. We convert the sharing of personal information, demonstrated performance, and length of mutual history into trust.

Type II Chaotic System
When we can't predict how an outcome would be affected by different past decisions because our options and the way we see them are altered by each previous choice.

Unconscious Mind
Scientists denote a difference between subconscious and unconscious thinking, but this book refers to both as subconscious for the sake of simplicity.

Unilateral Relationship
A one-sided relationship where an influencer shares information with many, and many people know or trust them in return. Those who follow an influencer don't know them personally but can sometimes feel a sense of trust or friendship similar to what they feel in bilateral connections. Other examples include authors, politicians, and thought leaders of the past.

Venn Diagram
A diagram that uses two or more overlapping circles to show the relationships among those dimensions.

Viral Ideas
A belief that passes rapidly from one person to another.

Weak Relationship
A connection that lacks high levels of trust. Weak relationships can be beneficial as they provide access to more people without the corresponding demands of time to maintain the relationships.

Worldview
The way we see our options and evaluate life.

ENDNOTES

3   **We change through relationships.** Goldfried, M. R., & Davila, J. (2005). The role of relationship and technique in therapeutic change. *Psychotherapy: Theory, Research, Practice, Training, 42*(4), 421.

16 **TV producers turned the story** Details about Eddy, Bobby, and David's stories included in this book were adapted in part from Wardle, T. (Director). (2018). *Three identical strangers* [Film]. Universal Pictures Home Entertainment.

17 **The twin study method** Galton, F. (1875). The history of twins, as a criterion of the relative powers of nature and nurture. *Fraser's Magazine, 12* (71), 566–576.

17 **Researchers frame the answer** Gazzaniga, M. S. (1992). *Nature's mind: The biological roots of thinking, emotions, sexuality, language, and intelligence*. Basic Books; Haldane, J. B. S. (1946). The interaction of nature and nurture. *Annals of Eugenics, 13*(1), 197–205; Kendler, K. S. (1993). Twin studies of psychiatric illness: Current status and future directions. *Archives of General Psychiatry, 50*(11), 905–915; Voracek, M., & Loibl, L. M. (2007). Genetics of suicide: A systematic review of twin studies. *Wiener Klinische Wochenschrift, 119*(15-16), 463–475.

18 **As we moved through** Qvortrup, J. (2000). Macroanalysis of childhood. *Research with Children: Perspectives and Practices*, 77–97.

19 **The impact people have on us** Stone, E. (1988). *Black sheep and kissing cousins: How our family stories shape us*. Transaction.

21 **At least ten varieties** Smithsonian National Museum of Natural History. (2021, March 13). *Human species.* https://humanorigins.si.edu/evidence/human-fossils/species.

21 **Humans are not unique** Rogers, L. J., & Kaplan, G. T. (2002). *Songs, roars, and rituals: Communication in birds, mammals, and other animals.* Harvard University Press.

21 **Soon we gained more advanced** McAnany, E. G. (2012). *Saving the world: A brief history of communication for development and social change.* University of Illinois Press.

21 **Yet, we are largely** Ellison, P. T., & Ellison, P. T. (2009). *On fertile ground: A natural history of human reproduction.* Harvard University Press; Wade, N. (2015). *A troublesome inheritance: Genes, race and human history.* Penguin.

21 **So our dominance as a species** Harari, Y. N. (2018). *Sapiens: A brief history of humankind* (illustrated ed.). Harper Perennial.

22 **Since your first breath,** Leach, H. M. (2003). Human domestication reconsidered. *Current Anthropology, 44*(3), 349–368.

22 **This programming process,** Bednarik, R. G. (2020). *The domestication of humans.* Routledge.

22 **is uncomfortably similar to** Brüne, M. (2007). On human self-domestication, psychiatry, and eugenics. *Philosophy, Ethics, and Humanities in Medicine, 2*(1), 21.

22 **In fact, over thousands of years,** Diamond, J. (2002). Evolution, consequences and future of plant and animal domestication. *Nature, 418*(6898), 700–707.

22 **Pruning plants is another form** Ross-Ibarra, J., Morrell, P. L., & Gaut, B. S. (2007). Plant domestication, a unique opportunity to identify the genetic basis of adaptation. *Proceedings of the National Academy of Sciences, 104*(Suppl. 1), 8641–8648.

22 **For many millennia,** Clear, J. (2018). *Atomic habits: An easy & proven way to build good habits & break bad ones* (illustrated ed.). Avery.

22 **Studies have shown how** Robinson, E., Tobias, T., Shaw, L., Freeman, E., & Higgs, S. (2011). Social matching of food intake and the need for social acceptance. *Appetite, 56*(3), 747–752.

22 **In one, researchers showed** Ashe, S. E. (1951). Effects of group pressure on the modification and distortion of judgments. In H. Guetzkow (Ed.), *Groups, leadership and men: Research in human relations* (pp. 177–190). Rutgers University Press.

22	**In another study, researchers quizzed**	Gladwell, M. (2005). *Blink: The power of thinking without thinking.* Little, Brown.
23	**This is peer pressure in action.**	Rosenberg, T. (2011). *Join the club: How peer pressure can transform the world.* W. W. Norton.
23	**Many religions and cults forbid**	Library of Congress. (2015). *Prohibition of interfaith marriage.* https://www.loc.gov/law/help/marriage/interfaith-prohibition.php.
23	**Some cults go as far as**	Stein, A. (2016). *Terror, love and brainwashing: Attachment in cults and totalitarian systems* (1st ed.). Routledge.
23	**Fortunately, we don't pick up**	Falk, A., & Ichino, A. (2003). Clean evidence on peer pressure. *Available at SSRN 391701.*
23	**Research shows that our peers**	Clasen, D. R., & Brown, B. B. (1985). The multidimensionality of peer pressure in adolescence. *Journal of Youth and Adolescence, 14*(6), 451–468.
23	**Having athletic friends can help**	Galuska, D. A. (1999). Are health care professionals advising obese patients to lose weight? *JAMA, 282*(16), 1576. https://doi.org/10.1001/jama.282.16.1576.
23	**a little bitterness goes a long way**	Baumeister, R. F., Vohs, K. D., & Tice, D. M. (2007). The strength model of self-control. *Current Directions in Psychological Science, 16*(6), 351–355. https://doi.org/10.1111/j.1467-8721.2007.00534.x.
23	**Academics have shown that**	Jauch, L. R., Osborn, R. N., & Glueck, W. F. (1980). Short term financial success in large business organizations: The environment-strategy connection. *Strategic Management Journal, 1*(1), 49–63. https://doi.org/10.1002/smj.4250010106.
24	**Humans use many tools**	Wentzel, K. R. (2003). Motivating students to behave in socially competent ways. *Theory into Practice, 42*(4), 319–326.
24	**In *The Communist Manifesto*, Karl Marx teaches**	Marx, Karl. (1996). *The Communist Manifesto.* Pluto Press. (Original work published 1848.)
24	**George Orwell wrote *Animal Farm***	Orwell, G. (1996). *Animal Farm.* Signet Classics.
26	**The stats on teenage pregnancy**	Gaudie, J., Mitrou, F., Lawrence, D., Stanley, F. J., Silburn, S. R., & Zubrick, S. R. (2010). Antecedents of teenage pregnancy from a 14-year follow-up study using data linkage. *BMC Public Health, 10*(1), 63.
26	**Fewer than half of adolescent parents**	Gyan, C. (2013). The effects of teenage pregnancy on the educational attainment of girls at Chorkor, a suburb of Accra. *Journal of Educational and Social Research, 3*(3), 53.

26 **Two out of three families** Cunnington, A. J. (2001). What's so bad about teenage pregnancy?. *BMJ Sexual & Reproductive Health, 27*(1), 36–41; *11 Facts About Teen Pregnancy*. (n.d.). DoSomething.Org. https://www.dosomething.org/us/facts/11-facts-about-teen-pregnancy.

26 **More than five hundred American teenagers** US Centers for Disease Control and Prevention (2021, November 15). *About teen pregnancy*. https://www.cdc.gov/teenpregnancy/about/index.htm.

26 **Internationally, that number rises** Darroch, J., Woog, V., Bankole, A., & Ashford, L. S. (2016). *Adding it up: Costs and benefits of meeting the contraceptive needs of adolescents*. Guttmacher Institute.

27 **And in the final 25 percent,** US Census Bureau (2020, May 13). *Custodial mothers and fathers and their child support: 2017*. Author. https://www.census.gov/library/publications/2020/demo/p60-269.html.

27 **During many decisions, our subconscious** Fülöp, J. (2005, November). Introduction to decision making methods. In *BDEI-3 workshop, Washington* (pp. 1–15).

30 **Many people believe college is** Reid, K. (2005). The causes, views and traits of school absenteeism and truancy: An analytical review. *Research in Education, 74*(1), 59–82.

30 **Programs or options may be available** Strand, M. A. S. (2014). "School—no thanks—it ain't my thing": Accounts for truancy. Students' perspectives on their truancy and school lives. *International Journal of Adolescence and Youth, 19*(2), 262–277.

30 **Not only does relationshift** Adler, P. S., & Kwon, S. W. (2000). Social capital: The good, the bad, and the ugly. *Knowledge and social capital, 89*.

32 **The human system is what** Liang, Q., & Mendel, J. M. (2000). Interval type-2 fuzzy logic systems: Theory and design. *IEEE Transactions on Fuzzy Systems, 8*(5), 535–550.

33 **We tend to make big improvements** Hardy, D. (2012). *The compound effect*. Vanguard Press.

38 **They were, of course, the Beastie Boys.** Details about the Beastie Boys included in this book were adapted in part from the following sources: Diamond, M., & Horovitz, A. (2018). *Beastie Boys book* (illustrated ed.). Random House; Hess, M. (2005). Hip-hop realness and the white performer. *Critical Studies in Media Communication, 22*(5), 372–389.

39 **You could dress flamboyantly** O'Brien, L. (2014). Not a piece of meat: Lady Gaga and that dress. Has radical feminism survived the journey?. In *Lady Gaga and popular music* (pp. 35–51). Routledge.

40   **No basketball team had ever**   Basketball-Reference.Com. *2016 NBA finals—Cavaliers vs. Warriors.* Retrieved December 11, 2021. https://www.basketball-reference.com/playoffs/2016-nba-finals-cavaliers-vs-warriors.html.

41   **As one negative example,**   Eisold, K. (2011, August 18). Understanding why people riot. *Psychology Today.* https://www.psychologytoday.com/us/blog/hidden-motives/201108/understanding-why-people-riot.

44   **The most outstanding leaders**   Rashid, B. (2017, May 2). 3 reasons all great leaders have mentors (and mentees). *Forbes.* https://www.forbes.com/sites/brianrashid/2017/05/02/3-reasons-all-great-leaders-have-mentors-and-mentees/?sh=293fcc413f9d.

44   **And those entrepreneurs who**   Taskdone. (2019, August 20). The coach behind Steve Jobs, Eric Schmidt, and Bill Gates. *Taskdone.* https://www.taskdonehq.com/2019/08/20/increase-productivity-with-the-help-of-an-accountability-coach/.

46   **Humans developed an intense instinct**   Richerson, P. J., & Boyd, R. (2001). The evolution of subjective commitment to groups: A tribal instincts hypothesis. *Evolution and the Capacity for Commitment, 3,* 186–220.

46   **You must become a member**   Junger, S. (2016). *Tribe: On homecoming and belonging.* Twelve.

48   **For instance, one reason**   Lovett, I., & Levy, R. (2020, February 8). The Mormon church amassed $100 billion. It was the best-kept secret in the investment world. *Wall Street Journal.* https://www.wsj.com/articles/the-mormon-church-amassed-100-billion-it-was-the-best-kept-secret-in-the-investment-world-11581138011.

48   **Mormons feel a sense of pride**   The Church of Jesus Christ of Latter-Day Saints. (n.d.). *Men's divine roles and responsibilities.* https://www.churchofjesuschrist.org/study/manual/eternal-marriage-student-manual/mens-divine-roles-and-responsibilities.

49   **We can use these principles**   Kingma, L. (2009). *What's your tribe?: An enneagram guide to human types at work and play.* Juta.

50   **Tully's on Main earned**   Blaney, J. (2015). *Famously helpful: The surprising results of flipping self-promotion, hype and marketing upside down.* Inkliss.

51   **In the back of a book**   Misner, I., & Hilliard, B. (2017). *Networking like a pro: Turning contacts into connections* (2nd ed.). Entrepreneur Press.

59   **Researchers have long wondered**   Details about the Jewish diamond trade in New York City were derived from multiple sources including

Coleman, J. S. (1988). Social capital in the creation of human capital. *American Journal of Sociology, 94,* S95–S120; Richman, B. D. (2006). How community institutions create economic advantage: Jewish diamond merchants in New York. In *The Global Diamond Industry* (pp. 44–86). Palgrave Macmillan; Berger, R., & Herstein, R. (2012). The limits of guanxi from the perspective of the Israeli diamond industry. *Journal of Chinese Economic and Foreign Trade Studies* 5(1), doi:10.1108/1754440121 1197940.

60 **Researchers have been studying** Portes, A. (1998). Social capital: Its origins and applications in modern sociology. *Annual Review of Sociology, 24*(1), 1–24.

60 **They mostly have focused on** Sandefur, R. L., & Laumann, E. O. (1998). A paradigm for social capital. *Rationality and Society, 10*(4), 481–501; Edelman, L. F., Bresnen, M., Newell, S., Scarbrough, H., & Swan, J. (2004). The benefits and pitfalls of social capital: Empirical evidence from two organizations in the United Kingdom. *British Journal of Management, 15*(S1), 59–69.

60 **Other benefits discovered include** Adler, P. S., & Kwon, S. W. (2002). Social capital: Prospects for a new concept. *Academy of Management Review, 27*(1), 17–40.

61 **New York's Diamond District** Lin, N. (1999). Building a network theory of social capital. *Connections, 22*(1), 28–51.

61 **The more closed a structure is,** Clawson, L. (2005). "Everybody knows him": Social networks in the life of a small contractor in Alabama. *Ethnography, 6*(2), 237–264.

62 **Some kinds of networks enjoy** Stolle, D., & Rochon, T. R. (1998). Are all associations alike? Member diversity, associational type, and the creation of social capital. *American Behavioral Scientist, 42*(1), 47–65.

62 **The opposite of a closed network** Walker, G., Kogut, B., & Shan, W. (1997). Social capital, structural holes and the formation of an industry network. *Organization Science, 8*(2), 109–125.

63 **Open networks are ideal** Nahapiet, J., & Ghoshal, S. (1998). Social capital, intellectual capital, and the organizational advantage. *Academy of Management Review, 23*(2), 242–266.

63 **A person who builds** Burt, R. S. (2002). The social capital of structural holes. *The New Economic Sociology: Developments in an Emerging Field, 148*(90), 122; Tan, J., Zhang, H., & Wang, L. (2015). Network closure or

structural hole? The conditioning effects of network-level social capital on innovation performance. *Entrepreneurship Theory and Practice, 39*(5), 1189–1212.

65 **Often referred to in academic literature** Parks-Yancy, R., DiTomaso, N., & Post, C. (2009). How does tie strength affect access to social capital resources for the careers of working and middle class African-Americans? *Critical Sociology, 35*(4), 541–563. https://doi.org/10.1177/0896920509103983.

65 **Given time's finiteness, the number** Friedkin, N. (1980). A test of structural features of Granovetter's strength of weak ties theory. *Social Networks, 2*(4), 411–422.

65 **Inversely, creating and maintaining** Granovetter, M. S. (1973). The strength of weak ties. *American Journal of Sociology, 78*(6), 1360–1380.

65 **Seven dimensions contribute to** Gilbert, E., & Karahalios, K. (2009). Predicting tie strength with social media. In D. R. Olsen & R. B. Arthur (Chairs), *Proceedings of the 27th International Conference on Human Factors in Computing Systems—CHI 09* (pp. 211–220). Association for Computing Machinery. https://doi.org/10.1145/1518701.1518736.

66 **the frequency of requests** Blaney, J. R. (2015). *Innovation and influence: How individuals and organizations make use of multiple network structures to increase creativity and diffusion* [Unpublished doctoral dissertation]. University of Maryland University College.

66 **This constricts our number** Baker, W., & Dutton, J. E. (2007). Enabling positive social capital in organizations. In J. E. Dutton & B. R. Ragins (Eds.), *Exploring positive relationships at work: Building a theoretical and research foundation* (pp. 325–346). Psychology Press.

67 **How we approach building** Yli-Renko, H., Autio, E., & Sapienza, H. J. (2001). Social capital, knowledge acquisition, and knowledge exploitation in young technology-based firms. *Strategic Management Journal, 22*(6–7), 587–613.

68 **He shouted that they had** Logan Paul hosts Dubai's biggest-ever meet-and-greet. (2017). *ITP*. https://itp.live/content/1343-logan-paul-breaks-the-world-record-for-the-biggest-meet-and-greet-in-dubai.

69 **Many businesses today prefer to** Ladhari, R., Massa, E., & Skandrani, H. (2020). YouTube vloggers' popularity and influence: The roles of homophily, emotional attachment, and expertise. *Journal of Retailing and Consumer Services, 54*, 102027.

69 **The difference comes down to trust.** Blaney, J., & Fleming, K. (2020). *Will post for profit: How brands and influencers are cashing in on social media.* Post Hill Press.

69 **As the case of Logan Paul illustrates,** Chapple, C., & Cownie, F. (2017). An investigation into viewers' trust in and response towards disclosed paid-for-endorsements by YouTube lifestyle vloggers. *Journal of Promotional Communications, 5*(2).

69 **When an author, vlogger,** Marôpo, L., Jorge, A., & Tomaz, R. (2020). "I felt like I was really talking to you!": Intimacy and trust among teen vloggers and followers in Portugal and Brazil. *Journal of Children and Media, 14*(1), 22–37.

70 **Unilateral relationships are responsible** Scheer, L. K., & Stern, L. W. (1992). The effect of influence type and performance outcomes on attitude toward the influencer. *Journal of Marketing Research, 29*(1), 128–142.

70 **When we come to trust someone** Lou, C., & Yuan, S. (2019). Influencer marketing: How message value and credibility affect consumer trust of branded content on social media. *Journal of Interactive Advertising, 19*(1), 58–73.

71 **When we add unilateral** Blaney, J. R. (2015). *Innovation and influence: How individuals and organizations make use of multiple network structures to increase creativity and diffusion* [Unpublished doctoral dissertation]. University of Maryland University College.

79 **Long before he became** Details about Frederick Douglass's life were adapted from several sources, including Douglass, F. (2018). *Narrative of the life of Frederick Douglass.* CreateSpace Independent Publishing Platform; and Blight, D. W. (2020). *Frederick Douglass: Prophet of freedom* (reprint ed.). Simon & Schuster.

83 **The best managers see** Townsend, K., Wilkinson, A., & Burgess, J. (2014). Routes to partial success: Collaborative employment relations and employee engagement. *International Journal of Human Resource Management, 25*(6), 915–930.

84 **Many experts who study** Kaufman, S. B. (2018, March 1). *The role of luck in life success is far greater than we realized.* Scientific American Blog Network. Retrieved February 7, 2022, from https://blogs.scientificamerican.com/beautiful-minds/the-role-of-luck-in-life-success-is-far-greater-than-we-realized/.

87 **For most of us,** Stephney, S. (2015, October 19). *Why are parents such a powerful agent of socialization?* Ministry of Education, Guyana. https://www.education.gov.gy/web/index.php/parenting-tips/item/1752-why-are-parents-such-a-powerful-agent-of-socialization.

88 **Make the most of these** Raboteg-Saric, Z., & Sakic, M. (2014). Relations of parenting styles and friendship quality to self-esteem, life satisfaction and happiness in adolescents. *Applied Research in Quality of Life,* 9(3), 749–765; Dubow, E. F., Boxer, P., & Huesmann, L. R. (2009). Long-term effects of parents' education on children's educational and occupational success: Mediation by family interactions, child aggression, and teenage aspirations. *Merrill-Palmer Quarterly,* 55(3), 224.

90 **Counselors are a gift.** Eisenberg, D., Golberstein, E., & Hunt, J. B. (2009). Mental health and academic success in college. *The BE Journal of Economic Analysis & Policy,* 9(1).

90 **If you've attempted therapy** Luborsky, L., McLellan, A. T., Woody, G. E., O'Brien, C. P., & Auerbach, A. (1985). Therapist success and its determinants. *Archives of General Psychiatry,* 42(6), 602–611.

91 **As with managers, you should** Bozionelos, N. (2004). Mentoring provided: Relation to mentor's career success, personality, and mentoring received. *Journal of Vocational Behavior,* 64(1), 24–46.

91 **Studies prove that church attendance** Hallowell, B. (2016, October 5). Researchers explored more than 1,100 church budgets—and here's what they discovered. *Deseret News.* https://www.deseret.com/2016/10/5/20597502/researchers-explored-more-than-1-100-church-budgets-and-here-s-what-they-discovered.

92 **A good mentor would love** Goldner, L., & Mayseless, O. (2009). The quality of mentoring relationships and mentoring success. *Journal of Youth and Adolescence,* 38(10), 1339; Young, C. Y., & Wright, J. V. (2001). Mentoring: The components for success. *Journal of Instructional Psychology,* 28(3), 202; Jacobi, M. (1991). Mentoring and undergraduate academic success: A literature review. *Review of Educational Research,* 61(4), 505–532; Crisp, G. (2010). The impact of mentoring on the success of community college students. *Review of Higher Education,* 34(1), 39–60.

93 **A romantic partner's advice frequently** Ocampo, A. C. G., Restubog, S. L. D., Liwag, M. E., Wang, L., & Petelczyc, C. (2018). My spouse is my strength: Interactive effects of perceived organizational and spousal

support in predicting career adaptability and career outcomes. *Journal of Vocational Behavior, 108*, 165–177; Murphy, J. K., Williamson, D. A., Buxton, A. E., Moody, S. C., Absher, N., & Warner, M. (1982). The long-term effects of spouse involvement upon weight loss and maintenance. *Behavior Therapy, 13*(5), 681–693.

97 **We receive different kinds of support** Goodenow, C., & Grady, K. E. (1993). The relationship of school belonging and friends' values to academic motivation among urban adolescent students. *Journal of Experimental Education, 62*(1), 60–71.

98 **Without force pushing a person** Slim, A., Heileman, G. L., Kozlick, J., & Abdallah, C. T. (2014, December). Predicting student success based on prior performance. In *2014 IEEE Symposium on Computational Intelligence and Data Mining (CIDM)* (pp. 410–415). IEEE.

100 **People are great at sniffing** Gersick, C. J. G., Dutton, J. E., & Bartunek, J. M. (2000). Learning from academia: The importance of relationships in professional life. *Academy of Management Journal, 43*(6), 1026–1044. https://doi.org/10.5465/1556333.

104 **One must have off-the-charts self-discipline** La Place, J. P. (1954). Personality and its relationship to success in professional baseball. *Research Quarterly. American Association for Health, Physical Education and Recreation, 25*(3), 313–319.

104 **In this way, all great athletes** Guenzi, P., & Ruta, D. (2013). *Leading teams: Tools and techniques for successful team leadership from the sports world.* John Wiley & Sons.

105 **Saban's teams have won** Hildebrandt, A., & Marr, J. (2020). Nick Saban—a case study for recruitment methods and application of Tuckman's model of team development. *Global Journal of Business Pedagogy, 4*(1), 214.

107 **Simply stated, we survive by** Miyazawa, H., & Aulehla, A. (2018). Revisiting the role of metabolism during development. *Development, 145*(19), dev131110.

107 **If we don't give our body** Georgieff, M. K., Ramel, S. E., & Cusick, S. E. (2018). Nutritional influences on brain development. *Acta Paediatrica, 107*(8), 1310–1321.

108 **Nutritionists can help you understand** Adamski, M., Gibson, S., Leech, M., & Truby, H. (2018). Are doctors nutritionists? What is the role of doctors in providing nutrition advice?.

111 **The higher paid or more** Granovetter, M. (2018). *Getting a job: A study of contacts and careers*. University of Chicago Press.

111 **Yet, in the end,** Galaka, M. (2019). Networking: the strength of weak ties and the medici effect.

116 **If you know the story** Nanos, J., (2022). *Good Will Hunting: An Oral History*. [online] *Boston Magazine*. Available at: https://www.bostonmagazine.com/arts-entertainment/2013/01/02/good-will-hunting-oral-history/ [Accessed March 4, 2022].

120 **If you want to become wealthy** Fagereng, A., Holm, M. B., Moll, B., & Natvik, G. (2019). *Saving behavior across the wealth distribution: The importance of capital gains* (No. w26588). National Bureau of Economic Research.

142 **When he returned to civilization,** This story is based on a number of sources including the following: History.com Editors (2020, July 22). *Buddhism*. https://www.history.com/topics/religion/buddhism#section_11; Przyluski, J. (1934). Origin and development of Buddhism. *Journal of Theological Studies*, 35(140), 337–351; Sarao, K. T. S. (2010). *Origin and nature of ancient Indian Buddhism*. Munshiram Manoharlal.

143 **Today, five hundred million Buddhists** Johnson, T. M., & Grim, B. J. (2013). *The world's religions in figures: An introduction to international religious demography*. Hoboken, NJ: Wiley-Blackwell.

146 **Yet, these instincts are** O'Connor, L. E., Berry, J. W., Lewis, T., Mulherin, K., & Crisostomo, P. S. (2007). Empathy and depression: The moral system on overdrive. In T. Farrow & P. Woodruff (Eds.), *Empathy in mental illness* (pp. 49–75). Cambridge University Press.

147 **From the very first time** Dawkins, R. (2016). *The extended selfish gene* (4th ed.). Oxford University Press.

147 **For instance, harmful bacteria** Drexler. M. (2010). *What you need to know about infectious disease*. National Academies Press.

147 **So, despite possessing the world's** Paula, A. J., Hwang, G., & Koo, H. (2020). Dynamics of bacterial population growth in biofilms resemble spatial and structural aspects of urbanization. *Nature Communications*, 11(1), 1. https://doi.org/10.1038/s41467-020-15165-4.

147 **Humans have been expanding** Simberloff, D. (1996, January). [Review of the book *Extinction rates*, by J. H. Lawton & R. M. May]. *Journal of Evolutionary Biology*, 9(1), 124–126. https://doi.org/10.1046/j.1420-9101.1996.t01-1-9010124.x; Estes, J. A., et al. (2011). Trophic downgrading of planet earth.

Science, 333(6040), 301–306. https://doi.org/10.1126/science.1205106; Tilman, D. (1999). Global environmental impacts of agricultural expansion: The need for sustainable and efficient practices. *Proceedings of the National Academy of Sciences, 96*(11), 5995–6000. https://doi.org/10.1073/pnas.96.11.5995; PETA. (2020, May 1). *Factory farming: Misery for animals.* https://www.peta.org/issues/animals-used-for-food/factory-farming/.

148 **The goals of the game** Buck, R. (1985). Prime theory: An integrated view of motivation and emotion. *Psychological Review, 92*(3), 389; Hart, D., & Sussman, R. W. (2008). *Man the hunted: Primates, predators, and human evolution.* Westview Press.

148 **And within each species is** James, P. (2006). *Globalism, nationalism, tribalism: Bringing theory back in.* Pine Forge Press.

148 **I call this *evolutionary capital*,** James, P. (2006). *Globalism, nationalism, tribalism: Bringing theory back in.* Pine Forge Press.

149 **See *12 Rules for Life*** Peterson, J. B. (2018). *12 rules for life: An antidote to chaos* (illustrated ed.). Random House Canada.

149 **There are three components** Aunger, R., & Curtis, V. (2013). The anatomy of motivation: An evolutionary-ecological approach. *Biological Theory, 8*(1), 49–63.

149 **Our conscious mind is capable** Kantor, J. R. (1920). A functional interpretation of human instincts. *Psychological Review, 27*(1), 50.

149 **They act like three** Tooby, J., Cosmides, L., Sell, A., Lieberman, D., & Sznycer, D. (2008). Internal regulatory variables and the design of human motivation: A computational and evolutionary approach. *Handbook of approach and avoidance motivation, 15,* 251.

150 **The folks who didn't get** Bernard, L. C., Mills, M., Swenson, L., & Walsh, R. P. (2005). An evolutionary theory of human motivation. *Genetic, Social, and General Psychology Monographs, 131*(2), 129–184.

152 **We want to spread** Ehrlichman, H., & Eichenstein, R. (1992). Private wishes: Gender similarities and differences. *Sex Roles: A Journal of Research, 26*(9–10), 399–422. https://doi.org/10.1007/BF00291551.

152 **We compel ourselves to innovate,** Emmons, R. A. (2005). Striving for the sacred: Personal goals, life meaning, and religion. *Journal of Social Issues, 61*(4), 731–745.

153 **Though all organisms share** Dutton, D. (2009). *The art instinct: Beauty, pleasure, & human evolution.* Oxford University Press.

153 **Humans in particular utilize** Maslow, A. H. (1958). A dynamic theory of human motivation. In C. L. Stacey & M. DeMartino (Eds.),

Understanding human motivation (pp. 26–47). Howard Allen Publishers. https://doi.org/10.1037/11305-004.

153 **— sex,** Bauman, Z. (1998). On postmodern uses of sex. *Theory, Culture & Society, 15*(3–4), 19–33.

153 **— acceptance,** Ferguson, E. D. (1989). Adler's motivational theory: An historical perspective on belonging and the fundamental human striving. *Individual Psychology, 45*(3), 354.

153 **— resources,** Neave, N., Jackson, R., Saxton, T., & Hönekopp, J. (2015). The influence of anthropomorphic tendencies on human hoarding behaviours. *Personality and Individual Differences, 72,* 214–219.

153 **— influence,** Markey, R., Ravenswood, K., Webber, D. J., & Knudsen, H. (2013). Influence at work and the desire for more influence. *Journal of Industrial Relations, 55*(4), 507–526.

153 **— and novelty.** Pearson, P. H. (1970). Relationships between global and specified measures of novelty seeking. *Journal of Consulting and Clinical Psychology, 34*(2), 199.

155 **Sex sells, but fear sells even better.** Wildavsky, A. B. (1988). *Searching for safety* (Vol. 10). Transaction.

155 **If you choose the smallest dog** Harleman, J. (2019, May 16). Where do small dogs come from? *The Dog People by Rover.Com.* https://www.rover.com/blog/small-dogs-origin-2/.

155 **Fear has been so effective** Bauman, Z. (2013). *Community: Seeking safety in an insecure world.* Wiley.

156 **We seek out fears** Berkowitz, R. L., Coplan, J. D., Reddy, D. P., & Gorman, J. M. (2007). The human dimension: How the prefrontal cortex modulates the subcortical fear response. *Reviews in the Neurosciences, 18*(3–4), 191–208.

158 **Any number of fears can** Keller Institute (2015, February 16). *Learn how to embrace your fears.* https://www.kellerinstitute.com/content/embrace-your-fears.

158 **In this game of life** Aztec Animal Clinic (2016, August 24). *Dominance, alpha, and pack leadership—What does it really mean?* https://www.aztecanimalclinic.com/resources/pet-care-library/canine/dominance-alpha-pack-leadership-really-mean/; Lippa, R. A. (2009). Sex differences in sex drive, sociosexuality, and height across 53 nations: Testing evolutionary and social structural theories. *Archives of Sexual Behavior, 38*(5), 631–651; Sefcek, J. A., Brumbach, B. H., Vasquez, G., & Miller, G. F. (2007). The evolutionary psychology of human mate choice. *Journal of*

Psychology & Human Sexuality, 18(2–3), 125–182. https://doi.org/10.1300/j056v18n02_05.

159 **However, one factor that** Baumeister, R. F. (2004). Gender and erotic plasticity: Sociocultural influences on the sex drive. *Sexual and relationship therapy, 19*(2), 133–139; Beach, F. A. (1965). *Sex and behavior.* Wiley; Sallee, D. T., & Casciani, J. M. (1976). Relationship between sex drive and sexual frustration and purpose in life. *Journal of Clinical Psychology, 32*(2), 273–275.

160 **Some value money more** Kenrick, D. T., Keefe, R. C., Bryan, A., Barr, A., & Brown, S. (1995). Age preferences and mate choice among homosexuals and heterosexuals: A case for modular psychological mechanisms. *Journal of Personality and Social Psychology, 69*(6), 1166–1172. https://doi.org/10.1037/0022-3514.69.6.1166; Stulp, G., Buunk, A. P., & Pollet, T. V. (2013). Women want taller men more than men want shorter women. *Personality and Individual Differences, 54*(8), 877–883. https://doi.org/10.1016/j.paid.2012.12.019; Wang, G., Cao, M., Sauciuvenaite, J., Bissland, R., Hacker, M., Hambly, C., Vaanholt, L. M., Niu, C., Faries, M. D., & Speakman, J. R. (2018). Different impacts of resources on opposite sex ratings of physical attractiveness by males and females. *Evolution and Human Behavior, 39*(2), 220–225. https://doi.org/10.1016/j.evolhumbehav.2017.12.008.

161 **Every person alive has** Baumeister, R. F., & Leary, M. R. (1995). The need to belong: Desire for interpersonal attachments as a fundamental human motivation. *Psychological Bulletin, 117*(3), 497; Davidson, L., & Stayner, D. (1997). Loss, loneliness, and the desire for love: Perspectives on the social lives of people with schizophrenia. *Psychiatric Rehabilitation Journal, 20*(3), 3; Baumeister, R. F., & Leary, M. R. (1995). The need to belong: Desire for interpersonal attachments as a fundamental human motivation. *Psychological Bulletin, 117*(3), 497.

161 **This evidence was enough** Blumberg, J. (2007, October 23). A brief history of the Salem Witch Trials. *Smithsonian.* https://www.smithsonianmag.com/history/a-brief-history-of-the-salem-witch-trials-175162489/.

162 **Yet cults persist** Singer, M. T., & Lalich, J. (1995). *Cults in our midst.* Jossey-Bass.

162 **For example, devout QAnon follower** Hayes, C. (2021, September 10). California QAnon follower indicted on charges of killing his 2 kids

with speargun in Mexico. *USA Today*. Retrieved February 26, 2022, from https://www.usatoday.com/story/news/nation/2021/09/09/california-qanon-indictment-charges-children-killings-mexico/8266562002/.

162 **Perhaps the most remarkable** Coltheart, M. (2007). Cognitive neuropsychiatry and delusional belief. *Quarterly Journal of Experimental Psychology (2006)*, 60(8), 1041–1062.

162 **If you need proof** Fisher, M. (2010, February 1). "The Shining" = confession to moon landing hoax. *The Atlantic*. https://www.theatlantic.com/culture/archive/2010/02/the-shining-confession-to-moon-landing-hoax/341407/.

164 **We can develop additional masks** Kelley, R. L., Osborne, W. J., & Hendrick, C. (1974). Role-taking and role-playing in human communication. *Human Communication Research*, 1(1), 62–74.

164 **Above almost anything else,** Burger, J. M. (1984). Desire for control, locus of control, and proneness to depression. *Journal of Personality*, 52(1), 71–89.

165 **We want to control our emotions,** Hornsey, M. J., Greenaway, K. H., Harris, E. A., & Bain, P. G. (2018). Exploring cultural differences in the extent to which people perceive and desire control. *Personality and Social Psychology Bulletin*, 45(1), 81–92. https://doi.org/10.1177/0146167218780692.

166 **Examples of our insatiable desire** Rindfleisch, A., Burroughs, J. E., & Wong, N. (2009). The safety of objects: Materialism, existential insecurity, and brand connection. *Journal of Consumer Research*, 36(1), 1–16; Briers, B., Pandelaere, M., Dewitte, S., & Warlop, L. (2006). Hungry for money: The desire for caloric resources increases the desire for financial resources and vice versa. *Psychological Science*, 17(11), 939–943.

166 **If you ask people why** Wansink, B. (2007). *Mindless eating: Why we eat more than we think*. Bantam.

166 **They could be eating to distract themselves** Mead, M. (2012). Why do we overeat? In C. Counihan & P. Van Esterik (Eds.), *Food and culture* (3rd ed., pp. 33–36). Routledge.

166 **We spend a lot of energy** Sadrieh, A., and Schröder, M. The desire to influence others (December 2012). FEMM Working Paper No. 12027. Available at SSRN: https://ssrn.com/abstract=2180760 or http://dx.doi.org/10.2139/ssrn.2180760.

168 **In a recent study,** Lane, L. (2019, May 5). Percentage of Americans who never traveled beyond the state where they were born? A

surprise. *Forbes.* https://www.forbes.com/sites/lealane/2019/05/02/percentage-of-americans-who-never-traveled-beyond-the-state-where-they-were-born-a-surprise/?sh=42678fff2898.

170 **Overcoming our inherited compulsions** Khantzian, E. J., & Mack, J. E. (1983). Self-preservation and the care of the self: Ego instincts reconsidered. *Psychoanalytic Study of the Child, 38*(1), 209–232.

173 **The country had long been isolated** Schmidt, C. (2012). As isolation ends, Myanmar faces new ecological risks. *Science, 337*(6096), 796–797, doi:10.1126/science.337.6096.796.

176 **Ideas are like viruses.** Dawkins, R. (1993). Viruses of the mind. In B. Dahlbom (Ed.), *Dennett and his critics: Demystifying mind* (pp. 13–27). Blackwell.

177 **Ideas are formed just as** Sawyer, R. K., & DeZutter, S. (2009). Distributed creativity: How collective creations emerge from collaboration. *Psychology of Aesthetics, Creativity, and the Arts, 3*(2), 81.

177 **Einstein's crowning achievement** Howell, E. (2019, August 15). The genius of Albert Einstein: His life, theories and impact on science. Space.com. https://www.space.com/15524-albert-einstein.html.

177 **More than two centuries earlier,** Thompson, H., & Havern, S. (n.d.). Gravity. *The Thompson home page.* https://web.stanford.edu/%7Ebuzzt/gravity.html?.

179 **And God certainly didn't pay** McMillan, B. R., & Price, M. J. (2003). *How much should we pay the pastor? A fresh look at clergy salaries in the 21st century.* Durham, NC: The Divinity School at Duke University Pulpit & Pew Report Series.

179 **(the average pastor earns** Payscale.com. (n.d.). Average salary for International Church of the Foursquare Gospel employees. Retrieved December 8, 2020, from https://www.payscale.com/research/US/Employer=International_Church_of_The_Foursquare_Gospel/Salary.

180 **Other viruses, like Pegivirus C,** Mathew, C. T. C. (2019). Not all viruses are bad for you. Here are some that can have a protective effect. *ScienceAlert.* https://www.sciencealert.com/not-all-viruses-are-bad-for-you-here-are-some-that-can-have-a-protective-effect.

180 **But 2,500 miles north** America's Health Rankings: Vermont. (2020). *America's Health Rankings.* https://www.americashealthrankings.org/explore/annual/measure/Health_Status/state/VT?edition-year=2020.

180	**Comparably strong correlations exist**	Gallup, Inc. (2020, August 31). *State of the States* [Dataset]. https://news.gallup.com/poll/125066/State-States.aspx.
180	**Rural, southern states are**	Graham, D. A. (2017, February 2). Progressive cities vs. conservative states. *The Atlantic.* https://www.theatlantic.com/magazine/archive/2017/03/red-state-blue-city/513857/.
180	**Some posit the reason for**	*The Economist* (2014, August 6). Urban ideologies. https://www.economist.com/graphic-detail/2014/08/04/urban-ideologies.
182	**All those nerds stuffed into**	Kenney, M., & Von Burg, U. (2000). Creating Silicon Valley. *Understanding Silicon Valley: The anatomy of an entrepreneurial region.* Stanford University Press.
184	**Some estimate as many as**	European wars of religion (2007, December 17). In Wikipedia. https://en.wikipedia.org/wiki/European_wars_of_religion.
184	**The variety of what constitutes sin**	Grey, M. (1994). Falling into freedom: Searching for new interpretations of sin in a secular society. *Scottish Journal of Theology, 47*(2), 223–244.
186	**This is why arguing**	Krugman, P. (2020). *Arguing with zombies: Economics, politics, and the fight for a better future.* W. W. Norton; Curtis, K. T., & Ellison, C. G. (2002). Religious heterogamy and marital conflict: Findings from the National Survey of Families and Households. *Journal of Family Issues, 23*(4), 551–576.
187	**But over time, the habit-forming**	Duhigg, C. (2014). *The power of habit: Why we do what we do in life and business.* Random House.
188	**Our lens is fashioned from**	Naugle, D. K. (2002). *Worldview: The history of a concept.* Eerdmans.
189	**In the same way**	Yzerbyt, V., Corneille, O., & Estrada, C. (2001). The interplay of subjective essentialism and entitativity in the formation of stereotypes. *Personality and Social Psychology Review, 5*(2), 141–155.
189	**In 1968, the famous**	Bandura, A., & Menlove, F. L. (1968). Factors determining vicarious extinction of avoidance behavior through symbolic modeling. *Journal of Personality and Social Psychology, 8*(2, Pt.1), 99–108. https://doi.org/10.1037/h0025260.
191	**If a polarized lens is tilted**	Ling, S. J., Sanny, J., & Moebs, W. (2016). Polarization. *University Physics Volume 3.*

191   **But gradual exposure to new ideas**   Boysen, G. A., & Vogel, D. L. (2008). Education and mental health stigma: The effects of attribution, biased assimilation, and attitude polarization. *Journal of Social and Clinical Psychology, 27*(5), 447–470; Doosje, B., Moghaddam, F. M., Kruglanski, A. W., De Wolf, A., Mann, L., & Feddes, A. R. (2016). Terrorism, radicalization and de-radicalization. *Current Opinion in Psychology, 11*, 79–84.

193   **The reality is that truth**   Dorsey, D. (2011). Objective morality, subjective morality and the explanatory question. *Journal of Ethics and Social Philosophy, 6*, 1–25.

198   **Researchers may disagree on**   Strawbridge, H. (2020, January 30). Going gluten-free just because? Here's what you need to know. *Harvard Health Blog*. https://www.health.harvard.edu/blog/going-gluten-free-just-because-heres-what-you-need-to-know-201302205916.

208   **Given her influence and impact,**   Details of Gertrude Bell's story have been adapted from Howell, G. (2008). *Gertrude Bell: Queen of the desert, shaper of nations*. Sarah Crichton Books; and Wallach, J. (1996). *Desert queen: The extraordinary life of Gertrude Bell, adventurer, adviser to kings, ally of Lawrence of Arabia*. Nan A. Talese/Doubleday.

213   **As part of my research for**   The books I consulted were: Guinness, O. (2018). *The call: Finding and fulfilling God's purpose for your life*. Thomas Nelson; Dolan, P. (2014). *Happiness by design: Finding pleasure and purpose in everyday life*. Penguin UK; Shetty, J. (2020). *Think like a monk: Train your mind for peace and purpose every day*. Simon & Schuster; Ekstrom, J. (2019). *Chasing the bright side: Embrace optimism, activate your purpose, and write your own story*. Thomas Nelson; Goff, B. (2020). *Dream big: Know what you want, why you want it, and what you're going to do about it*. Thomas Nelson; Raynor, J. (2020). *Master of one: Find and focus on the work you were created to do*. WaterBrook; Winfrey, O. (2020). *Oprah Winfrey 3 books collection set (The path made clear, What I know for sure, Words that matter)*. Bluebird/Macmillan USA/William Morrow; Schooler, J., & Kearns, K. (2019). *Find your purpose in 15 minutes: Your shortcut to a meaningful life*. BoomerMax; Brown, L. (2021). *The power of purpose: How to create the life you always wanted*. G&D Media; Kentgen, L. (2018). *An intentional life: Five foundations of authenticity and purpose* (1st ed.). Stryder; Losier, M. J. (2017). *Your life's purpose: Uncover what really fulfills you*. RosettaBooks; Young, B. (2020). *No passion or too many passions to focus on?: The secrets to find your passion and life purpose, find the one passion that you meant to work on your lifetime*. Author; Robinson, K. S., & Aronica, L. (2014). *Finding your element: How

to discover your talents and passions and transform your life (reprint ed.). Penguin; Heyland, R. (2020). *Live your purpose: A step by step guide on how to live your best life.* CI4life; Warren, R. (2013). *The purpose driven life: What on earth am I here for?* (10th anniversary ed.). Zondervan; Tolle, E. (2020). *Power of now, A new earth, and Practicing the power of now: 3 Books Collection Set.* New World Library/Penguin Random House; Strecher, V. J. (2016). *Life on purpose: How living for what matters most changes everything.* HarperOne; Sunfellow, D. (2019). *The purpose of life as revealed by near-death experiences from around the world.* Author; Millman, D. (2018). *The life you were born to live (Revised 25th anniversary edition): A guide to finding your life purpose.* HJ Kramer; Cole, A. (2020). *The purpose playbook: Design your life around what matters most.* Wise Ink Creative Publishing; Paquette, J. (2018). *The happiness toolbox: 56 practices to find happiness, purpose & productivity in love, work and life.* PESI.

224 **Research shows that this is** Craske, M. G., Treanor, M., Conway, C. C., Zbozinek, T., & Verviliet, B. (2014). Maximizing exposure therapy: An inhibitory learning approach. *Behaviour research and therapy, 58,* 10–23.

242 **You don't have to believe** Allen, P. M., Edwards, J. A., & McCullough, W. (2015). Does karma exist? Buddhism, social cognition, and the evidence for karma. *International Journal for the Psychology of Religion, 25*(1), 1–17; Obeyesekere, G. (2002). *Imagining karma: Ethical transformation in Amerindian, Buddhist, and Greek rebirth* (Vol. 14). University of California Press.

244 **Growing up as a conservative Christian,** Fuchs, E. (1983). *Sexual desire and love: Origins and history of the Christian ethic of sexuality and marriage* (p. 143). J. Clarke.

246 **the Bible says homosexuality is wrong.** Leviticus 18:22: "Do not practice homosexuality, having sex with another man as with a woman. It is a detestable sin." *Holy Bible: King James Version, 1611 Edition* (2006, 400th anniversary ed.). Hendrickson.

246 **In another example, the New Testament** 1 Timothy 2:12: "But I suffer not a woman to teach, nor to usurp authority over the man, but to be in silence." *Holy Bible: King James Version, 1611 Edition* (2006, 400th anniversary ed.). Hendrickson.

246 **The Bible has many other** Deuteronomy 22:28–29: "If a man meets a virgin who is not engaged, and seizes her and lies with her, and they are caught in the act, the man who lay with her shall give fifty shekels of silver to the young woman's father, and she shall become his wife. Because

he violated her he shall not be permitted to divorce her as long as he lives." *Holy Bible: King James Version, 1611 Edition* (2006, 400th anniversary ed.). Hendrickson.

246 **women should dress modestly,** 1 Timothy 2:9–10: "In like manner also, that women adorn themselves in modest apparel, with shamefacedness and sobriety; not with broided hair, or gold, or pearls, or costly array; But (which becometh women professing godliness) with good works." *Holy Bible: King James Version, 1611 Edition* (2006, 400th anniversary ed.). Hendrickson.

246 **women are responsible for** 1 Timothy 2:11–12: "Let the woman learn in silence with all subjection. But I suffer not a woman to teach, nor to usurp authority over the man, but to be in silence." The author's rationale: "For Adam was formed first, then Eve, and Adam was not deceived, but the woman was deceived and became a transgressor." *Holy Bible: King James Version, 1611 Edition* (2006, 400th anniversary ed.). Hendrickson.

246 **women should not be allowed to teach men,** 1 Timothy 2:12: "But I suffer not a woman to teach, nor to usurp authority over the man, but to be in silence." *Holy Bible: King James Version, 1611 Edition* (2006, 400th anniversary ed.). Hendrickson.

246 **men may divorce their wives** The Bible's Book of Deuteronomy (22:13–21) says that if a man marries a woman and then decides that he hates her, he can claim she wasn't a virgin when they married. At that point her father must prove she was a virgin. If he can't, then the woman is to be stoned to death at her father's doorstep. *Holy Bible: King James Version, 1611 Edition* (2006, 400th anniversary ed.). Hendrickson.

251 **Scientists have recently discovered** Harvard University Graduate School of Arts and Sciences (2019, March 27). No, it's not just you: Why time "speeds up" as we get older. *Science in the News* (blog). http://sitn.hms.harvard.edu/flash/2019/no-not-just-time-speeds-get-older/.

251 **When you recall something,** Antic, V. (2020, November 25). Memory recall/retrieval: Types, processes, improvement & problems. *The Human Memory*. https://human-memory.net/memory-recall-retrieval.

252 **Though we lose conscious recollection** Reber, P. (2010, May 1). What is the memory capacity of the human brain? *Scientific American*. https://www.scientificamerican.com/article/what-is-the-memory-capacity/.

252 **Some, like *The Hobbit*,** Laforet, V. (2013, June 17). *The Hobbit:* An unexpected masterclass in why 48 FPS fails. *Gizmodo*. https://gizmodo.com/the-hobbit-an-unexpected-masterclass-in-why-48-fps-fai-5969817.

252 **Einstein's theory of relativity proves** Einstein, A., Gutfreund, H., & Renn, J. (2019). *Relativity: The special and the general theory—100th anniversary edition* (Annotated ed.). Princeton University Press.

254 **You leave a seventh of your body behind** Opfer, C. (2020, June 30). Does your body really replace itself every seven years? HowStuffWorks. https://science.howstuffworks.com/life/cellular-microscopic/does-body-really-replace-seven-years.htm#:~:text=What%20Frisen%20found%20is%20that,to%20a%20decade%20or%20so

INDEX

A

Abdelnour, Ziad K., 178
abusive relationships, 19
acceptance, 22–23, 161–164. *See also* peers; tribal affiliation, shared
access, 259
accomplishment, need for, 209. *See also* purpose
Adams, Douglas, 236
Adams, Scott, 28, 150
addiction, 108, 130–131
advice. *See also* mentors
   about purpose, 213
   asking for, 242
   of authors, 182–183, 191
   harmful, 175
   ignoring, 179, 182–183
   from romantic partners, 93
   trusting, 92
   unilateral relationships and, 182–183
advisers. *See* mentors
advising relationships. *See* mentors
Affleck, Ben, 116
Alabama, University of, 105
Alder, Shannon L., 154
Alexander, David, 51
Altig, Rick, 216
ambition, 213. *See also* goals; paths; purpose
default. *see* instincts
Animal Farm (Orwell), 24
Arden, Paul, 204
artistic success, 117–120
athletes, 104–105
authors, 182–183, 191. *See also* relationships, unilateral
autism spectrum, 6–7

B

background, common, 67. *See also* tribal affiliation, shared
Bad Brains, 37–38
Band of Brothers (film), 62
Bandura, Albert, 189, 192
Barker, Scott, 75
basketball, 40–41, 42
Beastie Boys, 38–40, 43–44, 258
behavior, acceptable. *See* acceptance
beliefs, 134, 162. *See also* religion; worldview
   exposure to ideas and, 181

beliefs (*continued*)
  physical location and, 180–181
  shared, 67
Bell, Gertrude, 4, 207–209, 258
Bellow, Saul, 163
belonging, sense of, 62. *See also* acceptance; tribal affiliation, shared
Beyoncé, 242
biases, 35
Biz Enrich, 75
bloodlines, 67
body image, 109–110
book, blank, 18–20. *See also* relationships
boss. *See* supervisors
Brady, Maureen, 191
Brown, H. Jackson, Jr., 94
Brown, Les, 219
Bryan, Mark, 114
Buddha, 142–143, 254, 258
Buscaglia, Leo, 229, 260
Bush, George W., 69–70
business, starting, 125–130, 231

C
capitalism, 231
Cardi B, 24
careers. *See* job; paths
Carroll, Pete, 83, 84
celebrities, 115. *See also* relationships, unilateral
challenge, constant, 201
change, 43. *See also* worldview
Cher, 230
choices, 25–27. *See also* decisions; instincts; options
  fear and, 165
  intuition and, 226–227
  pleasure and, 28
  previous, 16, 27, 31–34, 35, 220–221
  responsibility for, 220–221
Christensen, Clayton M., 177

circle, inner. *See* inner circle
circumstances, 17–18. *See also* nurture
civilization, influence and, 21
climate change, 198–200
clique, 61
coaches, 90–91, 105. *See also* mentors
  fitness goals and, 109
Coker, Frank, 75
Coleman, Matthew Taylor, 162
colleagues, 97. *See also* peers; supervisors
college education, 128
common sense, 261–262
commonality, clues of, 49–50
communication, 21
Communist Manifesto, The (Marx), 24
competition, 231
complacency, 56
confidence, 8
connections. *See also* influences; mentors; relationships; tribal affiliation, shared
  gaining, 76. *see also* networking
  importance of, 39, 73, 75
connectivity, 259
contentment, 56
control, 164–166, 210, 211
Coolidge, Calvin, 54
Cotton, Will, 166
counselors, 89–90, 110, 131
COVID crisis, 133, 137–139
creators, 24–25. *See also* relationships, unilateral
cults, 162
Curry, Stephen, 40, 41

D
Dalai Lama, 255
Damon, Matt, 116
Darrow, Clarence, 233
dating, 133. *See also* romantic partners
decisions, 221–222. *See also* choices; options

desires and, 30
    weighing options in, 27–31
DeMann, Freddy, 38–39
depression, 245. *See also* mental health
desires, 28, 30, 163–164, 210. *See also* instincts
Diamond, Mike, 37–40
diamond business, 59–61, 67
direction, 210, 212, 215, 226, 236. *See also* purpose
divorce, 244–250
dogs, 163
dollar-cost averaging, 122
domestication, 22
doors, closed, 229
Douglass, Frederick, 4, 79–82, 87, 101–102, 258
dreams, childhood, 227
drive, lack of, 265–266
Du Bos, Charles, 56
Dyer, Wayne W., 187

E
Earhart, Amelia, 266
e-capital (evolutionary capital). *See* evolutionary capital (e-capital); instincts
Einstein, Albert, 151, 177
empathy, 138–140
employees. *See* protégés
emulation, 7–8
energy, fame and, 114–115
environment. *See* nurture; relationships
epidemics, 181–182. *See also* COVID crisis
eugenics, 15n
evolution, 21, 22, 24, 165, 169. *See also* instincts
evolutionary capital (e-capital), 148, 175, 195. *See also* improvement; instincts; reproduction; survival
    acceptance, 161–164
    components of, 149–152
    influence, 166–167
    novelty, 167–169
    rating people on, 263–264
    resources, 164–166
    safety, 155–158
    sex, 158–161
    strategies for obtaining, 153–169
exercise, 106. *See also* fitness goals
expectations, 215, 217–218. *See also* peer pressure
experience, openness to, 168
exposure, incremental, 190, 192

F
facial expression, 7
failure, 156, 218–219, 228
faith. *See* religion
fame, 103, 114–117, 118
family, 87–88. *See also* genetics; parents
family connection, 67
famous people, 115. *See also* relationships, unilateral
fears, 146, 155–158, 165, 189, 223–224
Ferriss, Tim, 118, 196
financial crisis (2008), 202–204
fitness goals, 106–110
fitting in. *See* acceptance
food, 107–108
friends, 97. *See also* peers; relationships
    addiction recovery and, 130–131
    fame and, 116–117
    worldview and, 136–140
future, 33, 259

G
Galland, Edward "Eddy," 13–14, 15, 16, 17, 257
Galton, Francis, 14, 17
game. *See* evolutionary capital (e-capital); instincts

Gates, Bill, 181
generosity, 242
genetics, 14–16, 35–36. *See also* instincts; nature
George Mason University, 198, 199, 200
ghostwriting, 120
giving attitude, 230
giving circle, 100
Gladwell, Malcolm, 179, 192
global warming, 198–200
goals, 146. *See also* paths
  writing down, 223
Goethe, Johann Wolfgang von, 23, 217
Good Will Hunting (film), 116
Goodfellas (film), 24
gratitude, 56
gravity, 42–45, 115, 211, 265. *See also* high-gravity individuals (HGIs); mentors; peers
Green, Draymond, 41, 97, 258

H

habit-forming ability, 187
Habyarimana, Bangambiki, 165
Hall, Barbara, 223
Hall, Doug, 75
Hamid, Mohsin, 158
happiness, 56, 102, 217. *See also* worldview
hard, vs. impossible, 54–55
Hasty, Collins, 157
hate, 157
Hawking, Stephen, 173
Heinlein, Robert A., 145
helpfulness, 50–53
Hemingway, Ernest, 152
heredity. *See* genetics; instincts; nature
high-gravity individuals (HGIs), 45–56, 59, 86. *See also* gravity; mentors; peers
Hilliard, Brian, 51
Hiukka, Kristiina, 75

Holmes, Oliver Wendell, Sr., 232
Hootie and the Blowfish, 114
Horovitz, Adam, 38–40
human connection, 113
humanity, 157. *See also* instincts
humility, 114

I

ideas. *See also* worldview
  evaluating, 175, 193
  exposure to, 175, 180–181, 192
  formation of, 177–178
  geography and, 180–181
  harmful, 175
  incorrectly categorizing, 189
  rejecting, 183, 186. *see also* mental immune system
  relationships and, 178–180
  spread of, 174, 176, 180–184
  subjective, 194–202
ignorance, 204
imitation, 7–8
impossible, vs. hard, 54–55
improvement, 148, 152. *See also* instincts
income. *See also* wealth
  artistic success and, 119–120
  purpose and, 231
  vs. wealth, 121, 124–125
influencers, 69. *See also* relationships, unilateral
influences, 18–20, 30, 166–167. *See also* connections; nurture; relationships; religion
information, reacting to, 32
inner circle, 77
  gaps in, 82
  intentionality and, 93
  mentors, 89–93
  parents, 87–88
  peers, 97–99
  protégés, 99–101
  romantic partners, 93–96
  supervisors, 83–86

instincts, 143, 146, 175, 210, 264.
    See also desires; evolutionary
    capital (e-capital);
    improvement; nature;
    reproduction; rules; survival
  improvement, 152
  overcoming, 169–171, 176
  overriding, 154
  reproduction, 151–152
  survival, 150–151
intentionality, 93
interaction, human, 6–7
interests, shared, 49–50
introductions, 51
intuition, 226–227
investing, 120, 122, 123–124. *See also*
    wealth
iPhone, 177

J
James, LeBron, 41
Jami, Criss, 24
Jews, Orthodox, 59
job, 231. *See also* paths
  separating purpose from, 227
job hunting, 110–114
Jobs, Steve, 177
Jung, Carl Gustav, 79

K
Kahoutek, Titus, 109
Keller, Helen, 98
Kellman, David, 14, 15, 16, 17, 257
Kenyon, Sherrilyn, 147
King, Stephen, 222
knowledge, gaps in, 175
Koomson, Dorothy, 163
Kreger, David, 26
Kübler-Ross, Elisabeth, 228
Kubrick, Stanley, 162

L
Lao Tzu, 156
Lawrence, T. E., 208

Le Guin, Ursula K., 207
leaning, 211–212, 215
lens. *See* worldview
Leventhal, Eric Micha'el, 216
Lewis, C. S., 32
life, listening to, 226
life situation, curating, 8
LinkedIn, 111, 113
literacy, 82
Lombardi, Vince, 220
loss, 228
love life, 131–134. *See also* romantic
    partners
loyalty, 84
luck, 57–59, 84, 91, 211, 227

M
Madonna, 38–39, 44, 258
Maluleke, Tshepo Koos, 156
managers, 83–86
Mandela, Nelson, 155
marketers, 175
Marx, Karl, 24
masks, 163–164
Maugham, W. Somerset, 162
Maxwell, John C., 30, 182
mediocrity, 221
Megan Thee Stallion, 24
memories, 251
mental health, 15, 89–90, 95, 110, 131,
    245
mental immune system, 183,
    184–186, 190–191, 192
mental toughness, 220
mentors, 42–45, 83–86, 89–93.
    See also advice; gravity; high-
    gravity individuals (HGIs)
  access to, 182
  advice from, 179
  choosing, 57–58, 91, 230
  making most of relationship
    with, 85–86
  for pillars, 240–243
  unilateral relationships and, 89

mindsets. *See* worldview
Misner, Ivan, 51
money, 165, 166. *See also* income; wealth
Moneyball (film), 41
Moning, Karen Marie, 13
Monroe, Marilyn, 251
motivations, 210. *See also* instincts; purpose
multiplication, 148, 151–152, 165. *See also* instincts
Murdoch, Iris, 194
music, 24
Myanmar, 173, 178

N
Naskar, Abhijit, 152
nature, 16, 17–18, 27, 35–36. *See also* genetics; instincts
NBA, 40–41
negativity, overcoming, 94
network structures, 71
networking, 51, 73, 76, 111–113, 129
Networking Like a Pro (Misner), 51
networks, bridge, 63–64
networks, closed, 61–62
networks, open, 62–63
Neubauer, Peter, 15, 16, 17
newness, 167–169, 176. *See also* ideas
Newton, Isaac, 37, 177
nirvana, 142
Norris, J. Loren, 141
novelty, 167–169, 176. *See also* ideas
nurture, 16, 17–18, 22, 27, 30, 35, 36. *See also* connections; influences; relationships
nutrition, 107–108

O
Obama, Michelle, 226
objections, to relationshift philosophy, 261–266
Ogunlaru, Rasheed, 103
opportunities, 3, 56

options. *See also* choices; decisions
  awareness of, 30
  evaluating, 27–31
  fear and, 165
  previous choices and, 31–34
  view of, 25
Oregon Institute of Science and Medicine, 198, 199
Orwell, George, 24

P
pain, 228
Panwar, Nishan, 234
parents, 87–88. *See also* genetics; nature; nurture
Parrish, Tony, 104
Pascal, Blaise, 194
passions, childhood, 227
paths, 103. *See also* goals; job
  artistic success, 117–120
  athletic success, 104–105
  developing new worldview, 134–140
  fame, 114–117
  fitness, 106–110
  improving love life, 131–134
  job hunting, 110
  overcoming addiction, 130–131
  starting business, 125–130
  wealth building, 120–125
Paul, Logan, 69, 70
pause to reflect
  attracting HGIs, 59
  blank book, 20
  changing worldview, 193
  e-capital, 171–172
  inner circle, 86, 88, 93, 96, 99, 101
  leaning, 212
  mentors, 93
  options, 34
  parents, 88
  paths/goals, 140
  peers, 99
  pillars, 243

protégés, 101
purpose, 235
romantic partners, 96
social capital, 72
supervisors, 86
transformational gravity, 45
worldview as obstacle, 206
peer pressure, 19, 22–25, 42, 107, 209
peers, 44, 97–99. *See also* acceptance;
    gravity; relationships
    addiction recovery and, 130–131
    artistic success and, 119
    business and, 128–129
    evaluating, 97–99
    fame and, 116–117
    goals and, 108–109
    wealth and, 124–125
    worldview and, 136–140
people, relating to, 7
Perry, Tyler, 101
perseverance, 54–55
personality, 8. *See also* traits
personas, alternative, 164. *See also*
    acceptance
Peterson, Jordan B., 149
Picasso, Pablo, 224
pillars
    defining, 236–240
    mentors for, 240–243
Pirsig, Robert M., 197
pleasure, 28. *See also* desires
Plinko, 210–212, 265
plus/minus statistic, 41, 42, 55
Poe, Edgar Allan, 202
politics, 136, 186. *See also* worldview
positivity, 94, 177
possibilities, 3, 215–222
pregnancy, teenage, 26–27, 30, 34
preparation, 55
present moment, 254
Price Is Right, The, 210–212
procreation, 148, 151–152, 165. *See also* instincts
Proctor, Bob, 90

programming, 22–25. *See also*
    nurture; peer pressure
protégés, 99–101, 129–130. *See also*
    employees
psychologists, 89–90. *See also*
    therapy
purpose, 209, 210, 213. *See also*
    direction; pillars
    advice about, 213
    changing strategies for, 225
    defining, 215, 225–226
    income and, 231
    need for, 212
    redefining, 205
    relationships and, 230
    separating from job, 227
    spirituality/religion and, 232–234
    starting and, 234
    strategies for moving toward,
        222–225

Q
QAnon, 162

R
rapport, building, 49–50
Ravindra, Ravi, 164
reactions, 219–220
readiness, 55–56, 82
reality, 194, 198, 202, 215
reciprocity, 242
recruiters, 113
regrets, 220
rejection, 55
relationships. *See also* influences;
    inner circle; mentors; peers
    blank book and, 18–20
    effects of, 3
    ending, 262–263
    importance of, 39, 73, 75, 77
    number of, 65
    opportunities from, 3
    power of, 23
    speed of development, 54

relationships (*continued*)
    strength of, 61, 65–67, 71
    value extracted from, 40. *see also* social capital
relationships, unilateral, 69–71, 89, 182–183, 191
reliability, demonstrated, 70
religion, 25–27, 35, 162, 184–185, 244–250. *See also* worldview
    arguing about, 186
    purpose and, 233
religious leaders, 91–92
reproduction, 148, 151–152, 165. *See also* instincts
requests, relationship strength and, 66
resistance, overcoming, 224
resources, 164–166
results, slowness of, 54
riot, 41–42
risk, 228–229
Robbins, Anthony, 31
Rogers, Jeff, 50–51, 74, 75
Rohn, Jim, 23, 215
romantic partners, 93–96
    building wealth and, 122
    goals and, 108–109
    improving love life, 131–134
Roosevelt, Eleanor, 239
Rubin, Rick, 38, 44, 258
rules, 146, 211, 248. *See also* instincts
    choosing, 205, 209
    ignoring, 217–218
    playing by, 204
Run-DMC, 39
Runyon, Joel, 200
RuPaul, 48

S
Saban, Nick, 105
sacrifice, 85
safety, 155–158. *See also* survival
St. Maarten, Anthon, 218
Salem Witch Trials, 161–162
samples, 53
saving, 122–123
self-control, 163
self-deception, 162–163
self-preservation. *See* survival
self-worth, 217–218
sex, 158–161. *See also* instincts; reproduction; romantic partners
Shafran, Robert, 14, 15, 16, 17, 257
Shaw, George Bernard, 175
Shining , The (film), 162
shortcuts, 183
Siddhartha (Buddha), 142–143, 254, 258
Simmons, Russell, 38, 44, 258
slavery, 79–82
smiling, 7
social capital, 40
    network structures, 61–65
    relationship strength and, 61, 65–67
    unilateral relationships and, 69–71
social climbing, 262
social networks, 162
societal messaging, 24. *See also* expectations
socioeconomic situation, mental health and, 16
speed, 42–43
spiritual leaders, 91–92
spirituality, purpose and, 232–234
sports, 104–105
Stone, W. Clement, 29, 239
striving, 56
substance dependency, 108, 130–131
success
    helpfulness and, 51
    reasons for, 84. *see also* luck
suicide, 245. *See also* mental health
supervisors, 83–86. *See also* mentors
support, 103

survival, 148, 150–151, 155–158, 165. *See also* instincts
synapses, 251–252

T
teaching, 86, 100. *See also* protégés
teenage pregnancy, 26–27, 30, 34
Teya, Joshua, 51
therapy, 89–90, 95, 110, 131
Thoreau, Henry David, 168, 174
Three Identical Strangers (documentary), 16
tie strength, 65–67, 71
time, perception of, 251–255
traits
 curating, 36
 emulating, 8
 genetics and, 14–16
 peer pressure and, 22–25
tribal affiliation, shared, 46–50. *See also* acceptance
triplets, 13–14, 15, 16, 17, 254, 257
trust
 bridge networks and, 65
 changing worldview and, 192
 closed networks and, 62
 demonstrated reliability and, 70
 similarities and, 67
 spiritual leaders and, 91–92
 spread of ideas and, 176
 tribal affiliation and, 49
 unilateral relationships and, 69–70, 191
truth, 176, 181, 193, 197–202
Tully's Coffee on Main, 50, 74
Twain, Mark, 19
12 Rules for Life (Peterson), 149
twin studies, 14–16, 17
type II chaotic system, 32

U
understanding, 138–140
unhappiness, 196. *See also* mental health

V
value, adding, 53. *See also* helpfulness
values. *See* pillars
velocity, 42–43
Villars, Gebru, 240
viruses, ideas as, 180–184
vloggers, 69, 70. *See also* relationships, unilateral

W
Washington, Denzel, 11
wealth, 103, 120–125
"Wet Ass Pussy" (song), 24
Wilde, Oscar, 258
Winterston, Jeanette, 161
wisdom, 183. *See also* advice; mentors
Wooden, John, 86
work, 231. *See also* job
work relationships, 83–86. *See also* colleagues; supervisors
worldview. *See also* happiness; ideas
 changing, 134–140, 176, 243–250
 choosing mentors and, 58
 deconstructing, 204
 formation of, 188
 like-minded people and, 201–202
 as obstacle, 187–189
 precedent and, 189
 rebuilding, 205
 retraining brain, 189–191
 subjectivity of, 200
 trust of influencer and, 191
 understanding origin of, 27

Y
Yauch, Adam, 38–40

Z
Zhang Yimou, 149
Zimmerman, Berry, 75

ABOUT THE AUTHOR

Justin Blaney, D.M., is a professor, serial entrepreneur, and author of 12 books with 100,000 copies sold, including *Will Post for Profit: How Brands and Influencers Are Cashing in on Social Media*. Justin has founded and sold multiple companies in industries ranging from advertising to consumer goods. Currently, Justin runs a digital marketing agency that has generated more than $250 million in revenue growth. He teaches at Foster School of Business at the University of Washington and created the first course on influencer marketing at a major university. One million people follow him on social media, and his work has received over one billion views. He created an app that features daily meditations on living well, which you can find along with all his other links at Blaney.app. Justin lives in Seattle with his wife, Anya, and the world's cutest mini Bernedoodle, Arlo.